THE A–Z OF SURVIVAL STRATEGIES
FOR THERAPEUTIC PARENTS

THE A–Z
OF SURVIVAL
STRATEGIES FOR
THERAPEUTIC PARENTS

FROM CHAOS TO CAKE

Sarah Naish

Illustrated by Kath Grimshaw

Jessica Kingsley Publishers
London and Philadelphia

First published in Great Britain in 2022 by Jessica Kingsley Publishers
An imprint of Hodder & Stoughton Ltd
An Hachette Company

1

A CIP catalogue record for this title is available from the
British Library and the Library of Congress

ISBN 978 1 83997 172 3
eISBN 978 1 83997 173 0

Printed and bound in Great Britain by TJ Books Ltd

Jessica Kingsley Publishers' policy is to use papers that are natural,
renewable and recyclable products and made from wood grown in sustainable forests. The logging and manufacturing processes are expected to
conform to the environmental regulations of the country of origin.

Jessica Kingsley Publishers
Carmelite House
50 Victoria Embankment
London EC4Y 0DZ

www.jkp.com

For my parents, who gave me the most precious gift,
that of secure attachments.

Contents

Introduction

If *The A–Z of Therapeutic Parenting: Strategies and Solutions* is your roadmap of strategies through to successful adulthood for your children, this book is your hot flask of tea or coffee, and a cosy blanket which will keep you warm, safe and well on your journey, ensuring you reach the other side, mentally and physically well.

I have written a great deal to help therapeutic parents, to manage the difficult and puzzling behaviours we frequently face, but, so often, we all overlook caring for *ourselves*. In this book, I deliberately avoid the use of the phrase 'self-care', as our knee-jerk response to that is, 'I don't have time'. So here, you will find survival strategies for essential maintenance.

Therapeutic parents are people who are caring for children from trauma or who have additional developmental and/or emotional needs. I've been quoted as saying that 'therapeutic parenting is the hardest, most worthwhile thing you'll ever do'. What I meant was, 'therapeutic parenting is the most excruciating, dreadfully difficult, wonderful, awful, painful, worthwhile, gut-wrenching, heart-rending, and rewarding thing you'll ever do'. I needed to water it down a bit though. Those of you who are some way along the journey will know this.

As therapeutic parenting becomes more mainstream, more and more parents find that they can use firm boundaries with empathy, and reflective parenting, to help their children become more secure and develop enhanced levels of empathy. For this reason, increasing numbers of parents are looking for ways to navigate the school and social care system, and need real-life strategies to answer the difficult, some might even say nosey, questions of others.

So, how do we find time for ourselves? Are we really alone in the way we think and deal with other people? Do other parents feel the same levels of anxiety, rage and indignation?

The answers are all here for you. Having walked a few miles in your shoes with my own five adopted children, here I am providing you with insight into why we may struggle at times, and, most importantly, what we can do about it.

FOR HELP WITH BEHAVIOUR MANAGEMENT STRATEGIES

In this book, I mainly steer clear of behaviour management strategies for our children, as these are comprehensively covered in my book *The A–Z of Therapeutic Parenting*. I do, however, insert some relevant reminders where there may be a slight crossover.

HOW TO USE THIS BOOK

The best way to use this book is as a handy quick reference, to access practical help and guidance for your immediate issue. All the topics are listed alphabetically, and for each letter you will find entries that relate to issues and feelings, along with some useful strategies.

The 'issues and feelings' entries describe feelings we often struggle with, as well as challenges we are likely to experience. I use anecdotes drawn from my life as well as those of others to reassure you that you are *not* the only therapeutic parent who ever felt this way. I also suggest other closely related topics, to ensure that you find the 'best fit' for you.

The strategies included relate to the issue or feeling. So, for example, if you are feeling very anxious, you may read about

'Anxiety', what it feels like, why it happens, and then choose a suggested strategy (perhaps 'Protecting Self') from the selection which best fits your circumstances.

The strategies are also highlighted with a light bulb icon, so you can jump straight to the ones you need which deal directly with the problem you are facing.

Above all, laugh at some of the stupid/rude things I have shared (sorry about some necessary swearing), feel free to indulge with a glass of wine or cup of tea. Revel in the knowledge that others are treading the same path as you, and you are not alone.

ABOUT THE AUTHOR

Sarah Naish is an adopter of five siblings, Rosie, Katie, William, Sophie and Charley, who are now all adults. At the beginning of her journey, Sarah adopted the children with her ex- (practice) husband, who did not remain with the family. Later, Sarah met her husband, Ray, who became the adoptive stepfather to the children and remains an integral part of the family.

Sarah has fostered over 40 children, worked as a social worker and owned therapeutic fostering agencies. She is now Chief Executive Officer at the Centre of Excellence in Child Trauma, which helps parents, social workers, teachers and health professionals to find the best solutions when caring for children from trauma.

OTHER SOURCES OF SUPPORT – RESOURCES AND ORGANIZATIONS

We all have favourite books, friends or communities we lean on for strength.

Below, I've listed some of my other publications which I hope you'll also find helpful, as well as some of the organizations I run to help support therapeutic parents.

- *The A–Z of Therapeutic Parenting* was written to be a one-stop reference providing solutions to common pitfalls and challenges faced by therapeutic parents.
- *The Quick Guide to Therapeutic Parenting* is an easy-to-read, visual guide to therapeutic parenting principles and strategies, fully illustrated with fun cartoons and graphics. It is ideal if you are new to therapeutic parenting or if you're a more experienced parent after some fresh inspiration.
- *Therapeutic Parenting Jumbo Cards* use the images and key messages from the *Quick Guide* in a high-quality pack of 56 full-colour, jumbo playing cards which come with an accompanying booklet. The cards are ideal for starting tricky conversations about parenting, or for sticking on your noticeboard to keep your mind on the mission!
- *Therapeutic Parenting Essentials: Moving from Trauma to Trust* was written to guide the reader through the experience of parenting therapeutically, including the perspectives of both parents and children, and draws on my own life and experiences.
- *The Complete Guide to Therapeutic Parenting* (lead author Jane Mitchell) is for readers who want to dig deeper into the theory and research that lie behind therapeutic parenting.
- Finally, *The A–Z of Therapeutic Parenting Professional Companion* is a resource for social workers and related professionals with tools to help support therapeutic parents and their children.

The Centre of Excellence in Child Trauma (COECT) is the umbrella organization for all our services. This includes the National Association of Therapeutic Parents (NATP) which supports over 10,000 parents of neuro diverse children in the UK, and Inspire Training Group which delivers training, qualifications and change in the field of child trauma, adoption and fostering.

A

ACCEPTANCE

Also see Boundaries, Catastrophic Thinking, Controlling, Expectations (Managing), Letting Go, Overwhelm

I must be honest and say there are still some things I do *not* accept. I don't accept my adult daughter moaning that 'no one ever helped her'. This is good, as we definitely should not be accepting and encouraging this type of dismal victim-wallowing.

The feeling of *having to* accept something that we find goes against everything we believe in or desire can be really challenging. I think it can be one of the toughest aspects of parenting a child from trauma, or with additional needs.

I found life got much easier when I began to accept all the things I could not change. For example:

- The time my teenagers came in after an exciting night out at the amusement arcade.
- The amount of food my children stole from others while claiming hunger.
- The friends my children made as they became older (being particularly drawn to the local neighbourhood thugs and drug dealers).
- My children's aversion to homework and studying and their general resistance to engaging in any type of academia.
- The thoughts and opinions of others about my parenting.

- The weather.
- The fact that I was going to be fat for quite a long time.
- The fact that social workers who understood trauma were a rare find – and I hadn't found one...yet!

We can waste so much time planning and strategizing. Sometimes this is really useful and sometimes, frankly, it's a completely pointless waste of everyone's time. The skill is in working out what falls into which category. When we feel overwhelmed, it's a good idea to start off by looking at what we *need* to accept.

At times, we may feel that if we accept a situation it means we've given up. This is not the case. I've often talked about the difference between 'letting go' and 'giving up'. When we accept that we're unable to change something, it doesn't mean that we give up forever. It means that we look for an alternative way to make things better. Sometimes, right now, this course of action isn't going to work. (See 'Letting Go'.)

It's useful to ask yourself what you're trying to achieve. At times, we are just stuck in a mindset that says a child has to behave in a certain way because that's our belief system. But if you're repeatedly banging your head against a brick wall, you're only going to get a very bad headache. Much better to accept that your head is making no impression on the wall and make yourself a nice cup of tea instead.

Nothing stays the same. Think of your life five years ago, it was different. It will be different again in five years' time. Whatever the challenge or difficulty you are trying to change now, it will change anyway.

See strategies: Natural Consequences (Allowing), One Step at a Time, Picking Your Battles, Protecting Self

☼ ACRONYMS

On the social media groups for therapeutic parents I have developed, we are often asked what some acronyms and language mean. It should be noted that at the Centre of Excellence in Child Trauma we actively discourage some of the terms used by some agencies and local authorities which we feel is discriminatory and outdated. These include:

- Placement (instead of child or home)
- Respite (instead of break or planned sleepover)
- Cases or case load (instead of families).

However, therapeutic parents do need assistance in navigating all the shorthand and jargon used within the sector, so I have inserted a current list of acronyms below. Please note that these do change fairly frequently and often the use of the term 'disorder' is discouraged.

ACE	Adverse childhood experiences
AD	Adopted daughter/Attachment disorder
ADD	Attention deficit disorder
ADHD	Attention deficit hyperactivity disorder
AD-UK	Adoption UK
AO	Adoption order
AS	Adopted son
ASD	Autism spectrum disorder
AT	Attachment therapist
BD	Birth/biological daughter
BP	Birth/biological parent
BS	Birth/biological son
CA	Child abuse
CAF	Common Assessment Framework
CAMHS	Child and Adolescent Mental Health Services

CF	Compassion fatigue
CIC	Child in care
CIN	Child in need
CIW	Care Inspectorate Wales
COECT	Centre of Excellence in Child Trauma
CPS	Child Protection Services
CPV	Child to parent violence
CSA	Child sexual abuse
CSE	Child sexual exploitation
CSW	Child's social worker
CYPS	Children and Young People's Services
DA	Domestic abuse
DD	Developmental delay
DDP	Dyadic developmental psychotherapy
DT	Developmental trauma
DTD	Developmental trauma disorder
DV	Domestic violence
EHA	Early Help Assessment
EHCP	Education, Health and Care Plan
ELSA	Emotional literacy support assistant
EMDR	Eye movement and desensitization therapy
EOTAS	Education otherwise than at school
EP	Educational psychologist
FASD	Foetal alcohol spectrum disorder
FC	Foster carer
FD	Foster daughter
FII	Fabricated induced illness
FP	Foster parent
FS	Foster son
GD	Granddaughter
GDD	Global developmental delay
GS	Grandson
ICPC	Initial Child Protection Conference
IFA	Independent Fostering Agency

IRO	Independent reviewing officer
LA	Local authority
LAC	Looked after child
LC	Listening circle
LO	Little one
MBP	Munchausen's by proxy
MVB	Managing violent behaviour
NATP	National Association of Therapeutic Parents
NPD	Narcissistic personality disorder
ODD	Oppositional defiance disorder
OT	Occupational therapy/therapist
PACE	Playfulness, acceptance, curiosity, empathy
PAD	Post-adoption depression
PARENTS	Pause, assess, reflect, empathize, nurture, think, self-care
PC	Panel chair
PDA	Pathological demand avoidance
PEP	Personal Education Plan
PIE	Patronizing Ignorant Expert
PMH	Perinatal mental health
PND	Post-natal depression
PNS	Pre-natal stress
PP	Perfect Parent
PPD	Post-partum depression
PTSD	Post-traumatic stress disorder
RAD	Reactive attachment disorder
RM	Registered manager (adoption and fostering, England)
SALT	Speech and language therapy/therapist
SENCO	Special educational needs coordinator
SG	Special guardian
SGO	Special Guardianship Order
SI	Sensory issues
SPD	Sensory processing disorder
SS	Social services
SSW	Supervising social worker

SW	Social worker
TA	Teaching assistant
TFP	Therapeutic foster parent
TP	Therapeutic parent
VH	Virtual head
VS	Virtual school
YP	Young person

ADULT CHILDREN

Also see Acceptance, Catastrophic Thinking, Conflicted Feelings, Empty Nest, Grief, Rejection

When our children are little, they can be very annoying. When they are bigger, they are usually much more annoying. I found that the level of annoyingness grew in direct proportion to their feet. I think this is because their feet are bigger, they make bigger footprints, and the bigger shoes are smellier, making more mess when discarded all over the place. In any case, their shoes serve as a reminder for the problems coming our way.

It can be really painful watching our children trying to transition to adulthood, especially as, often, they are so much younger emotionally. As parents, we struggle to know when to step in and when to step back. In *The A–Z of Therapeutic Parenting* I give you strategies for managing issues like gambling, addictions and drugs and so on. In this book, I am talking more about *our feelings* around sitting on the sidelines and watching our children make catastrophic decisions. We can see where they're heading. I mean, let's face it, some of us may have made similar ludicrous decisions ourselves. It's very distressing knowing we can't stop our children making these choices. We can advise them, and we can be ready to step in when needed, but often it's more about accepting what we *can't change* and keeping our expectations realistic.

Technically, as adults they might move out. Their bodies move out, but their brains don't usually. Naive parents may think that is the end of their problems. But no, whether they are still living at home or newly, proudly independent, a whole new raft of issues approaches with train-crash horror. As adults access more power, they are allowed to make their own choices in life; and if that means that they want to take a car and drive it through a farmer's field, then set light to it so they can watch fire engines, then so be it! It is their choice.

They eat more food (sugar) and they can do more damage. They might have an income of their own which they have control over. This means the deep joy of new addictions, an endless stream of useless tech purchases (quickly abandoned), and being able to ignore most of what we advise. Horror of horrors, frequently it also means access to their brand-new, shiny credit rating. Although our children often destroy this in about three working days and two mobile phone contracts, the repercussions land at our door in the guise of bailiffs coming to collect goods on account, with the phrase, 'Well their registered address is here, so therefore you have to prove that you own everything in the house.' Top tip. Keep receipts for everything.

There is not much that is more painful than looking at your child and seeing the little child behind their eyes, seeing their fear masked by belligerence and arrogance, but knowing that you cannot reach them.

This won't last forever; you will be able to reach them again. The little child is still in there, you haven't lost them. Let them know that you are there and that although you may not necessarily always agree with their life choices, you can help them sort it out.

See strategies: Expectations (Managing), Natural Consequences (Allowing), Picking Your Battles, Protecting Self, Self-Regulation

 **ALCOHOL**

I did think carefully about whether or not to put alcohol in as an actual strategy. The problem is, if I ignore it then I'm pretending that millions of TPs, all over the world, don't fall into a vat of gin most evenings. It would be false to claim that I've never had the odd glass of wine in order to escape into a lovely fog of 'not caringness'. It's much easier to sit and have a meal in a restaurant on Mother's Day with five arguing children when you're floating in a pleasant fug of wine, than it is to stick to the diet coke, immersed in the full horror of the latest fork stabbing and under-table kicking.

Obviously, it's all about proportion. It isn't a problem to have that lovely glass of wine or gin and tonic when the children have gone to bed. It doesn't matter if you treat yourself when things are tricky and there are other adults around who can take charge if needed. It's not a good look, though, to be honest, to drink so much that you're a snivelling heap on the floor and the children use your prostrate body to catapult themselves up onto the breakfast bar to reach the biscuits.

When my children were growing up, I rarely drank alcohol because I worried that I'd be too tempted to drink more than was healthy. I wasn't sure I was strong enough to ignore the over-whelming urge to drink myself into oblivion on Sundays. If you have stronger willpower than I do, and can stop at the pleasant fog stage, and if that's what gets you through, why not? Of course, there are lots of pious things I could say here about setting good examples to your children, but this is *the survival guide for therapeutic parents*. The odd glass of wine helps us to *survive*, and probably makes us a temporarily nicer parent for our children. I know that I was perhaps more fun when I'd had a glass of wine and was more relaxed about the latest transgressions. I always knew what I was doing, and I was always fit to drive.

Well, that's my story and I'm sticking to it…

See strategies: Brain Breaks, Cake, Coffee, Essential Maintenance, Tea (Cups of, Cream)

ALLEGATIONS/FALSE ALLEGATIONS
Also see Anxiety, Betrayal, Catastrophic Thinking, Doubt, Empathy, Isolation, Overwhelm, PIEs, Relationship Problems, Sexualized Behaviour (Impact of), Sleep Problems

Being faced with an allegation your child has made against you is a truly terrible experience. Feelings of disempowerment and over-whelm are frightening. Often, we don't know where the allegation has come from or even what it contains. Furthermore, we have the added fear of knowing that people may be handling the allegation who don't really understand the circumstances surrounding it, or even how our children's minds work.

As we become more skilled, we learn that sometimes an allegation or false allegation can come from a place where a child believes what they are saying, but the impact of their trauma confuses memory. It can help us as parents to understand that *in these circumstances*, the child is not lying but they are not telling the truth. In *The A–Z of Therapeutic Parenting*, I explain about memory and how, as my co-author Sarah Dillon says, 'children can confuse what has *happened* with what is *happening*'.

When your child makes an allegation, it can feel really personal, almost like a personal attack and a betrayal of trust. Making sure that we really understand where it came from is the first step in our own healing. During an investigation, the child may not be living with us or we might not feel like talking to them! As parents, we need to keep central our knowledge around the impact of trauma on memory, and the fact that it is *likely* that the child did not do it to us deliberately. I know it feels that way, but if we can put those feelings to one side, it helps us to stay connected to the child, which is better for all of us.

When we're facing an allegation, all the feelings of isolation and fear are magnified. We worry about what people might be thinking about us. It's difficult to confide in family and friends for fear of judgement. Suddenly the supporting professionals that we trusted or confided in can no longer be trusted or may not even be around. Worse, sometimes the child is removed or leaves, and we are dealing with feelings of abandonment, loss and rejection, as well as fear for the future – ours and theirs! What will happen to us? What will happen to our child? How did we get here? These are all real feelings which might last for some time.

Sometimes, local authorities do not manage allegations swiftly and skilfully. There is still a remarkable lack of knowledge around the link between trauma and memory, and this is compounded by the way in which allegations are received. We do need to be brave, and we need to be strong, as often, sadly, it is a case of fighting our corner and educating others about where the allegation has come from.

Know that you are not alone. Know that thousands of people have been through this before you. Know that this will end. If you hold in your heart that there is a reasonable explanation for what has happened, stick to your truth, say your truth. If you cannot think of a reasonable explanation, you will need to put your detective hat on. Putting yourself in the child's place and thinking about past triggers and how they are interpreting events can help us to make sense of what is happening.

Often, huge positives can come out of allegations. We reach a new understanding of the child, and sometimes a new understanding with supporting professionals too.

Luckily, we are now able to offer you lots of practical strategies for how to deal with those terrible times when you are facing an allegation.

At times of course, a parent may have overstepped the line and the allegation is founded in fact. We know that the feelings and experiences of the child must be held in our hearts and are protected in law.

Whatever the facts of the matter are, you will be feeling over-whelmed and frightened. This is a normal response. Put your feelings of anger or shame to one side and look at the strategies suggested in this section, to ensure that your family is not left isolated.

See strategies: Empathic Listening, Havening, Protecting Self, Responding to Allegations, Switching Off, Training, Triggers (Managing)

ANGER

Also see Disempowerment, Family, Friendships, Frustration, PIEs, Relationship Problems, Resilience

There can be so much anger around us. There's the kind of simmer-ing resentment which often bubbles up as bad temper or a mini rant, and then there's the anger that is *always* on the surface. I mean, let's face it, we have a lot of things to be angry about, don't we? It's hardly surprising that we spend a lot of time feeling angry, but to be honest it's just a bit of a waste of energy.

Here are some of the things I used to get angry about:

- My children lying to me in a 'mad lie' type of way.
- People stealing my precious treat.
- The teachers metaphorically patting me on the head.
- The local authority having no clue on any level how to deal with almost anything I ever asked them.
- Stupid things said by family and friends.
- Seeing my hard work destroyed in multiple different ways, ranging from broken furniture to a failure to attend a hard-fought-for school.
- The utter incompetence and lies about the way my children's early life was (not) managed.

- Just being angry because I was so tired.
- Other parents, any of them – just because.
- Thoughtlessness in others – always trying to minimize the reality of our difficulties, simply because they couldn't cope with the magnitude of them.
- My practice husband walking into the house, oblivious to any dynamics at play, clumsily making everything a million times worse without a care in the world.

There are some positives that come out of anger. Anger often drives us to action. I used to find it handy to use the power from the anger to change into a force for good.

It did take me a long time to lose the angry feelings. They are so debilitating, and you literally can't think straight when you're angry. The problem is that when we're angry, our cortisol levels are high and it fogs the brain. That's why we can never think of the clever, witty responses when someone makes us furious, but always think of the great retort afterwards.

You can't sit and write an angry email (and it be skilled and meaningful), without lowering your cortisol levels (and therefore anger), first. This is how I managed to end up writing a furious email to the local authority one Christmas. The poor administrator had sent out a benign little email to all the adopters saying that they were organizing a Christmas get-together. Unfortunately, she also said we would need to bring various craft objects with us to 'make table decorations'. My anger went from 0 to 90 (at least it wasn't 100 – that would have been 'rage'). Without thinking, I sat down and wrote a response along the lines of:

> *So! Even though I've got five children and they're all dysregulated approaching Christmas, you actually think it will somehow be lovely for me to go shopping for craft objects to take to a 'support group', and instead of having cake and coffee (and actually getting some relief), you think it's a good idea for us to sit there like we are in preschool, trying to*

create yet another thing that my children will destroy! Well guess what? That isn't my idea of a support group. I won't be coming.

Before I could think straight, I pressed send. I *did* regret that, because it wasn't her fault, and she did mean well, but at least the local authority did not ever suggest it again.

One of the most useful things we can do is actually *recognize* that we feel angry. Sometimes we feel as if we might be in a bad mood and we just kind of get on with that, without really stopping and thinking about *how* we feel and *why* we might feel that way. When we recognize that it is anger we feel (and then think about where it comes from), we can start to do something about it.

Seething anger will make you tired. It's understandable but it damages your health, and if you can lose it, do so.

So, to summarize, you have four choices about what to do with your anger:

1. Hold on to it, accepting you are angry and embrace your new life as a resentful seether.
2. Tackle the *cause* of the anger.
3. Take action to reduce the *feelings* of anger.
4. Let it go.

See strategies: Badminton, Breathing, Cake, Chocolate, Crying, Empathic Listening, FFS, Pausing, Screaming, Self-Regulation, Swearing, Understanding, Views, Walking

ANTI-SOCIALISM

Also see Friendships, Isolation, Perfect Parents, Support, Top Trump Parenting

Are you worried that you have become anti-social?

As a therapeutic parent, I did not have time for small talk, I used to think of this as 'pond life'. Gradually my social interactions fell away, in direct correlation to the uninformed opinions shared by ignorant people with astonishing regularity. Coffee mornings, or so-called 'support groups', and family gatherings quickly became events to be endured, not enjoyed.

It's unsurprising that we may become anti-social. This is due to the difficulties in communication and the lack of time. I did not have the time or inclination to talk about other people's children's joyous achievements. Neither did I have the time to join parent–teacher association (PTA) groups or school fete committees. It seemed to me as if these kinds of things took place in a parallel universe, behind a glass screen. I didn't look through the glass screen and wish I could join in; rather, I looked through, drew the curtains, and wished it was soundproof.

Now I'm not saying that this is healthy, but it is a normal coping mechanism. The chasm that exists between our lifestyles and the lifestyles of parents of neurotypical children makes us withdraw and seek out the company of others who 'get it'. Initially, you might feel that you tried your best to 'educate' others or to communicate the difficulties you are dealing with in your life, or that your child is experiencing. After a year or two it's just quicker not to bother.

Hence, if you feel as if you are intolerant and anti-social – oh well, it's kind of to be expected. You will find that as your children grow up you may become more sociable again. But by then, your friendship circle will have changed, and you will be using cackling shorthand with your therapeutic parenting peers, for all the ridiculous things that happen in your life. You still won't want to join the PTAs and talk about baking.

It is easy for anti-socialism to tip over into isolation. Then, things have gone too far, and we don't know how to get them back (see 'Isolation').

The extent of my anti-socialism only became apparent to me during the Covid crisis. I embraced lockdown with glee. I cherished the solitary walks, the lack of social interaction and the sudden release of pressure forcing me to engage with people I did not want to engage with. Luckily, after eight months, even I started missing social interactions. I concluded that the antidote to anti-socialism is to deprive yourself of nearly all social contact and see how you get on. I can see this is difficult for parents of school-age children, as home schooling may not be an attractive idea.

The other difficulty with socializing is that when we *have to* socialize, this takes up time. This could be time well spent staring vacantly into space trying to process the latest traumatic event that has happened in our lives. 'Staring vacantly into space, open mouthed' is seriously underrated.

I don't think it's about being anti-social anymore; I think it's about connecting to the right group. Therapeutic parents want to talk about the important things in life: how they're going to get their child from where they are now to where they need to be, how they can stop their son urinating all over the house or, failing that, the best way to get rid of the smell of piss. It's tricky to have these conversations at the PTA, so we stop bothering.

See strategies: Dogs, Protecting Self, Space, Useful Phrases

ANXIETY

Also see Catastrophic Thinking, Overwhelm, Resilience, Sleep Problems

Breaking news! Most parents feel anxious quite often. It's all about managing the levels and also thinking about how reasonable it is to feel anxious about something. If you're naturally quite an anxious person, something which may not even be noticed by a more confident parent may consume you and keep you awake at night.

It's okay for different parents to have different levels of anxiety. It's all relative! Do not allow others to minimize your issues by having a little competition about how trivial it sounds. How you feel is real. There is an actual cause for why you are feeling that way, and it's not up to others to tell you how you should be feeling about that or showing off about how well they managed a similar situation. Your feelings are valid. It's how you manage them that counts.

In the strategies for this section, we give you ways to manage levels of anxiety, but here I think it's key to just acknowledge that we all have those feelings. They may range from a constant, low-level, gnawing anxiety, to an all-consuming bout of catastrophic thinking.

If we are not anxious it would mean we don't care, so let's think about what an acceptable level of anxiety is. I think it's about what is:

- manageable
- relevant
- proportionate.

Here are some of the things that used to make me anxious:

- When my children were out late, and I didn't know where they were.
- Whether Rosie would find the Easter eggs I had hidden.
- When the children were at school and I knew the school was about to make a disastrous error.
- When I was trying to complete a task, but I could feel the tensions going up between the children and I needed to complete the task.
- What other people thought about my parenting (luckily this faded very quickly and I stopped caring).
- Fear of the future and what might happen to the children.
- Whether I was getting it right.
- Whether I was good enough.
- Whether I'd spend the rest of my life on my own.
- Whether my children would ever be able to live independently.
- Whether I'd ever get my life back.

- Whether my child would ever heal.
- What would happen if there was an allegation made against me because I'd followed a certain course of action which I knew to be right.
- Whether I could get everything done in time and still get to work.
- Whether I could make a good representation of myself in an important meeting.
- Whether I could get to the meeting without bits of sweet wrapper stuck to my hair.
- What would happen if my practice husband left?
- What would happen if my practice husband didn't leave?

We have so many choices of things to feel anxious about. As therapeutic parents, naturally a great deal of the worry comes from issues relating to our children and the supporting professionals around them, but of course there's all the other life problems as well! Things like paying the bills, juggling work, relationship issues – that's just the stuff that everyone else has to deal with too!

If you feel that you are overly anxious a lot of the time, use some of the strategies here to get a perspective on that. You need to be able to lower your immediate stress levels, so you can take a step back and look objectively at the things that are making you feel anxious. Often, it's about recognizing that it is anxiety. If we don't recognize the anxiety, we can sometimes overcompensate. Just sitting down and saying, 'I'm feeling anxious about...', and exploring it with someone kind, can be hugely beneficial and help to put worries into context.

See strategies: Brain Breaks, Breathing, Empathic Listening, One Step at a Time, Protecting Self, Self-Regulation, Switching Off, Tech Control, Therapy (For Parents)

ARGUING

Also see Anger, Controlling, Family, PIEs,
Refereeing, Relationship Problems

Often there is a lot of tension around us. Sometimes the arguing can be almost unnoticeable as a constant kind of background noise. In my book *The A–Z of Therapeutic Parenting*, I give you strategies for managing arguing in children. Here, I'm looking at the *impact* that has on us.

I remember feeling as if there were lots of bees attacking my head, with the constant sniping that I heard going on around me. The music of my children's life became the instrument of torture for me. There was also the added frustration of the ridiculousness of the arguments. Was it really important if someone's dinner had two more peas on it? Did I really care if one child looked at another child in a horrible way? No, I didn't. I'd never cared, and I was not going to care.

We also get into arguments with other people. This is really draining when we're trying to make a point and explain why our strategies *work* with our children.

Arguing is closely related to anger, of course, and it's often just a habit that we fall into. As we become more confident, and know that we are right, this comes through in our actions and behaviours and makes arguing less necessary. In the related strategies, we give you some useful phrases to help you step away from arguing and save you some time!

See strategies: Brain Breaks, Co-Regulation, Pausing, Picking Your Battles, Self-Regulation, Smug Smile, Useful Phrases

ASKING FOR HELP

*Also see Blame, Doubt, Forgotten, Inadequacy
(Feelings of), PIEs, Valuing*

There are several reasons why it can become increasingly difficult to ask for help. This does depend a bit on the situation and the reason that you're asking for help, but it also depends largely on your character and past experiences. I stopped asking for help when I found that it invariably led to frustration for me. Now I'm not saying that this is a good idea, but I do understand why it happens. I think it's all about looking for help in the right places. For example, sometimes we expect someone to be an expert with no actual evidence of that being the case. Social workers go to university to learn to be social workers, because they want to make a positive difference – they *want* to help. In many universities, training in child trauma and therapeutic parenting is simply absent. Therefore, when we get to a point when we really need help (and let's face it, we usually wait too long), we might be asking somebody who is still learning, or who knows a lot less than we do. For this reason, we can become disenchanted and frustrated. Next time we are less likely to ask for help.

The other reason we sometimes don't ask for help is because if we've been assessed to foster or adopt, we may have inadvertently painted a very rosy picture of ourselves! I don't mean that we actually *lie*, but if you're trying to convince the social worker that you are a fit and able person to look after a child from trauma, you're unlikely to share some of your darker secrets or confide that you enjoy a bit of mad dancing in the shoe shop. This is a failing in the system.

For all parents, there is that deep-seated fear that if we ask for help, we are exposing ourselves as 'struggling'. Our ultimate fear is: 'Will they take my children away?' This is a huge stumbling block in accessing help.

The main reason that parents stop asking for help is because too frequently we are met with 'blaming judgement' rather than actual help. It can be *so* hard to ask in the first place, and then if the person you have reached out to panics (because they think you need them to solve the complex problem), then blame and judgement with a bit of minimization and denial thrown in are much easier to offer than solutions.

Ironically, we don't really want them to *solve* the problem, we want them to listen to us, so we don't feel so damned alone, but that is a secret that almost no one finds out – until it's too late.

Once rebuffed, rejected or sidelined, we're less likely to ask for help again. So, stop and think. Who are you asking for help? Are they equipped to help you? What do you want the outcome to be? Make sure you match the 'asking' with the correct 'receiver'. There is no point asking a question in Spanish to a native French speaker. Not without a very good interpreter.

Know that you have a difficult issue and that you are doing your best. You *deserve* to be listened to. Whether it's talking about your child's additional needs and trying to find the right strategies for them, or it's around behaviours or relationships, or even just the fact that you've had a bad day, you *deserve* to be heard.

In the strategies related to this topic, we help you to find the right person to hear you and the right way to go about it to make sure you are heard. That way you won't end up a bitter old woman like me. 🙂

See strategies: Empathic Listening, Protecting Self, Useful Phrases, Vanishing Helpers

ATTACHMENT STYLE

Some parents have told me that they find it really helpful to think about their own attachment style, in order to understand their reactions to stress and therefore to their children. I'm sad to report that during the entire time my children were growing up, I did not give my own attachment style a second thought. I don't know if this is because I'm securely attached (so didn't think about it), or I was just too busy getting the poo marks out of the carpet.

I'm delighted to report I have now discovered that I apparently have a 'secure' attachment style. This is astonishing considering I clearly remember my mum pretending to be dead, lying on the lounge floor in the middle of the summer holidays. (As a twenty-something, naturally I paraded this about as evidence of a traumatic childhood; as a forty-something adopter of five, I seriously considered using this as a strategy.)

I'm also quite amazed that complex PTSD arising from caring for children from trauma didn't affect my secure attachment either. Yay! Further proof that if you're okay early on, you can get over anything.

If we understand whether our attachment style is anxious, avoidant, secure or disorganized, it can help us to make sense of why we respond and feel the way we do. When we use this knowledge alongside feelings about triggers, it can be a very powerful insight.

In order to help you with this, I have devoted tireless hours on the internet to find the best attachment style quiz which is free. You will have to give your email address, but The Attachment Project website gives you a very interesting report and directs you to how you can get help if needed. The quiz is found at https://quiz.attachmentproject.com.

See strategies: Reflecting, Therapy (For Parents), Triggers (Managing), Understanding

 **AUDIO BOOKS**

Audio books are a great way to help our minds enter into a parallel (calmer) universe. If you've got good boundaries with your children, you might even be able to get away with playing them in the car so you can zone into the audio book, rather than the bashing and screeching noises emanating from the back of the car.

I used to enjoy listening to books in the car, while just giving the odd interested 'Hmmm' or nod to create the effect that I was listening to the children. You might need to team this up with in-car entertainment systems for the children (an investment worth its weight in gold in my opinion).

I also use audio books to help me switch off at the end of the day and to go to sleep. Top tip though, if you do this make sure you keep a note of where you started playing, as I've lost count of the times that I woke up in the morning and the book had finished! It can be a challenge finding where you started from.

Even though *The A–Z of Therapeutic Parenting* is available as an audio book, I wouldn't recommend listening to this late at night as it will remind you of all the behaviours you hadn't thought of yet, and you will start to worry about when they might surface.

See strategies: Podcasts, Reading, Switching Off

B

🔅 BABYSITTERS

Get one. Right now!

You need someone who you can train up in the early days to understand developmental trauma and your child's special or additional needs. Get them knowledgeable about more or less anything you know. If they are mature enough, this also handily makes them an unwitting empathic listener.

If you do not have a reliable babysitter, you are destined to lose not only yourself, but also any semblance of how things work in the normal world.

If you are in a couple relationship, cherish it, preserve it. Keep some times just for you. You will need a babysitter to achieve this. Waiting for the children to grow up is not a sensible option. I know it can be draining organizing it all, but trust me, the initial investment will pay dividends forever.

It does not matter if the babysitter does not do things *exactly* as you would want when you are out. This is the pay-off. Your free time is more important than whether or not the babysitter got reeled in and gaslit by your child. You can put this right later when you are refreshed. You have a babysitter. You can think straight. Your child cannot trick you. Well, not today anyway.

When planning for a night out, do not share your excitement about this with your children. It is much safer to suggest you are going to a boring meeting, while they have the excitement of a less strict babysitter, than it is to celebrate your forthcoming night out. This will be sabotaged. You will be sad.

See strategies: Brain Breaks, Essential Maintenance, Holidays, Protecting Self

BAD DAYS

Also see Catastrophic Thinking, Doubt,
Guilt, Inadequacy (Feelings of)

What do we mean by 'having a bad day'? Some of us might mean shouting and screaming in a rage like a banshee, and belatedly noticing our children looking horrified. For some of us, it might be throwing the sandwiches out of the back door (like I did on one memorable occasion). Sometimes it's worse than this, sometimes it's not as bad.

When we say 'bad days', we're not talking about the days when things have been a bit tough, because, let's face it, that's most days. We usually mean the days when we feel that we have failed in some way.

Let's have a reality check here. We all have bad days. It's not possible to swan through life as a therapeutic parent, getting everything right all the time like some kind of Stepford Parent. I know that lots of you think I somehow did this, but I can assure you that's not the case.

Well at least my children didn't die, in fact they've got to adulthood and they're actually okay! Mostly. We've got quite good relationships most of the time and we're pretty much like most other families I would say.

Interestingly, when I talk to my adult daughter Rosie about bad days that happened when I lost it, she doesn't remember them. The other children don't either. I'm not suggesting that's always the case, but I think it's crucial that we have a sense of perspective here. What was a 'bad day' to me may not have been a 'bad day' to my children. Sometimes, a bad day is not actually bad at all. If you have needed to be very firm and used your 'stop it now' face rather than your kind, nurturing one, this may have been what your children actually needed!

Sometimes a lot of the 'bad day' is internalized. We might just do a fair bit of huffing and stamping about. In the case of children who have experienced abuse before being removed from their birth family, a bad day may have meant that they didn't eat, or that somebody punched them or abused them. So that puts quite a different perspective on things, doesn't it?

Every time we use therapeutic parenting we help our children to think about things in a different way, and we light up lots of synapses in their brain, creating new pathways. When we have a bad day, those synapses haven't gone out. If you have a bar of chocolate after losing three stone, you don't put on three stone, do you? No, you've just had a bad day and you have to start again tomorrow.

Bad days are normal. Of course, we can repair. Most of the time we repair with our children because it makes *us* feel better... And if it makes us feel better then it's a good thing to do.

I wonder why my children's favourite positive saying is, 'Oh well, no one died!'

Yes, so at least that was lucky anyway.

See strategies: Alcohol, Cake, Celebrating, Dogs, Forgiving Yourself, Krispy Kreme Donuts, One Step at a Time

 BADMINTON

Why not? All that jumping about and hitting things? Very cathartic, and there's bound to be a café nearby.

BATH BOMBS

As a strategy, this is completely pointless, unless you can take a load with you when you go for a weekend away or a night in the local Travelodge. If we don't even have time to actually run the bath, then there is zero chance of there being time for the bath bombs to actually *dissolve* in the bath before a child-related intervention is necessary.

I found it astonishing that the very people who make it their business *never* to offer any practical help whatsoever are the same ones who would smilingly offer me bath bombs and pamper kits at birthdays and Christmas, with vacuous encouragements to 'spoil myself'. Well, I could have spoiled myself quite a lot by throwing the bath bombs at their annoying heads.

I do still smile, though, when I remember the day that a friend gave me a packet of six bath bombs that looked like little fairy cakes. Oh how I laughed when my daughter Charley Chatty tried to steal a bite...

See strategies: Babysitters, Baths, Brain Breaks, Hot Tubs

 # BATHS

If you've ever read any books on self-care (or have urgently looked it up on the internet after a particularly fraught day), you will see that it won't be very long before someone suggests a nice, long, relaxing soak in (preferably) a big, deep bath. Well, how does that work? If you manage to achieve this, please share the strategy with me and the millions of other therapeutic parents, desperate to immerse themselves in this luxury.

For me, before I even turned the taps off, there would be children hammering on the door. The most I could hope for was a quick shower. People who advise us to soak in the bath either don't have children or spend a lot of time ignoring their children.

You can of course enjoy a lovely bath, but this will need to be one of the nights when you are escaping, and you are in the local Travelodge. The only problem then, of course, is you can hardly call the three-inch-deep baths 'luxurious.' But the silence! Oh the silence!... more than makes up for it.

See strategies: Babysitters, Bath Bombs, Brain Breaks, Hot Tubs

BETRAYAL

Also see Allegations/False Allegations, Anger,
Friendships, Relationship Problems

How many ways can I betray thee? Let me count the ways...

If I think of the word betrayal I immediately go back to my practice husband, and the day that I found him drinking a bottle of whisky at our children's christening party. As he was drunk and had promised me never to drink again, this was the beginning of the end.

Betrayal hits us hardest when it happens at high points in our lives, and I have found that to be fairly common timing. I don't know if that's to do with us being more susceptible to being betrayed when things are going well, but it's almost as if we set ourselves up to fail, inadvertently. The higher we climb the bigger the fall. This is different from sabotage, and the way that our children sabotage nice times. Betrayal feels deliberate, more thought out.

The betrayals that stick with us are those that happen at key moments, when we thought we could count on someone.

We might feel betrayed and let down by friends and family who said they were going to help us with our children, and then when the first sign of difficulty occurred, they ran for the hills.

Sometimes we feel betrayed by the actions of our children. It's at those times that I always tried to remind myself that, invariably, the children were not doing it *to* me, they were just doing it. They would have done it wherever they were, it wasn't personal. In some ways, with our children, therefore, it's easier. We can look at their trauma and find reasons for their actions. Yes, it still hurts, but when we understand, it can be a little easier.

If you feel you have been betrayed, someone has hurt you powerfully and profoundly. They may have taken your innermost hopes, thoughts and dreams and trampled on them. They may even have held up their 'tramplings' for all to see, with pity-seeking blame. Betrayal strikes at your very core. It can really knock you off balance and make you question everything you thought you knew about that person. You may have had one, trusted, true friend, only to realize, too late, that they were just in it for what they could get for themselves. When you confront them with this, they may indulge in a little blame fest. Maybe your strength, your success or your parenting has made them feel inadequate? Maybe you were the accidental victim of their thoughtless actions? Maybe your friend has a new friend or partner in their lives, and they have decided they want to re-invent themselves and that your services are 'surplus to requirements'.

When you feel as if you have been betrayed, it can take you a long time to recover. It may take you a *very* long time to trust people again. Give yourself time to heal and be kind to yourself. Accept that what has happened, has happened. Getting closure, or making a repair, even if the relationship is changed and cannot recover, will make you feel better.

See strategies: Alcohol, Cake, Havening, Protecting Self, Therapy (For Parents), Vanishing Helpers

BIRTHDAYS

Also see Disappointment, Forgotten, Resilience, Unappreciated

There might come a day when your children dance joyfully into your room, carrying armfuls of thoughtfully chosen beautifully wrapped presents. This will be the same day that those around you realize that what you *really* want is a break, and arrive triumphantly, telling you to 'go and enjoy your spa break' as they are taking over all care and responsibility for the children for the day.

This never happened to me.

That's not to say that when your children are older (and you've done tons of empathic modelling and nurture with them), that it won't happen. It's just that you're going to have to wait for a little while. Until that time, you have to take responsibility for your own birthday. I know this is very sad, but believe me it can save much disappointment and arguing and many accusations and tears all round.

You may be really lucky and have a thoughtful partner in your life, one who anticipates your every need and makes sure that your birthday is a day to be remembered. If not, spell it out to them. Tell them what you need in advance. Ever since 'The Peacock Incident' (see 'Forgotten'), my husband, Ray, particularly likes being told what the expectations are, because that way he can't disappoint. Sometimes we expect our other half to be psychic, giving us a lovely excuse to be furious with them when they fail.

Mostly, we approach our birthdays with a feeling of dread. We know that often our children can't cope with competing distractions and our birthdays can be a trigger for them, and us! I got in the habit of not mentioning my birthday and downplaying it. If your expectations are low, you are unlikely to be disappointed.

And yet... Why *shouldn't* we have a nice birthday? Why *can't* we have days when *we* are the centre of the world, and other people around us have the opportunity to show how much they care about us, or how important we are to them? You may be one of the lucky few where that actually happens, but if not, you're in the majority. At least now you know you *are* in the majority, and all the Perfect Parent Facebook birthdays you see are indeed Fakebook birthdays. You know the ones I am talking about? The ones where the children are presenting the handmade cards to the simpering parent, usually with vacuous emojis and a trite little comment like 'I've been so spoilt today!!!!' When I used to see those, it made me feel emptier and angrier. I wanted to stab the emojis, and frankly that is not a positive, or even logical, response.

See strategies: Alcohol, Babysitters, Brain Breaks, Cake, Christmas Survival (and Other Celebrations), Expectations (Managing), Protecting Self

BIRTH FAMILY ISSUES

Also see Anger, Anxiety, Boundaries, Catastrophic Thinking, Conflicted Feelings, Grief, Guilt, Honesty

When I first started fostering, the children's birth mother would come to see the children in my home. I would feed her along with the children. She was a lovely woman who was just overwhelmed by her children and couldn't manage them. She needed support and help, not judgement. She loved her children, and it was straightforward to help her *and* help the children. We were working towards a shared goal.

When we sign up to foster or adopt, we accept that the children's birth family are a big part of their lives. We are encouraged to facilitate communication and visits where appropriate and to be positive about the relationship. In an ideal world, we are able to do this. Where there have been temporary difficulties in the birth family, but there is love and a strong bond, it is straightforward. Sadly, this is not always the case for children from trauma.

It can be very difficult to manage the myriad of feelings which arise when dealing with your unique child's birth family. Some therapeutic parents, such as special guardians and kinship carers, are often a *part* of that birth family, and this brings its own set of complications and conflicts.

The types of problems which are frequently experienced by therapeutic parents relating to birth family are often minimized by others, without any due regard for the complexities of the deep feelings and responses provoked by these interactions. At the Centre of Excellence in Child Trauma, we challenge outdated policies and ideas which place the birth parents' needs above those of the child. We know that taking a child to see people who have terrified them makes it incredibly difficult to build trust with the child and we, as the therapeutic parent, are in the front line for the fall out.

Here are some reported problems:

- Having to take a child to see a birth parent who has abused the child, leaving the therapeutic parent to manage the fall-out in behaviours.
- Having to accept a plan where the child is to be sent back home to a family which the therapeutic parent understands to be abusive. This is especially difficult when this is happening multiple times.
- Differences in parenting style, which may undermine the therapeutic parent's methods. This often happens around unhealthy food choices, unsuitable toys and so on.
- Dealing with a birth parent in a situation which provokes aggression and anger aimed at the therapeutic parent.
- Managing the level of honesty when there are conflicts in advice and expectations.
- Having to attend meetings with the birth family where there is aggression, lying or other difficult behaviours.
- Having to help children to deal with the disappointment of a birth parent failing to show up or to send an expected letter or card.
- Having to deal with a supporting professional who is very entrenched in the birth parent's view and has lost sight of the needs of the child.

We might be left feeling like helpless bystanders. Watching on, as all our good work is unravelled before our very eyes. Bringing a child home from 'contact' where old behaviours resurface due to a reignited trauma is desperately sad. We feel that we are in a system that is broken and does not give any thought to the child's feelings. We know that children are often communicating clearly to us through their behaviour about how they feel, and of course any contact will provoke anxiety and feelings of loss. Wherever unification is the plan and we're all on the same page and working towards that, this is much easier to handle, as it is short term, and we can expect a positive ending.

When we are faced with a situation where we are forced to facilitate visits with people who we believe, or know, will harm the child, this is unmanageable. We are furious. We are terrified for the child, we are disempowered and we feel as if we have been silenced. The bewilderment in the child's eyes can feel like a knife to the heart.

For special guardians and kinship carers, there is a pre-existing relationship with the parent. They may love the birth parent. They may have raised them. Something has happened where, for whatever reason, the birth parent cannot care for the children. In these situations, the therapeutic parent has a special kind of hell. The special guardians I have worked with over the last few years all report that they are under-supported. So much is expected of them, more I think than foster parents and adopters, and yet there is little support. There is an expectation that because they have already parented the parent (or at least been closely involved with them), they are better equipped. The opposite is true of course. The conflict in that feeling makes the dichotomy ten times harder.

One special guardian who had unexpectedly taken on the children of his nephew described it like this:

One day I was looking at my retirement and making plans for some fairly extensive holidays with my wife. Literally within a week we had had multiple visits from social services and the three children suddenly came to live with us. They were aged between three and six. At first, we had a lot of visits from my nephew, their dad. I had always had a close relationship with him. But gradually these visits tailed off. I thought the children were going to go back and live with him. I didn't want to be negative about my nephew, but I knew he kept letting the children down. I was not prepared to be a full-time father again, and my wife was not prepared to be a full-time mother. We didn't feel able to confront their father because we didn't want him to be scared off completely, but we were angry with him. Over time, as we grew to love the children and accept that our lives were different, there were more problems which arose. We had no support and virtually no financial assistance. We never got a break. After two years, my nephew came back into the children's lives and started talking about taking them to live with him. We knew he was living a chaotic life and was taking drugs. We didn't know what to do for the best and there was no help for us. No one will make a decision and we have a court case pending. Our lives have more or less continued in the same way. It is chaotic, frightening, and very lonely. [At this point he broke down.]

See strategies: Brain Breaks, Empathic Listening, Having, Managing Visits (Contact), One Step at a Time, Pausing, Picking Your Battles, Protecting Self, Self-Regulation, Useful Phrases

BLAME

Also see Anger, Boundaries, Compassion Fatigue, Criticism, Disempowerment, Isolation, PIEs, Resilience

Blaming others

Blame is like chocolate. You know you shouldn't indulge, but it's too tempting.

At our office, we have a culture of 'no blame'. Well, that's all well and good, but when the photocopier runs out of paper, and 'no one' got any more, but it was clearly 'somebody's' job, everyone will stare or glance at the person they believe to be responsible, indicating that it certainly *was not them*, do not even *think* that...*this* is the person who is responsible. This little 'goat of scape' right here. So even though the starer is not *actually* responsible, instinctively they have to ensure that any blame missiles are not heading in their direction. This is despite the fact that there are no blame missiles on site, we have not sent any blame missiles for years, and there are no blame missiles being made.

Guilt is to be avoided, but blame is *so* rewarding. If we can unite in the blameyness, then it bonds us together – united, as the winners against the failing 'goats of scape'.

Blame is great for making us feel better, so, for example, if I find my jacket ripped it's going to make me sad, then quickly angry, as anger is safer (and less vulnerable) than sadness. I can then indulge in a nice bit of blaming as a channel for my anger. But what if I then discover that in fact the jacket was ripped accidentally, by *me*, as I took it off the peg? Nobody ripped it on purpose. Will that make me feel better? Well, it might do, I might be relieved, but I might also be a bit angrier as now I have all this blame stored up inside me that I cannot discharge. I can't blame anyone, only me. Oh dear, that's not very comfortable. I'd much rather keep muttering to myself that someone else must have at least *started* the rip. Much more rewarding.

The problem with blame is that it is like an infectious disease. It displaces accountability and entirely prevents us from looking at:

- why something happened
- what we can do about it
- how we can improve things
- how we can prevent this from happening again.

Instead, we obsess over:

- whose fault it is
- who we can blame regardless of fault
- who will pay
- how they will pay
- whether or not they did it deliberately
- how we can get out of this without looking bad or in any way partly responsible.

In an ideal world, we would always be looking at both sides of the story, in order to resolve issues and embrace accountability effecting positive change. When we blame, we are not looking at *why* something happened and fixing it. Rather we are looking at *who* is to blame, so we can metaphorically dust our hands and move on, secure in the knowledge that it wasn't *us* who failed. Oh no!

Being blamed

Much harder is when we are the *recipient* of the blame. Then it is unfair, and the people who are judging us are unskilled, stupid, ignorant or just plain wrong (in *our* view). In fact, we can even blame them for their stupidity.

We know that blame is really about self-protection, and in this risk-averse, blame-obsessed system we all now live in, with children from trauma, it is no wonder that it is so prevalent. Extended family, friends and supporting professionals lacking skills, knowledge, tolerance and experience are avaricious in their hunt for a nice bit of satisfying blame. Accountability and problem-solving skills are overlooked and sidelined, as participants and observers alike rush to point their vulgar, blamey fingers at anyone who looks as if they may have made a mistake: rushing to kick the person who looks as if they may stumble.

This type of blame can be really disempowering, especially when we know that we have done nothing wrong, and that the blamer is merely uneducated.

Sometimes it feels as if others just start from the perspective that it's all your fault. It's your fault that your child is in a bad mood, it's also your fault that it's raining or it's not raining. It's your fault that you didn't anticipate your partner's every need, and it's also your fault that your child has lost their socks.

Basically, everything that has ever gone wrong ever in the entire history of the universe is deemed to be 100 per cent your fault. It all comes down to you and everybody is happy.

Except you.

Everything that goes wrong is *not* actually your fault. Sometimes shit happens. In strategies for this section, I will help you develop your therapeutic parenting thick skin, which has a built-in blame-resistant lining.

I know! Let's all just stop blaming, shall we? I will start. I am *never* going to blame anyone *ever again*…just as soon as I find out who is responsible for making all the racket that is stopping me from concentrating. So bloody thoughtless.

See strategies: Jolliness/Jauntiness (Fake), Paddington Hard-Stare, Pointy-Eyebrow Death Stare, Protecting Self, Smug Smile, Understanding, Useful Phrases

BOREDOM

Also see Drained (Feeling), Perfect Parents, Single Parenting

Oh, my days, it is so boring sometimes! Well, that's a bit of a lie – it's so boring nearly all the time. The fact that we have to keep such a strong routine means that spontaneity is a dim and distant memory, so this contributes to the monotony. Our day-to-day tedium is broken only by the latest horrific behaviour tantrum, unforeseen damage/abscondment or school exclusion.

I realize now that when I was bored, it meant things were calm. In moments of crisis, I'd look back at the boring times and wish they would return.

So, if you find yourself hankering after exciting times, be careful what you wish for.

Happy news, though! Most parents feel like this. It's nothing to do with being a parent of a child with special needs or a parent of a child from trauma. Parenting is dull. (Or maybe that was just me? If so, sorry, just skip this bit.) Of course, as a family we did have non-traumatic times full of joy, excitement and stimulation. These were few and far between, though, and mostly happened on holiday. Normally, any variety in routine tended to stem from the latest shoplifting event, resulting in a quick trip to the police station. So okay, yes that was exciting, or at least interesting as I had had no previous experience of being a 'responsible adult' for a minor under police caution. Very interesting...and at least I had a sit down with a cup of tea. Stress free? No. We can't have it both ways.

Just think of all those Perfect Parents out there. Day after day of drudgery and boredom, with no trips to the police station or school exclusions, not even any exciting meetings full of people talking crap about your child. How do people manage? What do they do to vary their days? I mean there's only so many times you can do an interested face at your child, when they are telling you the same story for the 458th time. Imagine how terrible that is for Perfect Parents. They have to look interested all the time, *forever*!

With my securely attached grandchildren, it's been so liberating! I've got new phrases like, 'The thing is though, Arthur, that's not a very interesting thing to say, is it?' Or I might say, 'We've talked about interesting things and boring things. Do you think that's an interesting thing to say or a boring thing?' This is not a strategy I could have used with my children.

My children have all left home now (yes, I know I keep saying this, I'm not rubbing it in, I promise), but my life is not boring. They are able to keep me entertained with the odd little, long-arm crisis. This makes me feel needed and wanted as a mum... And at least it's not every day now.

See strategies: Audio Books, Brain Breaks, Hysterical Playfulness, Music, Queuing, Screaming, Switching Off

BOUNDARIES

Also see Birth Family Issues, Conflicted Feelings, Doubt, Family, Friendships, Perfect Parents, PIEs

I am sure you will be relieved to know that this part is nothing to do with boundary-setting for your children. There is quite enough of that in other books. Here we need to explore how we feel, and what we do, when other people seem intent on breaching our *own* boundaries. This might happen through clumsy questioning and a mistaken assumption that, somehow, the questioner is entitled to the information, due to the status or behaviours of our children. I struggled when friends asked me intimate details about my children's early life history, particularly if the children were sitting nearby. The school also seemed to have an expectation that they should know every little detail of the children's life.

In my book *But He Looks So Normal*, I wrote a list of some of the most annoying things people said, or questions they asked. Some of them (revisited below) constitute clear boundary breaches and are often heard by therapeutic parents:

- But s/he looks so NORMAL!
- Do you have any REAL children?
- What happened to their REAL parents?
- Why are they in care?
- They should be grateful.
- I can recommend a really great parenting course! (It isn't.)
- They will grow out of it.
- All children are like that/my (securely attached) children were just the same.
- Try using time out or a reward chart.
- They need a good slap.
- Can't you just send them back?
- They won't remember anything.
- They should be settling down by now.
- Just ignore them, they'll be fine.
- They are just attention seeking.
- You are too strict, lighten up a bit.
- I bet you wish you had never 'taken them in' (as if they were wandering about outside your house one night).
- Can't you *do* something?

For me, the other way boundaries were breached was in the form of patronizing explanation. It was as if the other person believed I was not 'a real parent' and therefore they were entitled to give me unsolicited and patronizing parenting advice. This is exceptionally undermining, as often the luddites would wax lyrical about my failings in front of the children. On one occasion, for example, I was at my parents' house with my children, and I had given the children a clear instruction to eat their tea at the table. My mum (wanting to spoil her new grandchildren) overrode this instruction and told them they could sit on the floor as she was 'in charge' in her house, and they 'didn't need to listen to Mummy'. The confusion in my children's eyes gave me all the courage I needed to challenge my mum and say, 'The children will sit at the table. I am their mother.' Later, out of earshot of the children, I made it clear that she must never again undermine me in front of the children and explained why. To her credit, she never did.

These kinds of interactions are exceptionally uncomfortable. We feel an internal tug pushing us to 'keep the peace'. There is a constant feeling of conflict where we genuinely want to keep everyone happy. But when it comes down to it, we *have to* roar for our children. This can leave us in a very lonely place.

In strategies relating to this section, I have developed a table for you with useful phrases to employ in reply to the above and almost any other boundary-breaching situation. This includes those times when the school gate mafia decide it is their divine right to give you parenting advice or to ask deeply personal questions about your child.

See strategies: Managing Visits (Contact), Protecting Self, Training, Useful Phrases

 ## BRAIN BREAKS

We don't use the word 'respite', instead we have 'brain breaks'. That's what is needed. A break for your tired brain.

A brain break can range from a whole, vacant, starey-eyed week, to zoning out for a minute when a child is talking shite at you. In between that is mindfulness, meditation and more formal approaches to brain breaks. A short brain break might just consist of playing a game on your phone or focusing on something in the distance in order to take your mind away from whatever horror is unfolding in front of you.

My longest ever brain break was following a stroke. I was hospitalized for one week. I quickly regained the power of speech and felt fine, so I spent the week wandering about the hospital, chatting to other patients and visiting the café. It was pure bliss. The social workers phoning me to check why I wasn't at meetings backed off fast. And do you know what? The children were absolutely fine. They even had regular meals.

My best *ever* mini brain break was when I broke down at the side of the motorway and found that nobody could make me do anything for quite a long time. I was without children and phone signal and spent a joyous hour sitting on a crash barrier playing Candy Crush and casually wondering if a police car might help me before it got dark (but not feeling very worried if they didn't).

Following this revelation, I asked a group of therapeutic parents to give me examples of how *they* had creatively made use of a particular time to get themselves a brain break. Here's what they said:

- Being in an MRI scanner and listening to the lovely music.
- Waiting in the doctor's surgery.
- Waiting in the dentist surgery and even being in the dentist chair having treatment. (I found this one quite astonishing, but I suppose at least you can't answer your phone there.)
- 'Gardening' (hiding in the shed).
- Supermarket shopping.
- Competitive hiding during a hide and seek game.
- Going back to work and having an actual lunch break.

You can even weave in a sneaky brain break at a dull school play. If you are a lovely parent who delights in watching your child perform in the school play every year, then you can skip this bit. If, like me, you are the parent of the child who either refuses to come onto the stage (see 'Embarrassment') or is always cast as 'emergency sheep' or 'understudy fourth shepherd', then you are *fully entitled* to use the school play time as brain-break time. Here are my tried and tested tips for achieving this:

- Make sure you sit in an inconspicuous place, once eye contact has been established with your child.
- Make sure you have emptied snacks into unrustley packets so you can eat them surreptitiously.
- If possible, bring in a massive coffee or something lovely in a coffee cup. I'm not *suggesting* you bring in alcohol, and just keep in mind that you may need to drive afterwards.
- Depending on the nosiness levels of the Perfect Parents around you, you can either use ear buds under a nice hat to listen to your latest audio book or podcast, or you can play a lovely game on your phone.

You can also slip in a really quick brain break by nipping into the garden or standing outside for a moment, fixing your gaze on the furthest point, and just concentrating on that for a few seconds. Similarly, a quick 'emergency' trip to the toilet can have huge brain-break benefits, especially if you take your phone in for a read or text chat.

Me: Help!
Friend: Where are you?
Me: In the toilet.
Friend: Are you ill?
Me: No, hiding.

Pause as friend digests this. (Luckily, she is a TP friend so responds.)

Friend: How long can you get away with it? Are there screaming noises yet?
Me: Not yet, but the nonsense chatter has basically exploded my brain.
Friend: And breathe in...count to 10...and out.
Me: Okay.
Me: 😃

Me: Right, thank you. Back to the front line.

Friend: Will send chocolate.

In desperate times, I would tempt all the children into a wonderful, cortisol-powered game of 'Hide and Seek in the Dark'. During the game, I had ample opportunities to creep off into cupboards and concentrate on my breathing. As an added bonus, my children still remember these games as real highlights! Their view was, 'Mummy is playing an exciting game with us.' My experience was, 'I can escape legally for five minutes.'

There are any number of mindfulness or meditation apps and videos available to assist us with this. I have found lots of free ones on YouTube. If you have a smart speaker, you can also ask it to play some mindfulness exercises. These are quite good for when you can't actually think straight.

Naturally, this does rely on your child being absent. Full-blown 'mindfulness' can't be achieved when your child is dancing in front of you demanding more sweeties.

At the Centre of Excellence in Child Trauma, we offer a wide range of online and face-to-face events, all incorporating relaxation techniques. You can also find one that suits your timetable at The Haven Parenting and Wellbeing Centre in Gloucestershire, UK, which provides direct support and therapeutic interventions to all parents.

See strategies: Audio Books, Babysitters, Gardening, Holidays, Hot Tubs, Music, Pausing, Queuing, Reading, Shopping, Switching Off

 ## BREATHING

It is important to remember to breathe as otherwise you will die. And yes, I know that sometimes that might be an attractive thought due to the possibility of a rest, but long term it's a rubbish plan.

Breathing at the right time and in the right way will also massively help you to relax or think straight. It may even stop you doing or saying something you will regret. It is a fact that taking a deep breath has physiological effects that *really* help you to calm. That's why, in therapeutic parenting, when we speak about 'pausing' we always add in 'taking a deep breath'.

If you are faced with a shocking/surprising event (as in, more shocking than normal), just inhaling slowly through the nose, then out through the mouth, may be enough to stop the stream of swear words from exploding. When you breathe in this way, your brain starts to trigger a relax response. Basically, we are tricking our brain. 'Nothing to see here. This tin of black paint spilled all over my new kitchen is in fact a lovely addition to the decor. Everything is calm.'

See strategies: Brain Breaks, Pausing, Switching Off

C

☼ CAKE

It is a simple fact that sometimes only cake will do. Preferably big, fat, soggy, heavy cake. My favourite was from the bakers – lardy cake. I realize now it was called lardy cake because it made me lardy.

Recently, I've had to settle for hot cross buns to try to stop the weight piling back on. I can tell you now that hot cross buns are a very poor substitute indeed for thick, heavy, sugary cake.

We spend so much of our time running about (on empty usually), and sometimes feel very unappreciated or unfulfilled. When we have a nice piece of cake it feels like a 'hug in your stomach'. That's how Rosie used to describe it when I made banana cake. This was lucky, because in the early days (the Rosie Rudey days), she used to say it was like a rock in her stomach.

I always made banana cake with the children. It's really easy to make and kids have great fun mashing up all the bananas. (NB: Supervision required. Once a child mashed in another child's chalks to 'see what colour it would be'.) Not only does it sit in a nice solid way in your stomach, but it also has melatonin to promote sleep. (Okay, let's just ignore all the sugar in it which will also keep you awake.)

In times of cake emergency, I can highly recommend chocolate sandwiches – naturally you will always have chocolate in the house. Cut some French bread into sections and put in a couple of squares of chocolate. This is surprisingly tasty and takes the average person longer to eat due to the chewiness. If you only have sliced bread, then you can wrap up the chocolate and call it a Swiss roll.

If you are lucky enough to go to a National Association of Therapeutic Parents' listening circle, there is *always* lovely cake!

See strategies: Chocolate, Coffee, Essential Maintenance, Krispy Kreme Donuts, Tea (Cups of, Cream)

CATASTROPHIC THINKING

Also see Adult Children, Anxiety, Compassion Fatigue, Controlling, Eeyore Parenting, Fear (of Child), Letting Go, Overwhelm

It's an odd thing you know, but when William nipped off out to take drugs and completely stopped going to school, no amount of bubble baths would make me feel relaxed about that! Who'd have thought?

When we get into catastrophic thinking, we fall into a bog of overwhelming anxiety. It can be virtually impossible to pull our sucky feet out. The most benign incident can lead us into the swamp-land of what-ifs. Here are some examples:

He's not doing any revision
Therefore, he will fail his exams
Therefore, he won't be able to get a good job
Therefore, he won't have any money
Therefore, he will start taking drugs
Therefore, he will fall into a life of crime
Therefore, he will die in prison from drugs and alcohol abuse
Therefore, my life is over

She is late home
Therefore, she has been kidnapped
Therefore, she will get abused by sex traffickers
Therefore, she will never recover

Therefore, she may well kill herself
Therefore, my life is over

She is being rude to the teachers
Therefore, she will be excluded
Therefore, I won't be able to manage anymore
Therefore, she will have to move
Therefore, she will unravel
Therefore, I will never forgive myself
Therefore, my life is over

And so we go on…

Catastrophic thinking never ends with anything, other than the child dying (or at least ending up in prison or on drugs) and our own lives basically being damaged beyond repair. When I think back, none of the catastrophic thoughts I used to have (see above) materialized. *Now*, it's easy to realize that they weren't lying in a ditch – of course they weren't! They were on a friend's sofa playing on the PlayStation. *Now*, I remember that my children are survivors – and they're brilliant at that. *Now*, I've come to terms with the extent of what I can and can't do. But *then* I hadn't. *Then*, everything was going to end badly for everyone, forever.

Catastrophic thinking starts with anxiety, so we have to get a handle on our anxiety and work out where it comes from in order to manage the catastrophic thinking. Time is a great healer, as every time a child didn't die, I got a little bit more hopeful that they *wouldn't* die.

A lack of control as our children grow older also leads us to catastrophize minor or moderate events. There's lots of things suddenly happening which we used to be able to control and now we can't. So, the only alternative is to use all that energy in a nice bit of catastrophic thinking.

In order to manage this, we need to break down our thought

processes and apply logic. The strategies related to this section will help you with this.

See strategies: Havening, More, Natural Consequences (Allowing), One Step at a Time, Pausing, Picking Your Battles, Self-Regulation, Switching Off, Therapy (For Parents)

CATS

I think cats are takers but that's just me. I used to own five cats when I was young and all they did was stare at me and want food. However, even if you have a 'taker cat', stroking a cat does create delta waves in the brain through touch on your hands, which generates a calming effect. (Delta waves are the nice slow brain waves which we have when we fall asleep and are relaxed.)

I know lots of people who have cats that do funny things and make them laugh. For this reason alone – this little bit of lightness and joy which may come into your life – I decided to let cats have a place in strategies.

See strategies: Dogs (for real rewarding pets), Kittens

CELEBRATING

It can be very easy to forget about all those little victories that we have. That's because often the little victories are overshadowed by yet another horrific event.

We have to celebrate those small bursts of joy, because that's what keeps us going! It's a good idea to keep a written note of positives. It doesn't have to be lengthy, it can just be a note on your phone. In the notebook on my phone, I had one section of notes called Sophieisms (see 'Humour'). In this section, I would write down all the funny little things she said, until quite recently (when she was 25) and I would look at them to make myself smile.

In the same way, you can record those little positives in your life. When I had had a bad day with William, and he had been caught shoplifting yet again, it was incredibly helpful to look back at my little 'William celebrations' and recall that he had indeed been able to mend his bike and had managed to make a joke recently. These little celebrations keep us moving forwards.

It's easy to dread events which should be celebrations. I used to make sure that my expectations were always low. This meant that when the children got it right, or when something nice happened that was unexpected, it was even more meaningful. This was then written down in my little 'celebration' section.

Sometimes we might get a bit trapped in our parenting and discover just as we cautiously hope that we might be having a lovely time, or we have made a breakthrough, we immediately start doing a bit of catastrophic thinking or wondering how we will pay for it. Okay, we *might* have to pay for it but for goodness sake let's live in the moment and enjoy it just a *little bit* sometimes. We deserve it. Our children deserve it.

These days, I still count little wins. When I succeed in eating my biscuit at night, without my dog *noticing* I am eating it, this does indeed feel like a small victory for me. I don't write it down in my little celebration book as, to be honest, I haven't got 'dog celebrations' in there, but it still gives me a little smug smile that I managed to eat the whole biscuit without Stumpy noticing and staring at me to guilt trip me.

This is tiny compared to the victories I had with the children. If I stop and think about it, piece by piece, bit by bit, they changed from traumatized, desperate, sad little children into the fully functioning, well-rounded adults they are today. The only way they got there is by succeeding in a million different ways, through thousands of different days. That's a lot of celebrations to record. Perhaps we should have a party...

See strategies: Christmas Survival (and Other Celebrations), Expectations (Managing), One Step at a Time, Protecting Self, Reflecting

CHOCOLATE

Obviously. However you *want* it, however *often* you need it, just go for it!

It's well known that chocolate has that lovely feelgood factor, stimulating handy little hormones to lift you. My only words of caution here are: first, hide it. Buy yourself a chocolate safe if necessary. Whatever it takes, make sure that no one can deprive you of your special treat. Buy yourself an Easter egg. Nobody else will, or if they do they'll eat it before they can give it to you due to stress.

Second, try not to eat any an hour and a half before bedtime because it can keep you awake, so you are tired and then you need chocolate the next day. Take it from someone who learned the hard way... But one tiny little square at bedtime just to lower your cortisol levels, well, that's okay.

See strategies: Cake, Coffee, Essential Maintenance, Tea (Cups of, Cream), Vanishing Treats

CHRISTMAS SURVIVAL (AND OTHER CELEBRATIONS)

When I look back at our Christmases, they seem much better in retrospect than they were at the time. I know from our therapeutic parenting Facebook page that Christmas and other celebrations or religious festivals are often times of the year when parents struggle. Any time there has to be lots of cooking, changes in routine and presents to be bought and wrapped results in additional challenges and stresses for parents. Once you add in the trauma triggers, low self-esteem and fear-based behaviours, you have a recipe for perfect disaster.

In my book *The A–Z of Therapeutic Parenting*, I give you lots of strategies to help manage *behaviours* at celebration times, so here are my top tips to help *you personally* manage your own challenges at these times.

Don't stress about presents that the children buy (or don't buy)

One year, Sophie proudly handed my dad and brother an identical box of Ritz crackers. She had wrapped them up carefully. When they smiled at having the same gift, she proudly said, 'Buy one get one free!' She was always known for a bargain. This caused much hilarity and every year we are still on the lookout for duplicate presents. The present she got for my mum was a lavender toilet freshener. I had not seen what she had bought before she wrapped it up, and it made me cry with laughter. Sophie was indignant. 'What's the problem? Granny likes lavender, you said.'

Read *The Very Wobbly Christmas*

I wrote *The Very Wobbly Christmas* a few years ago. This is a children's story and a culmination of all the problems and difficulties that can face us at this time of year. Everything in it is true, from horrendous school plays and activities to the destruction of presents on Christmas Day due to feelings of low self-worth. Reading this book with children helps them to regulate and helps *you* to anticipate what might be coming and to mitigate that.

Do what *you* want

If there is an expectation to visit family, and you know it will be a bloodbath, do not go. No one can make you; you are a grown-up. You can make different arrangements to go later, or at a different time. You can even split the family and go at separate times. *Now* is the time to put to one side all those ridiculous expectations about how we all have to fit in and behave like every other Fakebook family. Now, we do what we *need to do* to get through this time and ensure that our children manage to get through to the other side without having a major meltdown.

Get something for *you*

I recently discovered the most brilliant way to make sure I got the present I wanted. I ordered it off Amazon about three months before Christmas and made sure it arrived gift wrapped. I then put it away with the other presents. Once Christmas arrived, I had nearly always forgotten what I had bought and was delighted with the present. This ensured that I always had one thoughtful present for me. Now, I'm not saying that others didn't make an effort – they did – but I was always the winner.

Wrap presents prior

Get presents off eBay or any other second-hand site. This is great as they are usually no longer in boxes. Also, they cost loads less, so you don't mind so much if they get 'mislaid' or 'accidentally broken'.

Put in all the batteries and wrap them up as soon as you get them. This saves the horrific and lengthy wine-fogged tasks at 1am on Christmas Day morning.

Eat dinner out

If at all possible, go out for dinner. You deserve it. So what if there is a bit of arguing and fighting? There will be no washing up and it will take up most of the day.

Avoid school plays

No one should have to sit through a school play if:

- you have seen it before
- you have a million other things to do

- your child does not want to be involved and refuses to come out.

You can use the strategies in Brain Breaks to get through the play. Or maybe your child needs an emergency day off?

Avoid present dejection

Look, it's simple. Your children *think* they want that particular present, but they almost certainly want you to get it for them more than the actual item. Five minutes after they own it, they won't want to anymore. As long as you prepare yourself for this and do not expect to be rewarded with smiles of joy for the next six months, you should be okay. Get what you think is *right* for the children. What *they need* is different from what *they want*. Obviously, there will be chocolate and that always takes the edge off anyway. I always used to make sure I got one present that was going to give *me* some free time. Whatever it cost, it was worth it.

See strategies: Alcohol, Brain Breaks, Cake, Chocolate, Essential Maintenance, Expectations (Managing), Protecting Self

 COFFEE

There is one thing I do not understand. Why did they invent decaffeinated coffee? I mean, what is the point? You can't be a therapeutic parent and not have caffeine. Well, you can, but you would be so tired you would be like a slug dragging yourself along the floor.

Coffee can be our lovely treat. There's something quite nurturing about a big, fat, heavy cup of milky coffee. When we team that up with the cake it can keep us going for hours!

When I used to live in Paris, I would go into a café and ask for a coffee, and then almost need to replace the lining in my mouth when I took a sip. I now know as a therapeutic parent that this is the kind of coffee that keeps you going. The essential petrol to your engine.

See strategies: Cake, Chocolate, Essential Maintenance, Tea (Cups of, Cream)

COMPASSION FATIGUE

Also see Disempowerment, Eeyore Parenting,
Essential Maintenance, Overwhelm

Nowadays, many therapeutic parents and supporting professionals are familiar with the term 'compassion fatigue' in relation to parents caring for children from trauma. A large part of this may be due to the research I undertook with the Hadley Centre at Bristol University in 2016, entitled 'No One Told Us It Would Be Like This'.[1]

Compassion fatigue is a fancy title for feeling exhausted and disconnected from your child. It's different from depression in my experience. If I am speaking to a parent who has compassion fatigue, they will normally be quite positive and animated when talking about anything unrelated to the child. If the parent is depressed, there is an apathy and a general hopelessness concerning everything.

So how do you know if you have compassion fatigue? It often starts with the feeling of needing to distance yourself from the child. Our brains are good at protecting us, and when there is relentless stress there is a physiological change in the brain to try to relieve that stress. This is why a common way we can identify compassion fatigue is when a parent describes the feelings of dread they experience when they see or hear the child approaching.

Before I understood compassion fatigue, I just thought I had

---

1   Ottoway, H. & Selwyn, J. (2016) 'No One Told Us It Would Be Like This: Compassion Fatigue and Foster Care.' University of Bristol, UK.

turned into a monster parent. I didn't understand where my love had gone. If you have compassion fatigue, life looks pretty hopeless. You don't want to spend time with the child concerned and you can't find empathy for them even though you know you should. Take heart, you have not turned into a monster parent, your brain is just doing its job. Once you have identified the fact that you do indeed have compassion fatigue, and taken action to remedy that, balance will be restored.

A lot of the work we do at the Centre of Excellence in Child Trauma is around educating social workers and professionals who support therapeutic parents. We train them to recognize the symptoms of compassion fatigue. Too often, the understanding isn't there, and, instead, parents who have compassion fatigue find themselves blamed and judged for the feelings they are experiencing. Of course, we must hold the child at the centre of our thoughts, but almost always the best outcome is for the child and the parents to work through the compassion fatigue and to re-establish connections.

Occasionally people will also talk about 'secondary trauma', or 'blocked care', in relation to compassion fatigue. Secondary trauma, in this context, will normally be referring to the feelings a parent or carer has of being traumatized by the experiences of the child, and/or their resulting behaviours. Blocked care relates to the physiological changes in the brain of the parent who has compassion fatigue and is unable to access empathy.

If you are struggling to get a supporting professional to understand what you are experiencing, and you are worried that people may be making hasty decisions rather than helping you to exit compassion fatigue, you can refer them to *The A–Z of Therapeutic Parenting Professional Companion: Practical Tools for Proactive Practice*. This contains some great step-by-step practical tools which supporting professionals can use to tackle difficult behaviours and to resolve compassion fatigue. No prior learning is necessary.

See strategies: Babysitters, Brain Breaks, Dogs, Empathic Listening, Essential Maintenance, Forgiving Yourself, Havening, Holidays, One Step at a Time, Protecting Self, Routine, Self-Regulation, Space, Switching Off, Therapy (For Parents), Understanding, Walking, Zones

CONFLICTED FEELINGS

Also see Bad Days, Birth Family Issues, Catastrophic Thinking, Grief, Guilt, Kindness, Letting Go, Overwhelm, Refereeing

Sometimes, people who are going to adopt or foster, or even parents about to have their first baby, ask me what it's like to be a parent. The problem is, when you are in the non-parent club, you are standing on one side of a chasm. The day your child is born (or your children come home), you have crossed the chasm in one fell leap, never to return. No amount of discussion or explanation can help the non-parent to comprehend the parent side of the chasm, before they leap... And once they have crossed, they are similarly prevented from accurately conveying this change to their non-parent friends. The non-parent has high expectations, hope, positivity and joy in their heart. That's not to say that some of that might remain once they have crossed the parenting chasm, but these feelings now have to live alongside disappointment, fear, guilt and anxiety. This is what gives us conflicted feelings.

The feelings that our children can provoke in us at times can be very strong, conflicting and confusing. We may feel guilty and overwhelmed by these feelings. They preoccupy us and we worry that we are not good enough, not worthy of our children. It's normal to have conflicted feelings because our unique children can drive us to distraction! If we did not feel conflicted, that would mean there was no care there at all.

On a logical level, we know it is not their fault, but on an emotional level, if we have poured our heart and soul into getting a child to where they need to be and then they reject us or behave in relentlessly exhausting ways, it can be soul destroying.

At times, we may feel regret that we chose the path we did. This regret might be profound and then there's a ton of guilt with that. How could we think that way? What is wrong with us? These children deserve more, surely? What kind of person does this make me? We start looking at the choices we made, the impact that has had on others and on ourselves. Can we turn the clock back? Did we do the right thing for us, for the child, for our family?

No one can know the answers to these questions. Only time will tell.

While it's true that our children deserve our best, we are only human. There are only so many times that you can be pushed down before you *stay* down.

Sometimes our conflicted feelings relate to loss around the child we *thought* we were going to have and the child that we have ended up with. Whether this is a birth child with additional needs, or an adopted or fostered child, the feelings are similar. I know that when I adopted my children, I remember looking at my youngest as a baby, and thinking, 'Who are you?' I genuinely felt confused as to why I had not immediately fallen in love with her. But do you know what? That's pretty normal. It takes time to get to know a child, and sometimes it can take years for these feelings to adjust and readjust until we come to a conclusion within ourselves.

One of the things that helped me to cope was to always be aware of how I was behaving. The way I *felt* was kept to myself, and I behaved in a loving and caring way no matter what. This can help alleviate the guilt.

Occasionally, our conflicted feelings are on a much smaller scale, but worrying nevertheless. For example, if you have a child who is following you around, you know she is anxious, you know she needs to know where you are. This doesn't help you to stop feeling annoyed! It is a trigger for you. This trigger creates the conflict. The heart doesn't seem very interested in what the head knows.

In the early days of fostering and adoption, therapeutic parents may have very strong conflicting feelings. We might even feel as if we've been duped somehow! Don't worry, this is normal. Early on it might be that the children seem very compliant and 'easy', so when this changes, we may be left feeling as if we've been tricked, or we somehow missed something. We might feel as if we've made a mistake and we've overestimated our abilities. This is not the case. This is normal. Just keep going, reassure yourself that this is okay. The best way to help yourself through these times is to be very aware in the early days and to understand that the children are likely to be in survival mode. Kindness is the key – to yourself and to them.

In the same way, a child who is very anxious and 'fake smiles' or uses nonsense chatter as a way to keep themselves at the forefront of your thoughts can make you recoil emotionally at times. This is a natural, physiological response. It can be really hard to conceal that, and people on the outside do not see the impact of this behaviour, adding a bit of blame and criticism to your already bruised heart.

Some of the hardest conflicts to deal with are when we are re-parenting the child of one of *our* children. The dichotomy here is real and instinctual. Special guardians and kinship carers are frequently grandparents who have stepped in to care for a child when the parent cannot or will not. There may be pressures around visiting and parenting styles, and loyalties are swiftly divided. This often leaves the therapeutic parent in the role of a referee. This is not a comfortable place to be when you are trying to do the right thing for so many others.

In the strategies relating to this section, I explain how you can remove some of these triggers and help you to resolve your conflicted feelings.

See strategies: Brain Breaks, Dogs, Empathic Listening, Essential Maintenance, Forgiving Yourself, Havening, Jolliness/Jauntiness (Fake), Managing Visits (Contact), Natural Consequences

(Allowing), One Step at a Time, Protecting Self, Self-Regulation, Space, Therapy (For Parents), Triggers (Managing), Understanding, Walking, Zones

CONTROLLING

Also see Acceptance, Anxiety, Bad Days, PIEs

Okay, let's face it, we can all be a bit control freaky at times. Looking after children with additional needs or children from trauma can make us feel out of control. Life becomes unpredictable. When we wake up in the morning we don't necessarily know if we will go back to bed that night in the same state of mind! To be honest, there were days when I woke up in one place and didn't even know if we would be going back to sleep in the same beds!

Many of our children need very structured lives. It was never my plan to have meals timed to the nanosecond, but my children's needs demanded it. It wasn't that they were shouting at me and threatening me, it was just that life was much easier when things were predictable for them. This kind of thing means that to the outside world, we look controlling.

Unfortunately, it's really easy for that to be the thin end of the wedge, and as things feel more and more difficult, we start controlling more and more tiny things. This is exacerbated by the fact that many of our children are also controlling due to fear.

Sometimes it's useful to stop and think about where our need to control comes from. Is it due to our own fears for our children or for our own mental health? Is it because life is simply easier? There's a real dichotomy here. As the therapeutic parent you need to be the unassailable safe base. That means you're in control. Therefore, if one of the things you are worrying about is that you are too controlling, then stop and think what would happen if you were not in control. What would life look like? My guess is it would look like chaos.

The strategies in this section will help you to feel in control – to the extent that you need to be – for your family. It's not another thing you need to feel guilty about – you all have quite enough of that already.

See strategies: Brain Breaks, Expectations (Managing), Losing Things, Natural Consequences (Allowing), One Step at a Time, Pausing, Picking Your Battles, Routine, Self-Regulation, Timesavers

 ## CO-REGULATION

What is co-regulation? I think of it as 'everybody calming down'. Co-regulation is all about *appearing* calm (and then becoming calm; see 'Self-Regulation') to inspire calm and confidence in others. It is a skill we develop over the years.

My pinnacle triumph in co-regulation happened while trying to reassure my eccentric, often dysregulated friend Sarah Dillon that all was completely fine, while I was in mortal danger. Sarah spent a great deal of her childhood in foster care and is now a skilled attachment therapist. We work closely together and are very familiar with each other's strengths and weaknesses. While we were delivering conferences in the USA, Sarah was frequently dysregulated due to changes in routine, differences in expectations and changing plans. We expected this, and my job was to be the 'unassailable safe base'. I used co-regulation frequently to demonstrate that 'all was well' even if I was a bit worried that it might not be. Everything was always 'fine', everything was always 'under control', and I only had to shout at her once... But to be fair that *was* to stop us crashing on the motorway, so I think that was reasonable.

We were staying with our hostess Sonia, in Alabama. The place we were staying was very beautiful and surrounded by lakes. On Sonia's birthday, she said she would like us to go out on the lake in a boat with her. This sounded like a lovely idea.

At the appointed hour, I decided at the last minute to wear my brightly coloured trainers. I am very glad I made this decision in retrospect. Sonia arrived with the two-month-old baby she was currently looking after as he was joining us on the boat trip.

The first hurdle we had to overcome was getting Sarah *on* the boat. The boat moves at about 5mph and was on a calm flat lake, but Sarah announced that she had a fear of boats, exacerbated by the 'Warning! Crocodiles in Lake' sign at the edge of the lake. Much demonstrating of the calm flatness of the water and anecdotes of friendly crocodiles were necessary.

Initially, all went quite well. We had a lovely, serene, sunset boat ride, and the baby only cried a little bit. Sarah eventually stopped freaking out after much 'unassailable safe basing' in tandem from me and Sonia. It should have been the perfect end to a perfect day. Unfortunately, this was not to be.

As we approached the jetty, in the dark, Sonia told me I needed to jump off the boat and attach the rope to the jetty. Now, those of you who know me will know that I'm not likely to be famous for my light-footed jumping abilities. Not wishing to appear too worried, I agreed and got ready to make the small step onto the jetty.

As I jumped, the boat seemed to move backwards and I suddenly found myself with one leg on the jetty, one leg on the boat and both moving apart at a rapid pace. Naturally, I instantly fell into the water and went right under the lake. Under the water, I had three immediate thoughts.

1. This is surprisingly warm.
2. My phone is in my bra.
3. There are crocodiles and probably snakes in here.

I surfaced, laughing, to find Sonia standing on the jetty also laughing but the boat floating away with Sarah and the baby still on board. Sarah had frozen to the spot and was saying, 'This isn't funny.' I realized that Sarah would not move about in the boat, was not by the steering wheel and would just keep floating away. Through gasps of laughter, Sonia asked me to try to grab the rope trailing off the boat and drag it back to the jetty. I thought, 'Okay, I'll just do everything then. Drown, get boat, pull boat back to shore, calm Sarah down, avoid crocodiles.' It was quite difficult to remain upbeat.

As I pulled the boat in, I realized I was probably going to be crushed to death between the boat and the jetty, so I quickly chucked the rope to Sonia and swam out.

Sarah managed to get off the boat, but by now I had realized I could not get out of the crocodile-infested lake. There was no ladder, it was pitch black and I had three helpers. One was laughing so much I thought she might actually die, the other was on the verge of hysterical anger, pacing up and down telling us it wasn't funny (while holding the baby), and the third *was* the baby. I felt I might need to get out of the situation myself. (Sarah has asked me to insert here that she *did* manage to get the baby to stop crying. This was nice, as my drowning became a bit more relaxing.)

Sonia then went round identifying lots of helpful exit points. All of them required the strength of a burly man to lever me out. No burly men were available, so I decided to try to head for four separate sets of high steps along the pier.

The crocodile thought *did* keep coming into my head, but I knew it was at the top of Sarah's catastrophic thinking list, so I decided to ignore it. I *thought* I heard Sarah say, 'Nothing can happen to Sarah Naish. Who will I do conferences with?' But I am sure I misheard with all the water and boat noises.

By the time I got to the fourth set of high steps in my attempt to get out, I was a bit tired. I pulled myself up, landed heavily on my side and felt a rib crack before sliding back into the water with a screech. Sarah immediately tipped over into screaming hysterics, deciding that a crocodile had got me and I was going to die. As I was finding it difficult to breathe now (due to my cracked rib), I just managed to gasp that 'everything was fine', and I had 'just trodden on something'. This meant that Sarah calmed down again, and the baby was safe. Phew!

I jauntily explained that I would be 'swimming straight to the shore now, no more mucking about'. I had been in the water 20 minutes and the novelty was wearing off now. In my head, the crocodiles were surely drawing closer with all this screaming, splashing and falling back into the water. In order to get to the shore, I needed to get through yucky, sinky mud-sand, rife with snakes. This was when I was very glad to still be wearing trainers. Sarah helped enormously by catastrophically announcing in relation to the:

- number of snakes near the shore
- likelihood of approaching crocodiles
- continuing need for a burly man
- fact that this was not funny. (Sonia obviously disagreed with this as she was still almost unconscious with laughter.)

Eventually I rocketed over the last few feet to shore, after feeling 'something alive' move under my feet. I was greeted by Sonia, armed with camera, ready to take some lovely photos and thanking me profusely (through her tears of laughter) for giving her the 'best birthday ever'.

Yeah. Thanks for that.

Later, when Sarah realized I had broken my ribs she asked, 'Why didn't you say anything?' I asked her what she thought would have happened if I had. She said, 'I would have gone hysterical!' I was very impressed that obviously she had not reached her height of dysregulation. See? Co-regulation every time. And because I was keeping Sarah calm, I hardly thought about the danger I was in. I did later, but then the crocodiles couldn't get me.

We know as therapeutic parents we have to 'fake it till we make it'. The great thing about acting calmly in order to keep your children calm is that you *do* actually start to feel calm. There's a lot to be said for taking a second and sitting down under a tree, looking at the patterns and just breathing for a few moments. When our children see us behaving in a calm way, they will feel less anxious.

I always found it really useful to think 'air steward'. You know how you're on a plane and you're a bit worried that something might be going wrong with the plane? Well, we tend to look at the air stewards to see if their faces look worried. They nearly always look completely serene and calm. They are either faking it or maybe the plane is not crashing after all. Practise your calm face in the mirror. Practise breathing slowly so that your child notices. Trust me, they *do* see these things.

As we get better at pausing in therapeutic parenting strategies, so we get better at co-regulation, calming down and calming others. It is just practice. Using our strategies around pausing and self-regulation can assist with this skill.

See strategies: Essential Maintenance, Hot Tubs, Pausing, Self-Regulation

CRITICISM

Also see Blame, Doubt, Family, Inadequacy, Perfect Parents, PIEs, Schools

What's the difference between blame and criticism?

Well, blame is: 'Your child is very naughty because *you* don't have good enough boundaries.' Criticism is: 'Have you ever thought of toughening up your boundaries a little bit?' ('Yes I had, right after I thought about kicking you out of my house.')

If you think about it, a whole market has been created from our need to be critical or dissatisfied. Customer services departments employ thousands of people. Really, they are the Criticism Management Department, or the Office for Blame Avoidance and Reallocation. I wouldn't want to work there. A place where we *ask* for feedback, but don't really want it (not if it's just negative moaning).

Nor do I want 'constructive criticism'. How many people have said to you, 'I hope you don't mind...a little bit of constructive criticism...', then gone on to trash your parenting? Well yes, I do mind, actually. Shut up. That's not 'constructive criticism'. How is that even a thing? It's like saying 'polite rudeness'.

Criticism is subtle and weaves its way into the most benign of conversations. Sometimes it's a constant thread running through our relationships. Examples of criticism masquerading as pseudo helpful comments might be:

- Oh, you let the children choose their own clothes do you? That's interesting!
- You *are* brave! I could never allow my children to do *that*.
- Would you like a fact sheet about how to do a healthy packed lunch? You might find it *very* useful.
- We gave William extra for his lunch today, because he said he was very hungry. (This is usually accompanied by raised eyebrows.)
- Did you notice that your child has socks that don't match? How *funny*!

This kind of criticism can make us doubt ourselves. We may worry about what other people think, or just become hugely irritated listening to the 'patronizing wisdom' of others, often with *no clue whatsoever*.

Sometimes it feels as if there's a sliding scale. Criticism from family members can be harder to take, but easier to deal with, than criticism from supporting professionals. I mean, let's face it, with family we can just swear at them and storm out if we want to.

There is often a direct correlation between what we *think* the criticizer should know, and what they are saying. We might feel less inclined to dismiss the criticism of someone who we believe is normally wise, knows a lot about the subject and usually has our best interests at heart. Conversely (and reluctantly), we may *have* to give added weight or thought if the criticizer has a great deal of power or influence over our lives, or our children's lives – even if we know them to be an idiot.

We need to think about what *our instincts* are telling us and what has worked for us in the past. Speaking to other therapeutic parents and skilled supporting professionals is the most powerful antidote to criticism.

Criticism from others is one thing, but speaking to parents, I find the most powerful critic is *ourselves*. We constantly worry about if we did this properly or if we did enough. This can lead us to doubt everything about what we are doing and paves a destructive pathway – a pathway we need to step off.

See strategies: Jolliness/Jauntiness (Fake), Paddington Hard-Stare, Picking Your Battles, Pointy-Eyebrow Death Stare, Protecting Self, Smug Smile, Understanding, Useful Phrases

CRYING

Also see Compassion Fatigue, Grief, Overwhelm

We can spend an awful lot of time trying *not* to cry. Crying is a symptom of many things. It can be an expression of our anger, sadness or grief. I like that saying about 'anger being the overcoat of sadness'. We know with our children that when they cry, their anger often reduces. The same is true for us; we might find that after a good cry our anger vanishes or diminishes. In the long term, that's much healthier.

Sometimes we worry about crying in front of our children. I think it's important to put this in context. Obviously, if we're walking round making wailing noises with lots of snivelling and snot running down our face, not only is it not a good look but the children are unlikely to consider us an 'unassailable safe base'. Many a time I rushed off to the loo to have a good weep, and then came out saying I needed to take a hayfever tablet.

It's not that we're not entitled to cry. We are! Our lives are difficult, frustrating and sad at times, but we have to be careful how many of those feelings we share. At times, modelling appropriate crying is beneficial to our children. After all, what will they think of us if we do not show sadness when a very sad event has happened? How will they learn to show their sad feelings and understand when it is okay to do so? We don't need to conceal these sad moments from them.

It is a fact crying can make us feel better, but I always found it better to just keep going and have one massive cry in private later on. Although it was tiring, it was also cathartic and cleansing.

See strategies: Cakes, Dogs, Essential Maintenance, Pausing, Protecting Self, Screaming, Self-Regulation, Space, Swearing

D

 DANCING (MAD DANCING)

If you are having a difficult conversation with someone who is stressing you out, do some dancing. This keeps your cortisol and adrenaline lower and enables you to think straight. Now, I do realize that if you are in the middle of a meeting with a social worker and you suddenly leap up and start throwing some moves, eyebrows will be raised and 'assessments' started. If, however, you 'suddenly need to stretch your bad back', you can get away with any number of weird contortions, while continuing to (technically) be present in the conversation.

Recently, I was subjected to a very trying sermon from one of my adult children. I knew it was going to be difficult, and long, so I set the scene. I made sure that the table was set outside and lots of food was available. I had just enough alcohol to loosen my moves and numb the pain of the shite I had to listen to. As she started declaring all her latest excruciating nonsense I said, 'Ooh I haven't done all my steps yet.' I then leaped up, told Alexa to play 'Sarah's dance list' and I appeared to listen carefully, while actually losing myself in some happy sounds of the 1980s. After an hour, I had done 10,000 steps, she thought I had listened without interruption and with interest (I hadn't), and we were all slightly drunk.

Using 'mad dancing' is great fun for us and has the added bonus of helping the children to self-regulate fast. For some reason, when

I started doing little dances in public, my children didn't like it very much and never encouraged me.

*See strategies: **Hysterical Playfulness, Music, Self-Regulation***

DIAGNOSES

Also see Asking for Help, Boundaries, Catastrophic Thinking, Eeyore Parenting, PIEs, Top Trump Parenting

As therapeutic parents, we can get obsessed with diagnoses. I have seen so many parents on our Therapeutic Parenting Facebook group having a little competition about how many diagnoses their child has. Stop it, step away.

A diagnosis is only useful if it is:

- accurate
- timely
- helpful in unlocking resources.

A diagnosis does not define or limit our children, but it might help *us* as parents to understand why certain things are happening, and handily relieves a bit of guilt ('Phew! I didn't miss the fact that he was deaf, he is dissociating').

If you are feeling weighed down and worried about your child's diagnosis, fearful for their future, remember that nothing is set in stone. Therapeutic parenting helps us to overcome what can feel like insurmountable odds, and my children are living proof of that.

*See strategies: **One Step at a Time, Training, Useful Phrases***

DISAPPOINTMENT

Also see Birthdays, Conflicted Feelings, Forgotten, Unappreciated

I used to spend a great deal of time thinking about and organizing fun days out and treats for the children. I quickly discovered that 'fun days out' usually consisted of:

- lengthy journeys, in traffic jams with a car full of arguing children
- lengthy queueing with whining children having toilet accidents
- picnics on tiny patches of grass, with wasps and flies triggering hysteria in children, with lunch consisting of emergency Tesco shopping, wolfed down and simultaneously criticized
- punch-ups in the back of the car on the way home.

I quickly worked out that the 'treat level' was in direct correlation to the 'retribution' level, as the table below demonstrates:

Trip to park	Low-level arguing. Some toilet accidents. Some whining. Some wandering off.
Trip to restaurant	Tension about what to wear, with low-level sulking. Bored moaning in the restaurant. Laughing rudely at other diners. Gorging on dessert. Kicking each other under table. Punch-up in car on way home.
UK mini-break	Multiple attempts to sabotage chances of them going, including burglary. Eating too much food to make themselves sick on journey out. Multiple incidents of arguing, fighting and moaning. Toilet accidents which weren't accidents. Some wandering off on to beach, creating full-blown lifeguard alert. Arguing with each other at night due to the thinness of caravan walls.

Holiday to Disneyland	Most of previous row plus:
	Refusing to go into Disneyland due to there being people in costumes.
	Nearly drowning in pool, twice.
	Being held by police in Orlando airport due to 'running away swearing incident'.
	Child locking self in toilet at transition airport due to being told they had to wear a vest.
	Constant, relentless arguing during travel.

Even when we understand about *why* our children sabotage, the effect on us can still make us feel as if there is no point in bothering. It *is* so disappointing! It's also tempting to say, 'Right, well you ruined that, so we won't be doing that again!' Be careful about this. Try not to let your own disappointment spill out into a futile consequence which is likely to stop you having a nice time in the future.

See strategies: Christmas Survival (and Other Celebrations), Expectations (Managing), Holidays, Natural Consequences (Allowing), Pausing, Picking Your Battles, Protecting Self, Useful Phrases

DISEMPOWERMENT

Also see Allegations/False Allegations, Anger, Blame, Criticism, Forgotten, Frustration, Letting Go, Overwhelm, PIEs, Rejection, Resilience

A very familiar feeling for therapeutic parents is that of being disempowered. We have often done lots of research on what needs to happen for our children. When that is ignored, or we are patronized, it can be infuriating and terrifying. The day a social worker told me they 'didn't believe in attachment disorder' when I was trying to get help for my son made me literally feel as if I was physically falling. I had nowhere else to go. Nowhere to turn and I was being hung out to dry...by an absolute idiot.

It is more infuriating because we are pretty sure we have it right. We have done the training, read the books, studied the history, the reports and the documents. Then a 'PIE' (Patronizing Ignorant Expert) comes along. Because they do not want to put the effort in, or reveal their incompetence, some disempowering 'im-propaganda' is called for.

It can feel like gaslighting too. Gaslighting is defined by Relate as: 'a term that refers to trying to convince someone they're wrong about something even when they aren't. Most commonly, it takes the form of frequently disagreeing with someone or refusing to listen to their point of view.'

There may be no *intention* to coerce or undermine, but the fact is that therapeutic parents are often surrounded by 'experts' with varying degrees of skill and knowledge. I explain more about this in 'PIEs'.

What you need is one person – one person who gets it, who knows you are not going mad, and that you are talking sense. That one person can help you to link up with others and feel that sense of relief. 'Phew! I knew my child was going through that!'

Once you have been validated, it's much easier to push back and insist that you are listened to.

At the National Association of Therapeutic Parents, we join parents up together and link them with experts in the field. This can be really helpful for getting through difficult meetings or accessing resources which have been refused. If this is what you are experiencing at the moment, have a look at the help you can access.[2] You do not need to be alone.

See strategies: Empathic Listening, Essential Maintenance, Havening, One Step at a Time, Picking Your Battles, Protecting Self, Screaming, Useful Phrases

---

2   www.naotp.com

DISORGANIZED

Also see Overwhelm

We sometimes feel as if we are always rushing, losing things and just feeling generally disorganized. No time, always hurrying...

Therapeutic parents are often some of the most organized people I have ever met. Prepared for every eventuality, a bottomless Mary Poppins' carpet bag stuffed full of emergency items:

- Wet wipes
- Walkie talkie
- Drawing items for unexpected boredom
- Half a packet of biscuits in case of emergency stranding
- Last week's banana (black).

It's this last item that makes us look and feel disorganized. That isn't very fair, as we did such a good job with all the other items.

Sometimes the disorganization is absolutely not our fault. When I was travelling back from Florida with all the children, I did not know that Charley had repacked her flight bag. I did not know that instead of useful spare clothing and cuddly teddy, her overnight bag now consisted of headless Barbies and a cocktail shaker. So I'm sure that to the other passengers on the plane I looked very disorganized. But I *had been* organized. I had packed it properly myself, but my efforts had been sabotaged – yet again.

Looking back now, I don't think I was particularly disorganized, or at least no more than any other parent. I think we get to a point where we ask ourselves, 'How much do we care about it? Does it matter if they are wearing unmatching socks? Has anyone ever actually died due to not wearing a vest?' After all, the level of organization versus disorganization is only in the mind, and in the judgement of others (or our perception of that).

It's useful to think about how much the disorder matters if nobody notices it. Forgetfulness is only a problem if it causes you difficulties. I mean getting to school without the PE kit is not a big deal to be honest. They are not going to do PE anyway, if they can help it. In fact, you might even have done them a favour! But getting to a picnic and forgetting the actual picnic, yes, that could be problematic depending on how far away the nearest Tesco is.

In the 'X-ing Out (Crossing Out)' strategy in this book, I share the easy organization system I use, which means nothing is ever forgotten (at least not accidentally).

And yes, I did once walk to the school wearing my slippers, and I received a few funny looks. It's this kind of thing that helps us to build resilience and creativity. I stretched my socks over the top and pretended they were plimsolls. No harm done whatsoever, and the perfect school gate parents didn't speak to me in any case...

See strategies: Losing Things, Protecting Self, Routine, Tech Control, Timesavers, X-ing Out (Crossing Out)

 ## DOGS

I do understand that some people don't like dogs. I find this remark-able, but I have *evidence* of it. My mum wouldn't let me have a dog when I was a child, and my brother refuses to visit because I have dogs. I *do* have a sign on my front door that says, 'Dogs Welcome, People Tolerated', but people still keep visiting without dogs. What is more surprising is that my mum continues to visit, remarking every single time how annoying it is that I have dogs. Well, if she'd have let me have one or two when I was a child, maybe I wouldn't have so many now! I do tell her this, but she chooses to ignore it.

Since early adulthood I have owned many dogs, peaking at seven. Simultaneously. For this reason, I live in the woods and my whole life is geared around the best life for the dogs (now my children have left home naturally).

Why are dogs so important to me, to many of us in fact?

Well, dogs have the ability to *give back* when no one else can. When you are caring for children who are *unable* to reciprocate, your dog will be there, just waiting to make you smile, laugh and to warm your heart. My dogs would greet me with overwhelming joy, totally eclipsing the five sullen little faces, demanding to know when tea would be ready. We know that the bond between humans and dogs can be very powerful, creating and stimulating oxytocin and also having positive effects on our ever-spiralling cortisol levels.[3] (Oxytocin is the feelgood 'love' hormone, while cortisol runs at high levels when we are stressed.) This makes for a very different relationship with dogs from that with other animals. It is a rewarding, reciprocal relationship.

When my children were young, I would obviously be giving them a lot of my time, energy and attention. There were many days when I felt I had nothing left to give. At these times, I would take the dogs for a walk, play with them, or just sit quietly with one of them on my lap, stroking their little head. The healing that happens in our hearts when we allow this little spell of calm should not be underestimated.

Dogs also help us to create and keep to a routine. It's very difficult to decide not to go for a walk when a dog sits and stares at you resentfully all night. It's easier just to quickly go. Walking with dogs is also very therapeutic and grounding – the rhythm, the change of scene, the opportunity to think outside the house. Sometimes my dogs had lots of walks... (see 'Walking').

One of the other benefits of dogs, which I had overlooked, was the healing it gave to my children when they used to spend time speaking to the dogs. When Rosie was unable to make any relationships with adults, she learned to make a relationship with one of the dogs. As she noticed that this dog trusted me and loved me, so her own attachment grew. It was easier and quicker for me to get

3   Gee, N.R., Rodriguez, K.E., Fine, A.H. & Trammell, J.P. (2021) 'Dogs supporting human health and well-being: A biopsychosocial approach.' *Frontiers of Veterinary Science*, 8. doi: 10.3389/fvets.2021.630465.

the children sitting calmly, stroking a dog, 'to help Pogo feel happier because she was sad', than it was for me to dedicate ten minutes of parental presence while the tea burned.

I know that some therapeutic parents have issues about animal cruelty with their children. In my book *The A–Z of Therapeutic Parenting*, I give you strategies for this. Our pets and our children deserve our very best care.

See strategies: Cats, Co-Regulation, Kittens, Routine, Self-Regulation, Views, Walking

DOUBT

Also see Asking for Help, Boundaries, Catastrophic Thinking, Conflicted Feelings, Criticism, Inadequacy (Feelings of), Perfect Parents, PIEs

I approached the adoption of my children with the confidence of a puppy, bounding towards a fun game with a loving owner... Within one year, the Confidence Dog was overdue a visit to the vets to cross the Rainbow Bridge.

Confidence can be hard to catch once it starts to slope off. The enthusiasm and certainty we start off with seeps away when Fat Doubt joins the party, making itself comfortable, spreading out and blocking confidence.

Sometimes we seem to be surrounded by people who are *sure* they know a lot more than we do about our child! They don't have any Fat Doubt, but they are masters at creating it in others, crushing confidence in one fell swoop. The blame and judgement we are subjected to from others helps to erode our confidence, so I used to pretend that I had a force field around me and imagined the barbs, cruel comments and stupid, undermining 'advice' bouncing off the shield.

As our knowledge grows and we start seeing the results we need, our own confidence grows too. Confidence becomes a bit more settled, developing a nice bit of middle-aged spread to push Fat Doubt out of the way. The difficulty is that this can be a long time coming. We may be waiting for a very long time, years even, to see the results of our therapeutic parenting. At these times, we must keep looking forwards to the distant horizon – over the top of Fat Doubt's head.

That's why we have to fake it till we make it! If you show a lack of confidence to your children, you know they will eat you alive! They are watching your every move just in case you show doubt, worry or hesitation. So even if you're not *feeling* confident, practise it. Practise that confident, Mary Poppins, self-satisfied nod in the mirror.

Finding our confidence happens at the same time as we find our own self-belief. It's about readjusting our expectations, educating ourselves about our rights and our children's rights, and then standing up for those rights.

I didn't want to be a Warrior Parent, but Fat Doubt had to be vanquished somehow...

See strategies: Expectations (Managing), Jolliness/Jauntiness (Fake), One Step at a Time, Paddington Hard-Stare, Pointy-Eyebrow Death Stare, Training, Useful Phrases

DRAINED (FEELING)

Also see Boredom, Compassion Fatigue, Eeyore Parenting, Exhaustion, Forgotten, Rejection, Resilience, Unappreciated

You know you are feeling drained when you wake up in the morning already feeling as if you can't possibly go on. It's when the very last shred of mental energy slips out of your body, slithers along the floor and out of the door. You don't even have the interest to try and catch it.

When we feel drained, it may be in addition to the feeling of *physical* exhaustion. It's quite possible to have physical energy but be mentally drained simultaneously. I often woke up with physical energy for the tasks ahead but lacked the mental energy or enthusiasm for the tasks. The relentlessness of our daily grind is the main contributor to our mood depletion.

In the training we run at the Centre of Excellence in Child Trauma, we often talk about how therapeutic parents are always filling up other people's cups, and how we need to make sure that our own cup is replenished. When we are drained, everything has leaked out of all the holes and nothing is staying put anymore. Our cup is empty. We all know that 'you can't pour from an empty cup'.

I didn't resent it too much when I felt drained because of the lack of reciprocity from the children. We *expect* our children to be somewhat draining and we know that it isn't going to be forever (yes, I know sometimes it feels like it!). However, it's not always just about our children. It's all the things everyone else expects or needs us to do, the absolute cast-iron certainty that we are there to sort everything out and to service everyone else's needs. When we feel unappreciated and taken for granted, it exhausts us in every way. There is nothing more disheartening than phoning up a friend because you have had a terribie day and being instantly silenced by their tsunami of need. We are left more alone, more drained and pushed into hopelessness.

So, it's time to do a little audit! When we are dragging along more than we should be, it will wear us out. Our task is hard enough without hangers-on. Nowadays, when I notice people riding on my coat-tails, I take the coat off or get the scissors out! It appears to be some time before they notice they're clinging on to a dead coat, or just the tails. This can still leave you feeling worn out and needing to find a little input from elsewhere. That in itself can feel like a major task, which is why it helps to break things down and take one step at a time.

In strategies for this section, you can see how you can do little life audits to help you to find your own scissors or to refill your cup.

See strategies: Brain Breaks, Empathic Listening, Essential Maintenance, Faith, One Step at a Time, Protecting Self

E

EEYORE PARENTING

Also see Compassion Fatigue, Drained (Feeling),
Exhaustion, Forgotten, Overwhelm, Resilience,
Top Trump Parenting, Unappreciated

We are all guilty of a little Eeyore parenting at times. I call it 'Eeyore parenting' from the bit in the Winnie the Pooh film where Eeyore is floating down the river, about to go over the weir. Despite multiple offers of help and strategies offered, Eeyore is resigned to his fate and miserably pronounces that he's 'going to go over the weir anyway'.

When we do this as parents, we find there are *no* solutions. Our children's behaviours, issues and psychological problems simply cannot be improved. There is no point even trying anymore. If this feels familiar to you, you are probably in compassion fatigue. A little bit of self-pity never did anyone any harm, especially if we can liberally pepper it with doughnuts, nice cakes and the odd glass of wine. It helps us to get through. Eeyore parenting is a problem when it becomes entrenched and part of our normal dialogue in life.

I know sometimes it feels hopeless, but we *have to* take the opportunities that we are offered. You won't be able to hear solutions and strategies if you are overwhelmed and having compassion fatigue. It's at those times that you will be saying, 'There's no point, he's going to end up in prison anyway', and that type of thing. By tackling your triggers and compassion fatigue, you will be able to start making use of the strategies on offer.

If you are dealing with an Eeyore parent, this can be really draining. The best solution is to stop offering strategies and simply do some empathic listening. If the empathic listening does not help them to exit Eeyore parenting, start wearing your pac-a-mac and putting the hood up over your eyes whenever you see them. You really don't need them in your life.

See strategies: Cake, Empathic Listening, Havening, One Step at a Time, Therapy (For Parents), Triggers (Managing), Vanishing Treats, Walking

EMBARRASSMENT

Also see Doubt, Inadequacy (Feelings of), Resilience

I cannot list here all the ways in which my children have embarrassed me over the years. What I can say is that the worm has turned. *I* am now a source of embarrassment to my children. When I wear my neon clothing, they look at me as if I am an incontinent halfwit, dancing naked in the supermarket. They like to pretend that they never embarrassed me and that the following events never happened:

1. At the school play, Charley, aged five, behaved so appallingly that her teacher was traumatized, and I had to pretend the purple-faced, screaming, lumpen child was not mine.
2. At parents' evening, I had to explain why I was not sad the dog had died (he hadn't) and how I had recovered so fast from my heart attack (which I didn't have).
3. At the hospital, I had to explain to the paramedic that my child did not in fact suffer from epilepsy but that he had learned to mimic the effects. I then had to face three weeks of 'most dreadful parent' award, until they realized I was right after all.

4. Having an entire ski slope full of people watching my child hurl her skis off into the distance, screaming abuse, and thereby becoming stuck halfway up a mountain. Subsequently, she threw herself face down in the snow, pretending injury and inadvertently triggering Mountain Rescue.

5. Being called over the tannoy in two international airports on the same day, due to different children stropping off, screaming and swearing. Two ended up in the police station.

All I can say is, you learn to grow a thick skin. It's really useful when you simply stop noticing the aghast expressions on the faces of other people. In fact, I would say it's liberating.

Recently, I needed to take one of my adult children to task for some really terrible behaviour. As we were out in a public place, they had mistakenly assumed that I would tone it down. No such luck. Many years of hardened experience have made me oblivious to the starey-eyed horror of interested passers-by. I said what I needed to say (in an unfortunately loud and shouty voice), and left. This meant that my adult child quickly re-evaluated their thoughts and behaviour and everything was resolved well. Had I tempered what needed to be said, and the *way* it needed to be said due to 'what people might think', we would not have moved on so quickly.

People say to me, 'Well that's all very well if you are outgoing and confident. It's easier to stop caring about the reactions of others. What if you're a shrinking violet?' Well, it's difficult. We literally have to push through and *pretend* not to mind, not to care. I used to be very sensitive to what other people's views were, but one of the main things my children taught me was that I could either:

- *really care* what other people thought, and modify my behaviour and actions in order not to offend them, thereby creating more tricky problems with my children

or:

- do what my children needed and do what *I* needed, thereby staying sane and having fewer friends.

I chose the latter. At least this way, my few friends were a hardy, resilient bunch who understood what I was talking about in a heartbeat. I cannot remember the last time I felt embarrassed. My children on the other hand…well unfortunately, I just bought some bright, pink chequered shoes, which apparently make me 'look like a clown'. Oh well.

See strategies: Hysterical Playfulness, Jolliness/Jauntiness (Fake), One Step at a Time, Paddington Hard-Stare, Pointy-Eyebrow Death Stare, Protecting Self, Useful Phrases

 EMPATHIC LISTENING

Empathic listening is like magic! It is so essential that in our therapeutic fostering agencies we employ people to be empathic listeners. These are people who have first-hand experience of living with our unique children.

Empathic listening is powerful no matter who the 'listener' is. In a couple relationship, you might alternate the role, depending on need. A single parent might have a special, knowledgeable friend or relative. In any event, the empathic listener needs to be someone who has a clue; someone who understands what it feels like to walk in your shoes.

As a struggling parent, I rarely found anyone who could properly listen to me. There were lots of 'Oh dear that's a shame', moving swiftly on to problem solving and patronizing advice, but when I found someone who truly understood my sorrows and struggles, made the right faces and sad noises, maybe even touched my arm and said empathic phrases, it made me feel less alone. Empathic listening joins your heart to another. It lowers the stress levels in your brain and helps you to think straight.

So how do we do it?

To be an active empathic listener you need to think about:

- body language
- putting your phone away
- making the right faces
- saying the right things.

There are a few key phrases that are really useful to use for the empathic listener:

- I can't imagine how difficult that must be.
- I am here for you.
- I am not going to say anything, I am just going to listen and be with you.
- You are not alone.
- I will help you sort this out.
- Tell me all about it.
- What happened next?
- How are you feeling?
- What do you think might happen?
- Is there anything I can do to help?
- It sounds really frustrating.
- How terrible for you.

Some useful paraphernalia the empathic listener can use to shore up their empathic listening might be a hot drink, a cake, or just some nice toiletries. Even just touching someone on their shoulder, showing them that you're with them, is a nice, nurturing accompaniment.

Phrases to avoid:

- Why don't you try...?
- Oh dear, poor child!
- Anyway, I must be going...
- Is that the time?
- I only have five minutes (as I have to get back to my lovely 'normal family').
- Yes, that happened to me too...but worse!
- My child is just the same...

In a couple relationship, where the natural rhythm of the day means there is a lot of discussion and explanation, it's a really good idea to set time aside for some active empathic listening. It's important to avoid using the same phrases all the time in order to ensure you don't get punched in the face. It will just feel patronizing if you are constantly saying to your partner, 'Oh dear, that's a shame', for example.

My husband was always overjoyed to indulge in a bit of empathic listening with a cup of tea rather than full-on problem solving (see 'Relationship Problems').

When couples forget this golden rule, problems arise. Do *not*, under any circumstances, offer to solve any problems.

Sometimes it can be difficult to find an empathic listener who has similar experience. In these circumstances, education is key.

We have enjoyed a long and happy marriage because early on I sat Ray down and said, 'You know when you come home and see I've had a bad day? Well, I'm not asking you to solve it for me. Deep down I know the answers but I'm too angry to access them. What I need is for you to listen to me without interruption, without patronizing me and without referring me to parenting classes. If you just make me a cup of tea and listen to me, I can solve it myself. And if I can't solve it, at least I will feel as if you're in my corner.'

Ray was thrilled with this news. Subsequently he told me that he felt as if all the pressure was off, and making a cup of tea plus listening was much easier to do than trying to work out how to solve the complex problem of getting the poo marks off the wall or working out why someone had hidden wee in the bin (again).

If you can't think of anyone to be your empathic listener, at the National Association of Therapeutic Parents we run listening circles, both face to face and online. There is lots of empathic listening which takes place there. Parents tell us they feel so much better after offloading to like-minded others.

See strategies: Babysitters, Brain Breaks, Cake, Essential Maintenance, Tea (Cups of, Cream)

EMPATHY

Also see Blame, Criticism, Compassion Fatigue, Conflicted Feelings, Doubt, Pity, Relationship Problems

Empathy is a bit of a double-edged sword. We need to find it for our children, and we crave it for ourselves. People often misunderstand our needs; they think we need problems to be solved and practical help. Well, that would be nice of course, but a bit of empathy and understanding gives us the boost we need to sort things out for ourselves a lot of the time.

If you are looking at your child and worrying because you feel as if you've lost your empathy for their difficulties and problems, you are probably in compassion fatigue. Don't give yourself *too* much of a hard time but do look into resolving that (see 'Compassion Fatigue').

The difficulty is that we sometimes *run out* of empathy. We are only human, and in order to give we also need to *receive*. If no one is giving you any empathy, kindness or understanding, it can be very difficult to keep giving that out.

Usually, therapeutic parents are quite empathic people. We learn to mirror the feelings of others around us. This in itself can be really draining. People begin to expect us to be the go-to person to solve their problems and to be that sympathetic or empathic ear. Let's face it, caring for children when they are young, vulnerable, needing lots of care and/or recovering is a one-way street. This is not their fault, but it *is* the way it is. We are constantly giving empathy, understanding, nurture and our best therapeutic parenting (apart from the odd off-day!). We can find ourselves feeling a bit aggrieved. Why isn't anyone caring about *me*? Why can't anyone else see how hard it is?

The reason that many people struggle to offer *us* empathy is because from the outside, what we are doing can *look* easy. Our children are often smiling and compliant. How lovely they are! What a joy they must be to look after. So helpful... No need for any empathy here.

Where the behaviours are difficult, it's much easier for others to blame *us* for those problems, rather than looking at how complicated that situation is. Empathy is replaced with blame.

Then, of course, there is just the fact that what we do is extremely complex. If I saw a mechanic who had broken down at the side of the road trying to fix their car, I probably wouldn't bother to offer to help. It all looks a bit tricky to me, and the person fixing it seems like an expert. In the same way, maybe people don't offer us empathy because we are 'copers', or 'experts'. We *look* as if we've got this. Maybe we have...but maybe we haven't. I think I need to remember to offer the mechanic a cup of tea or a sympathetic smile at the very least.

Empathy is not just about someone sitting down and listening to you, it is also about having that feeling that someone is on the *same page*, by the little things they do. Ray has this down to a fine art. Silent cups of teas are placed in front of me when a tricky situation is developing. When I'm on the phone to one of my children, and they have decided it's time to have a massive argument, a bar of chocolate will appear next to me. These little actions say, 'I feel your pain, I know this is difficult.' We don't even need to talk about it afterwards, I just know that he's in it with me.

Many therapeutic parents I speak to interpret empathy for themselves as self-pity. This is not the same thing at all. Recognizing that you've had a hard time and deserve something back is very different to sitting wallowing in self-pity with no proactivity or idea about how things might change. When we give all of ourselves to others, we *must expect and engineer if necessary* something in return. It's the therapeutic parenting law.

See strategies: Empathic Listening, Essential Maintenance, Forgiving Yourself, Protecting Self

EMPTY NEST

Also see Adult Children, Grief, Letting Go, Rejection

Although I shed a tear when the children moved out (some, to be honest, not all), I soon realized that it is a joyful experience. Trust me. It's all about embracing it and going with it. Don't fight it. Look for the joy of new freedoms and welcome them.

The main pitfall to look out for is filling your deliciously shiny, white-carpeted, undamaged furnishings, emptied nest with adult child detritus and their offspring. It can be tempting. Keep a bit of damaged furniture to remind you. I refer you to the sections on Boundaries and Protecting Self!

Here's a list of all the things you can do when your children leave home:

- Have a long bath.
- Stop hiding chocolate.
- Leave the safe unlocked occasionally.
- Have a loud chat on the telephone without using coded language.
- Go on holiday – a lot.

- Have conversations about your children without worrying that they have sneaked downstairs to listen.
- Buy whatever food you want.
- Have white carpets.
- Leave money out, blatantly.
- Go to garden centres and wander about, just because.
- Drive past the school without breaking out in a cold sweat.
- Stay up late because you aren't going to feel like death warmed up in the morning.

See strategies: Essential Maintenance, Expectations (Managing), Holidays, Protecting Self

 ESSENTIAL MAINTENANCE

You will notice that throughout this book I have been very careful not to talk about self-care. The reasons for this are obvious. Many of us find it frustrating to be told by others that we 'have to look after ourselves' when often we just want someone to look after *us*! Sometimes, when we are told 'you make sure you look after yourself', by a person who never does a *single thing* to try and help us, it can be enraging.

It's much more appropriate to replace the idea of self-care with the crucial *need* for essential maintenance. We have very busy lives, and we are often giving more of ourselves than feels sustainable. Therefore, in order to continue giving out, something has to be going back in.

When my daughter Sophie allowed the oil light to come on in her car and do nothing about it, in due course the whole engine seized and the car needed a new engine. She had failed to carry out very simple cost-effective essential maintenance in order to avoid a complete breakdown. In the same way, it is your duty and *right* to carry out essential maintenance on yourself when your 'oil light' comes on, in order to ensure that you can keep going and feel, at least, okay (if not great) at times.

How do we do this? We follow the Essential Maintenance Rules.

Essential Maintenance Rules

1. The first rule of essential maintenance – nobody can make you stop. *You* have to stop. Only you can do this. It's a bad idea to keep waiting for someone to notice you are nearly dead before you take a break. If necessary, organize and pay for the help you need. You don't have to feel guilty about this. You are doing a critical job. Having someone to clean for you or do the garden (finances allowing) can feel like a virtual hug.

2. Stop making excuses. I can hear you saying, 'But I can't stop. I can't take a break...who will...' and so on. It's all in the planning. I know it's tiring and disheartening being the one who has to do the planning to *get* the actual break but it's worth it a hundred times over. If I could do it, as a single parent to five severely traumatized children with fairly outrageous behaviours (not to mention the four or five dogs, two goats and assorted hamsters), then so can you.

3. If you have a health issue, go to the doctor! You might think this is simple advice, but so many therapeutic parents put their own health needs at the bottom of the list. This is not a good strategy. You probably had a reasonably large problem before you even noticed it. If you ignore your own health issues, you will almost certainly end up with much bigger problems.

4. Lose the guilt! There is so much guilt associated with taking time out for ourselves. You are entitled to a break in order to continue with all that you do. In fact, it's a very bad idea to

decide to *not* take a break! If you find you come under pressure from a supporting professional about needing a break, ask them how they would feel if their manager cancelled all their holiday for the next year and said they would have to be on call every night. Not very reasonable really, is it?

5. Stop thinking about essential maintenance as yet another task! Sometimes when people tell us we have to practise self-care, it can feel like another job to do. It might be very low down in our priorities. If you do not put yourself on 'the important list' it is unlikely anyone else will. Not only that, but people will keep assuming that 'you don't mind' having to continue dealing with all the things you still keep dealing with.

6. Lose the negativity. 'There's no point caring for myself, no one else does!' Stop this Eeyore-parenting self-destruct process right now. You are likely to be suffering from compassion fatigue. It is almost certain that others do care for you, but you have stopped being receptive to receiving that care. It happens. If it really does feel as if no one gives a flying monkey about you, then all the more reason to put yourself first for a short while.

7. Eat lots of cake.

8. Forget about the pay-off. If the children are dysregulated because you had a break, then you have some making up to do. But with the right preparation (i.e. ensuring minimum disruption to the children's routine and also allowing them to think you are going somewhere dull), disturbances can be minimized. Also, you will feel relaxed and refreshed on your return, even after a short break, and more able to deal with crises.

9. Put a sturdy lock on the bathroom door.

10. Connect to people who get it. Yes! You can do this. I have made sure you can. Just go to the Centre of Excellence in

Child Trauma website and be brave. Reach out. There are thousands of parents just like you, struggling to connect with others. You can also go to the Therapeutic Parents Facebook group to see just how many parents are thinking the same thoughts and experiencing the same issues.

11. Play whatever music you want.

12. Where life is too hard, nominate someone else to be in the front line. This might be your partner, a close friend or a family member. Sometimes, people need to be asked directly to help and have it spelt out to them what they need to do. For example, if you have been bereaved, you deserve the right to have the time to grieve. People will be around you, wanting to help. Let them.

13. Do a stock check on your cart and your coat-tails. Who is sitting in your cart and making life more difficult? It should only be the children. You have to insist that hefty, lazy adults get out and help to push, or at least stop being dead weights. You deserve better. If you have people quite happily dragging along on your coat-tails... Cut. Them. Off. They need to get their own jacket. Your life is hard enough without people dragging you down, but sometimes, a little stocktake is necessary as we can forget to check.

14. Don't be afraid to make official complaints. There is nothing more depressing than feeling disempowered. Enlisting the help of your local Member of Parliament (MP) or someone who can advocate for you can be truly liberating and empowering. I did this several times while my children were growing up. It was amazing how words like 'What is your complaints procedure?' or copying in the local MP or the Minister for Schools suddenly made the responder much more polite and focused.

See strategies: Alcohol, Babysitters, Brain Breaks, Cake, Chocolate, Coffee, Holidays, Hot Tubs, Ice Cream, Looking Good, More, Music, One Step at a Time, Protecting Self, Vanishing Helpers, Walking

EXHAUSTION

Also see Boredom, Compassion Fatigue, Drained (Feeling), Eeyore Parenting, Motivation, Overwhelm, Sleep Problems

Do you remember the days when you used to bounce out of bed, eager to greet the new day? Those days might seem very long ago now. I think mine ended when I was about five.

I deliberately haven't put in a section about tiredness because 'tiredness' is what normal parents experience. That is the tiredness that morphs into exhaustion for a few weeks or months when the children are very small. In therapeutic parenting, that exhaustion can be an ever-present hazard.

Often, I used to find that the mental negativity I felt made me feel physically exhausted as well. It's really difficult to get on top of things when you just don't feel as if you have the energy anymore. Exhaustion doesn't go away on its own, we have to take action to get over it. The difficulty is we are too exhausted to do it! If you're waiting for somebody to notice that you're completely done, be prepared for a very long wait. People will be very keen to ignore the fact that you are exhausted because otherwise they might have to help.

The reason that caring for unique children can be so strenuous is because of the relentlessness of the task. Just as we think we have resolved an issue, and behaviours are improving, it feels as if a big trick has been played on us and we are suddenly back at square one! So, you thought your child was potty trained, did you? No such luck. And here we are 12 years later, still trying to sort it out, still feeling exhausted at the mountain of washing this one little problem produces.

The feeling of being back at square one is truly so tiring, because we know how hard it was to resolve the first time, and now we're more tired and we have to do it all again!

I know that sometimes we can just feel exhausted with life altogether. At times, it can all feel too hard just to keep going. Making sure we factor in little breaks for ourselves and oases of calm within the structure of our day can sometimes be *just about* enough to get us through.

See strategies: Brain Breaks, Coffee, Essential Maintenance, Holidays, One Step at a Time, Picking Your Battles, Protecting Self, Routine, Tea (Cups of, Cream), Timesavers, Vanishing Helpers

EXPECTATIONS (MANAGING)

When my children came home to me, I had built up years of excited expectations, culminating in how delightful it would be to skip, Julie Andrews-like, 'over the hills', clasping hands with beaming, loving children in matching, un-chewed clothes. The cold shower of reality dripped over my head for a number of years before I accepted this little dream was unlikely to come true.

In order to avoid 'holiday fury', we had booked to go in the summer to the same resort where we went skiing. This meant the children could stay in the same apartment and were familiar with the landscape (albeit that they were bit angry they could not ski on the grass). We took the chairlift up the mountain and started the walk down. On the way (thoughts of Julie Andrews playing in my head), I said to the children, 'Right, hold my hands, we're going to make a little video.' I will draw a veil over the next few minutes; suffice to say I am the proud owner of a video featuring me skipping about alone on a mountain, singing 'The hills are alive' and looking completely mad. The children are sitting nearby, gazing at me sullenly and commenting loudly about my general failure as a parent.

By this time, you see, I had got to a point where I had decided that I was going to do all the things I had dreamed about, regardless of whether or not the children joined in. This meant I had quite a nice time, and also, of course, the children could not help smiling and joining in sometimes.

One of the best ways to avoid feelings of disappointment and frustration is to lower your expectations. If you expect a dreadful day, and actually there is only one incident of your child calling you a 'bitch from hell' in the supermarket, then this can count as a good day in comparison.

By planning less, we achieve more. Simple but true. Far better to have a lovely day at the nearby coast than a traumatic journey and weekend in an unfamiliar villa in Spain.

With our children, it's simple self-preservation and *logic* to lower our expectations. This doesn't mean we don't *expect* our children to achieve. It doesn't mean that we have given up on them. It means we expect them to achieve later, or in a different way. This protects us and gives us hope for the future.

Here are some useful strategies to help you to reframe disappointment and manage expectations:

- Try to find a little part of the experience which will be nice for *you*. For example, 'I am taking the children for a picnic; they are likely to argue but at least I won't have any washing up to do.'
- Build in a treat for yourself for afterwards. Don't expect the actual day out, or experience, to be your treat.
- Look further ahead. If everything is looking a bit hopeless and bleak, fast forward to a time when things will have to have changed.

To manage expectations around your child's development it's essential that you give yourself little reality checks, and also remind yourself of how far you have come. You can do this by:

- referring back to videos, photos and diaries
- reminding yourself of the behaviours currently demonstrated and what age you would normally expect to see these
- spending time with other therapeutic parents who are not in a 'my child saved global warming' competition
- checking the expectations you have about our own performance. How realistic is it that another person in this same situation would have achieved more?

When we are struggling because there is no reciprocity, reward or feeling of the child 'loving us back', this can be very hard. We might have expected the child to fall in love with us instantly, and that has not proved to be the case. Be assured that this is relatively common. Things will change, but you have to keep your eye on the prize, the long game. During the nine years when Rosie considered me a vague annoyance in her life (and certainly not her mum), it was sometimes difficult to keep believing that one day it would be alright. But the thing is, if you stop thinking it will be alright, then you stop trying. And if I had done that, Rosie would not now be my one of my beloved daughters.

See strategies: Cake, Celebrating, Dogs, Essential Maintenance, Faith, Havening, One Step at a Time, Reflecting, Therapy (For Parents), Training

F

💡 FAITH

I rarely talk about my faith, although sometimes at conferences, the eagle-eyed among you will notice the cross and chain I wear.

Faith is not just about feeling a connection to an organized religion, it is about having faith in *something*. Something bigger than us, something with purpose.

As well as (or instead of) having faith in a religion, we might have faith in:

- the universe
- fate
- karma
- ourselves
- our dog
- others
- our children.

I have always found that having faith in something greater than myself was very liberating. I do not think it was a coincidence that my faith as a Christian renewed itself, almost by magic, during our darkest days.

Having faith in karma also takes away a lot of anger and a pressing need for revenge or consuming anger. I have always found that letting karma take its course evens everything out in the end and relieves me of another job.

I found it comforting to be able to go to sleep at night with a big worry, after having a final thought, 'God will help me to sort this out.' At times, God was the only 'person' listening. And boy did I need someone! It was very liberating to be able to think, 'God has got this.' I could almost feel the weight shifting off me. So even if you are reading this and scoffing at the sheer nonsense of it, that's okay. Everyone is entitled to their own view. I am just sharing what helped me, and I know helps many others.

Occasionally, we all need faith in someone or something stronger than we are. Sometimes I was not enough. In order to be a 'trailblazer' I needed direction for the trail to go in, and someone holding my hand along the way. God held my hand at the hardest times.

See strategy: One Step at a Time

FAMILY

Also see Anti-Socialism, Asking for Help, Birth Family, Boundaries, Criticism, Isolation, PIEs, Refereeing

I remember the day that I took my three youngest children to meet my parents. It was a joyous occasion. I dressed them all up in their best clothes and I didn't even mind that they were all sick in the car on the way. One of the happiest memories was taking my youngest for a walk in her pram with my mum. We had waited many years to share these types of experiences. After this day, it was basically downhill all the way.

Fast forward five years and my lovely dad was sitting under the table with my son, trying to coax him out after a pie-throwing incident. I know now that I was very lucky that my dad was naturally insightful and empathic and had a wonderful way with children.

The other members of my extended family were nowhere near in the same library, let alone on the same page. We did have a real breakthrough moment though, when 22 years in, my mum used the word 'attachment' in the right context.

Many therapeutic parents have told me how painful it is to receive the judgement and unhelpful comments they get from their extended family. I feel their pain. Some of the (quite unbelievable) things which have been said or reported to us are listed below:

- They're so naughty why don't you send them back?
- Don't bring them over for tea. My other grandchildren are coming, and your lot are a nightmare!
- I didn't bother buying them any Christmas presents because they always break everything.
- I don't know why you couldn't have just had some normal children.
- I don't want them at the wedding because they disrupt everything.
- I bet you're sorry you took them on now, I did try to warn you.
- I bought you a parenting manual for Christmas because I think you need it. (Said to adoptive mum who had had 18-month-old twins with her for three months.)
- They've been with you long enough now, they should have settled down. (Said about my adopted child with additional needs six months after adoption.)
- You should not mention their past. They won't remember it and you are just making it worse.
- I don't want them near my children, they might still have head lice. (Said about my adopted children after three years with us.)
- You're too soft with them.
- You should be firmer with them.

- They need a good slap; it never did me any harm. (Said in reference to my child having a sensory meltdown.)
- Send them to their room so we can enjoy Christmas dinner in peace. (Said about a foster child who had been moved in an emergency, two days earlier, and was expected to sit quietly and join in with a large family Christmas.)
- Your brother didn't send them a card because they are not blood, so they don't really count the same, do they? (Said about one of my adopted children not receiving a birthday card.)
- He doesn't try hard enough. You make excuses for him. (Said about a child with complex disabilities.)

It can be really painful when unhelpful comparisons are made to other children in the family. Invariably, these comparisons are to children *without* additional needs, or who have not experienced trauma. This is a bit like comparing a penguin to an eagle. I often say in my training, 'Traditional parents with securely attached children are teaching their birds to fly, and we have to teach our penguins to swim.' This phrase *does* help others to understand that our children learn and experience the world in a different way.

Usually, the problems arise because the experience we are having is so far removed from anything the family has ever experienced. Where there is a disability, initially there might be all kinds of offers of help and support, but, often, these offers melt away as the child grows.

Where we are looking after children who have experienced trauma, it is unlikely that our extended family will rush off to learn all about brain development. No, they are much more likely to look at the behaviours, see that you are struggling and want to try to solve the 'problem' quickly and easily. And herein lies the challenge. Our children are not 'problems to be solved', they are complex, all-consuming little beings who need our full attention and care.

The trick is to get our family to understand that and to spell out how they can support us. They really *don't know*, you see. A lot of the judgement, blame and hurtful comments come from a place of ignorance. It is our job to educate our extended family and tell them what we need from them.

I know that, often, we have done that already. We have tried. We really have, and we cannot get the movement, engagement and support that we crave. In those times, we must take steps for self-preservation. If you cannot get your extended family to see what is happening and how they can help, in order to keep going you will need to preserve your strength. It does not mean you lose your family, of course. You just might be engaging with them in a different way.

Sometimes, though, we have to put in some clear ground rules with a 'take it or leave it' approach. If you have input from your extended family that is damaging your child, and they cannot, or will not, understand, you *have to* take a step back. That relationship will still be there later, but naturally it will be changed. That's okay. Hurtful but okay. We have to learn to look for the support we need from those who are *capable* of giving it to us.

I only took my children to an extended family Christmas once. After that, it simply was not worth it. We celebrated special days quietly on our own. I still saw my family, but I saw them in a different way. Now my children have grown up, the dynamics have completely changed. It might be a long time coming. There might need to be an awful lot of explanations and even arguments, but you will get there in the end. And yes, I know. This is not another battle you need.

See strategies: Picking Your Battles, Protecting Self, Sarcasm, Training, Useful Phrases

FEAR (OF CHILD)

Also see Conflicted Feelings, Doubt, Letting Go, Relationship Problems

I remember when I was working in a children's home where there were high levels of violence from young people, I frequently felt afraid. One day, I was walking along the beach with a young woman who had a certain reputation. She was bigger than me and very strong. Unfortunately, the staff had wandered on ahead and had forgotten that they should have been watching us. She casually asked me what I would do if she was to push me in the sea and drown me. I knew that she was capable of this, and my insides turned to liquid. I wasn't sure the staff would hear me screaming in time. In order to survive, I just responded casually, 'Well I suppose I'd get wet', and then changed the subject. She would not have seen a flicker of fear on my face. As I showed no anxiety or concern, the young woman did not carry out any threat, and simply re-engaged in the conversation we were having. Had I shown fear, there would have been a different outcome. It's so hard to act unafraid, though, when we *know* that the child or young person could harm us if they chose to.

When I adopted, I knew by then that if I showed my children I was scared, it would make them feel afraid or unsafe and would make a bad situation worse. I was lucky though; I had had years of training in therapeutic children's homes in some very frightening situations. I knew my children would have the capacity to over-whelm me physically and to be physically frightening as they got older, so I put in some very firm boundaries and structure when they were still young enough (and small enough) for me to be unafraid. This held us in very good stead as they grew older.

It's so difficult when the children we have loved and nurtured become the source of our fear. As they grow and become stronger, the adrenaline-fuelled rages can give them superhuman strength.

Others may look at them, away from that moment, and wonder how on earth we could be frightened of them.

It can be very disheartening to recognize that we are frightened of our own child. Others may judge us harshly, and we might judge ourselves in the same way! It is a fact that many therapeutic parents are physically harmed through 'child to parent violence' and this issue is often minimized or ignored by others. This happens because it is indeed a very complicated problem and one that goes on behind closed doors.

Just as in domestic violence, a parent may feel deep levels of shame if they are scared of their child due to actual or threatened violence. It can be incredibly difficult to talk about. The trick is to find others in the same situation and to join together to explore feelings and strategies. By taking the lid off this fear, it helps to minimize it and give you a sense of perspective.

In couple relationships, where one person is frightened of the child due to actual or potential violence or aggression, the other partner may overcompensate. This can sometimes exacerbate the problem because the vulnerable parent may be targeted more when the assertive parent is absent.

No amount of talking to the child will solve the issue of child to parent violence. In my book *The A–Z of Therapeutic Parenting*, I give you some strategies to use with this particular behaviour, and information about why this happens. You can also find links and strategies directly linked to child to parent violence in the 'Protecting Self' section in this book.

See strategies: Brain Breaks, Co-Regulation, Empathic Listening, Havening, Protecting Self, Self-Regulation, Training

FFS

Swearing under your breath, in code, can be very cathartic. I used to say FFS until my children cottoned on. Then I switched to 'What the actual F?' As authentic swear words do pronounce themselves in your head, it feels quite satisfying.

I tried to avoid swearing, but as a tension release strategy it's brilliant. In the 'Screaming' strategy, I explain about finding remote places to screech to. It's so much more satisfying when the screaming contains some nice juicy swear words too.

I used to find shouting 'WHY!? Why the fuck did you do that? What the bloody hell is going on in my life?' on top of a nice hill released a great deal of tension.

This is a great strategy to use with children who swear too. I used to do it with my foster children. It completely removed any shock power, and we all had a picnic afterwards.

See strategies: Screaming, Singing

 FORGIVING YOURSELF

We're very good at repairing with the children and letting them know when we think we have made a mistake. We kind of *ask* for their forgiveness. Be careful, though, that when you do a repair, you're not handing your children a great big stick to beat you with. This does nobody any good. You can be sorry, let them know you made an error, and then move swiftly on. You don't have to pay for it in PlayStation games, trips to the zoo and endless pocket money.

Although forgiveness from the children and others is important, it's forgiveness from *ourselves* that can be elusive.

A big part of forgiving yourself is to decide what you are able to let go of. A useful exercise is to sit looking in the mirror and tell yourself, 'I did the best I could with what I knew at the time.' This will be true. We nearly always do our best for our children, nearly all the time. Occasionally, there are times when we bugger it up. Oh well, that's life. Let's get a bit of perspective here.

Over the years, I have found that I can keep a guilt tally of 'guilt owes'. In my mind, I have a little record of all the times when I think I messed up. The times when I was short tempered, when I didn't give the right responses, and when I felt like giving up. Now, with my adult children when they are very annoying and need me to *do* something for them (that I don't want to), I simply remember one of my guilt owes, tick it off and do them the good turn. This might put me to some inconvenience, but it makes me feel better because I've got one less thing to feel guilty about now.

It can be useful to think about what belongs to us and what doesn't. We can use up a great deal of energy in feeling responsible for things or feeling guilty and anxious about something we feel we missed. Well, we can either do that, and become very inward looking, or we can start looking outward. We put that worry and that energy into change. We look at what the mistakes were and make it our business to change things, so that the mistake doesn't happen again. This is a much better use of our energy than all that guilt and sadness.

See strategies: Essential Maintenance, Havening, One Step at a Time, Protecting Self, Views

FORGOTTEN

Also see Birthdays, Unappreciated

As therapeutic parents, we are of course used to our children suddenly becoming deaf or ignoring us, and we have strategies for that. It is far harder to manage when we seem to become invisible to other people around us. The grown-ups. This might be due to the overwhelming demands and needs of our children, or it might just be because we have become consumed by our tricky life in general. Either way, there is nothing more disheartening than the confirmation of our fears, that we are indeed a drudgey, tired, unseen mess, just labouring away in the background, making sure the world doesn't end and the fridge remains fully stocked. It can cut us to the heart when we are forgotten. It reinforces our isolation and sadness.

Therapeutic parents *have* to plan ahead. We have to plan with military precision because that is our life, but it is not the life of others. It's easy to forget that. We tend to be 'copers' who minimize our own wishes and feelings. It becomes easier for others to say, 'She won't mind.' In the last few years, I have become quite good at saying, 'I know you thought I wouldn't mind, but I do.'

The birthday peacock

I rarely bought myself anything when the children were young. I didn't have the time or the inclination. However, one day in the garden centre I saw a stunning life-size, wood-carved, hand-painted peacock. I was so taken with this I decided to buy it, even though it was quite expensive. I placed it proudly on the centre of our lawn.

First, my lovely husband Ray dropped a log on the peacock. Not wishing to upset me, he mended it badly (like a child with papier-mache). Then a tradesman dropped a wheelbarrow full of bricks on the peacock, snapping the neck off. I wondered where the peacock had suddenly gone. Ray had moved it in order to 'save my feelings'. I was somewhat aggrieved as I thought somebody responsible for the damage might have thought of replacing the lovely peacock. Naturally, I did not say anything, I just did some mysterious martyr-sighing. ('What's wrong?' 'Nothing. Everything is completely *fine*!')

As the martyr-sighing proved ineffective, I decided to be clear with Ray about why I was upset. After all, I reasoned, Ray doesn't know that this peacock was important to me, so I will tell him; so I did and Ray nodded, making appropriate 'sorry' noises.

This is a good strategy. When we feel we are being overlooked, it can make us feel better and prevent us being overlooked again in the future. And if it doesn't, at least we know for sure that we have been clear about our feelings.

My birthday was coming up, so I was quietly hopeful, but when Ray proudly handed me a package I could instantly see this was not peacock shaped.

It was a really ugly, plastic chicken.

I immediately realized that Ray had left 'present buying' till five seconds before the garden centre closed. I asked him why on earth he had bought me such a hideous thing and he said, 'Well, you liked the peacock.' This made things a hundred times worse. I stared in disbelief at the offending chicken. 'Yes, I liked the peacock. The one that you broke. The wooden, life-size, hand-painted peacock. This is a fucking plastic chicken!'

All my anger at being sidelined and 'she won't mind' cascaded out onto the unfortunate chicken's head with Ray as bemused bystander. I realized that at least he had *intended* to get a peacock, but I was furious that I hadn't been important enough to plan for. I felt forgotten.

Now we see the funny side. I realize that when all is said and done, he meant well, it was just poor planning. We've worked on his planning a bit, and the plastic chicken stands in pride of place as a constant reminder that forgetting my birthday is a *very bad idea*.

I bought myself a beautiful, new wooden peacock. It is in a separate part of the garden. Ray is not allowed to touch it. We have reached an understanding...

See strategies: Essential Maintenance, Expectations (Managing), Paddington Hard-Stare, Pointy-Eyebrow Death Stare, Protecting Self, Useful Phrases

FRIENDSHIPS

Also see Anti-Socialism, Betrayal, Boundaries, Criticism, Family, Grief, Inadequacy (Feelings of), Isolation, Perfect Parents

As we emerge blinking, into the bright light of the 'parent of adult children' new world, we realize that the friends who were there at the start of our therapeutic parenting journey don't appear to be around anymore. The ecomaps (showing our robust and supportive friendship network), so confidently completed during the assessment to adopt or foster, are now a source of amusement.

Many therapeutic parents find that their friendship group changes dramatically in the first few years of parenting their unique child or children. These friendships can be rediscovered later, but sometimes we feel a sense of betrayal that in our hour of need, the friend who we *really thought* would be there, simply wasn't. It's not their fault that they didn't get it, it's just that our lives are taking a different path.

I know it can be a painful process, but new friendships are there to be formed. There are other parents who are on the same journey as you and who can share in the highs and lows. We can also change our relationships and see friends *away* from the stresses of our everyday lives. I kept one of my very long-standing friendships alive by simply seeing that friend without my children and not really ever talking about them. That friendship is still thriving. If I had tried to enmesh my life with hers at the same level as we had *prior* to my children coming home to me, it could not have worked.

However, that *process* of changing friendships can be a difficult and lonely one. Our carefree and happier times might be bound up in those relationships, and the loss of those relationships can be heart-breaking. It may feel daunting too, to try to summon up the energy to start new friendships.

It can be useful to do a little stocktake and think about who is in our inner and outer circle. This may well have changed over time. I thought it would be handy to have a quick reference table, so you can see who an inner circle friend might be, and who may need to be demoted, or barred.

Inner circle friend	Outer circle friend (or barred)
Listens without judgement.	Listens and then says, 'Hmm, I think the children have changed you, and not for the best.'
Offers to babysit, and actively seeks to understand how to complete that task, without causing undue trauma.	Pressures you to come out with them when it's obviously not in anyone's interest apart from theirs.
Also has unique children.	Makes unfavourable comparisons between your children and other children without the same difficulties.
Is appropriately helpful and kind.	Does a pity face at you that you want to punch.
Works hard to make sure they use the right words in order to avoid causing offence.	Continues to use terms like 'real children' despite you explaining the correct terminology.
Only visits by arrangement and unexpectedly brings cake.	Arrives unexpectedly and requires you to feed them, even though it means the children are now all up in the air and screeching.
Remembers your birthday and makes sure something nice happens.	Expects you to take them out for dinner on your birthday. And pay.

See strategies: Babysitters, Dogs, Empathic Listening, Essential Maintenance, Paddington Hard-Stare, Pointy-Eyebrow Death Stare, Protecting Self, Useful Phrases, Vanishing Helpers

FRUSTRATION

Also see Acceptance, Anger, Crying, Disempowerment,
PIEs, Relationship Problems, Resilience, Schools

We are entitled to feel frustrated. Our lives are hugely frustrating! That's why we need so much wine and chocolate. I mean, let's be honest, there is no way a normal person moves from coffee, to cake, to chocolate, to wine, so relentlessly and with such precision and skill, is there?

No, it's frustration that drives us, and forces us to ingest all those little treats in our way.

Here are some common frustrating situations that you may find yourself in:

- A person saying yet another patronizing, nonsensical state-ment about your children.
- School, just about anything to do with school, but especially moronic reward charts and phoning you up yet again because your child is faking illness and they can't tell the difference.
- A child eating your precious treat.
- A child managing to pull the wool over everyone else's eyes and making you out to be a Hell Parent.
- A partner or relative blatantly undermining you.
- A social worker talking absolute shit with a patronizing face.
- A manager saying that as you have done so well with ther-apeutic parenting (and stabilized the child), obviously you don't need support anymore.
- The local authority deciding that it's okay for the child to go back to abusive birth parents now as they have learned their lesson (they haven't).
- The court ordering you to take your child to see their abusers three times a week for a nice visit (as it's their 'right'), thereby retraumatizing the child so frequently that you cannot build attachments.

- The team manager deciding that the child who has lived with you for four years, and made brilliant progress, has to be moved somewhere 'cheaper'.
- Being told your child is too unstable to access therapy, then when they are stable, you realize they don't need it anymore, but they are going to be forced to have it, thereby immediately destabilizing them again.
- Being unable to access resources that your child needs right now because you have not ticked 7234 boxes or completed the appropriate 489 page-long duplicating form.
- Being told your child has a condition which you know is 100 per cent wrong.
- Being told your child does *not* have a condition, when you 100 per cent know that they do.

This is why we have to look after ourselves. No one else is going to remove these frustrations from your life. There is not a magic Frustration Fairy just waiting to pop along to see you to say, 'Wow, that looks tricky, let me just quickly solve that for you.' No, that will be you. You, who solves the frustrations as you go along.

The good news is that frustrations diminish over time. Partly this is due to us stopping caring about tiny things which we can't change and partly that as we grow in knowledge, strength and assertion, people get a tiny bit nervous of us and stop doing things which annoy us.

See strategies: Brain Breaks, Breathing, Cake, Chocolate, Coffee, Empathic Listening, Pausing, Screaming, Self-Regulation

G

GARDEN/GARDENING

Gardening is great. You can pretend to be doing lots of outside things and be 'busy in the garden'. If the children want to help, make sure there are lots of dull, smelly jobs so they don't ask again. This way, gardening becomes a brain break. A cosy shed with a secure lock on the inside and a comfy garden chair can enhance the 'busy potting' experience.

See strategy: Brain Breaks

GRIEF

Also see Acceptance, Empty Nest, Guilt,
Loss of Identity, Overwhelm

Grief can knock you sideways. You never know when it's going to sneak up on you and for what reason, and worse, you don't know when it's going to go! Our heartache ranges from the deep-rooted, gasping heartache to just a kind of dull, miserable feeling which takes the edge off everything. Dulling everything down. Even when an anticipated, sad event happens, the accompanying grief is still debilitating, and sometimes accompanied by guilt.

Today I have the grief elephant sitting on my head. I woke up with him sitting there this morning. This was only to be expected as

I had to have my beloved dog put to sleep yesterday, after 16 years of his constant presence by my side.

Grief is easier to deal with when we understand where it's come from, but as therapeutic parents we can experience grief from so many different angles. It is always an unwelcome and debilitating visitor.

You may have a visit from grief due to:

- a close family bereavement
- the loss of the child you thought you would have (the ideal child/biological child and so on)
- pet bereavement
- losses that your children have suffered that you could not prevent
- lost futures
- an ending where a child has moved
- an estrangement from an adult child
- the couple relationship that you had, which is no longer there.

There are so many ways that grief affects our lives. In my book about the experience of therapeutic parenting, *Therapeutic Parenting Essentials*, I write about the grief we feel for the losses that our children suffered in early life which we could not prevent. My daughter Rosie has also spoken about the sense of grief *she* felt because I hadn't been there in her early life.

The other type of grief we experience as parents of our unique children is for the loss of the child we thought we would have. If your child has additional needs, it is normal to grieve for the child they might have been without those challenges. It does not mean you don't love and appreciate the child for who they are. Similarly, adopters in particular may feel grief or post-adoption depression, soon after their long-awaited child comes home to them. This may bring into sharp reality that a longed-for birth child is never going to materialize and can re-awaken grief linked to infertility.

If you are struggling with grief for whatever reason, name it. Place where the grief has come from. When we are grieving, we often feel very tired and lacking energy and enthusiasm for anything. It's easy to keep trudging on day to day, feeling down in the dumps, ignoring the fact that we *are* grieving for our lost contact with a loved one, child, pet or anything else.

When I lost my dad, I needed time and space to grieve. People asked what they could do to help, so I took them up on it. People want to be useful at these difficult times. I needed people to keep everything running like clockwork with the children, so I could take my foot off the pedal. I was still present physically, but emotionally I needed time out.

The grief and sorrow we feel for abuse or neglect our children have suffered is hard to handle. We have everyday reminders through their behaviours about the trauma they have experienced, but we cannot join them in their sorrow. We empathize with them, we reflect, but then it is our task to make sure our children become survivors, not victims. If we allow our circumstances to create a wallowing grief swamp, our children will join us within it. And then there's *a lot* more work to do.

I know this is very hard, so in the strategies for this section, you will find ways to help you to manage grief and carry on.

See strategies: Empathic Listening, Essential Maintenance, Havening, One Step at a Time, Protecting Self

GUILT

Also see Bad Days, Catastrophic Thinking, Conflicted Feelings, Doubt, Essential Maintenance, Inadequacy (Feelings of), Letting Go, Overwhelm

Someone once told me that when you give birth to a baby you give birth to an equal amount of guilt. On that basis, I must have acquired several stones of guilt when my children moved in with me. Yes, that feels about right.

The feeling of guilt, or being ashamed of oneself, is an uncomfortable one. As parents of our unique children, we are particularly lucky to have so many different reasons to welcome guilt and shame into our lives. Here are some of the most common reasons for guilt, related to therapeutic parenting:

- The impact of the unique child on other children living in our home.
- 'Giving up' on children.
- Taking time out for ourselves (essential maintenance).

- Changing relationships.
- Choosing the wrong school.
- Not believing a child.
- Believing a supporting professional who turns out to be wrong.
- Having a bad day and overreacting.
- Feeling as if you are failing to meet the child's needs.
- Feeling as if you don't connect to the child/don't love them.
- Feeling responsible for the cause of the trauma.
- Fearing that you are making things worse.
- Post-adoption depression/compassion fatigue or post-natal depression.
- Feeling bad that you are struggling, as compared to what the child has suffered, you have 'no right'.

The guilt we experience looks and feels different depending on our circumstances. For special guardians and kinship carers there is often an extra layer of guilt. They tell me that they sometimes feel responsible for the initial difficulties experienced by the child's birth parent, or that they were unable to salvage the situation earlier. This leaves therapeutic parents feeling that guilt is *magnified* due to the trauma occurring, which they believe was preventable. That is an uncomfortable, leaden visitor, sitting in your heart and weighing you down.

Birth parents of children who have additional needs or developmental trauma explain that their guilt is particularly hard to bear. Difficulties may have arisen from domestic violence, medical needs during pregnancy, a difficult birth, additional medical needs/ condition or hospitalization following birth. A birth parent with two children with developmental trauma describes her feelings about this:

Being physically ill for the duration of my pregnancies was at best an endurance test, at worst a living hell. At five weeks into my first pregnancy, I was diagnosed with hyperemesis gravidarum – severe pregnancy sickness which affects one in 100 pregnancies.

It was 38 weeks of constant worry – worry that I was harming our baby by not being able to keep any food down, worry about going to the scans and not being able to see our baby, having thrown up the required amount of water before even getting through the hospital doors. There was the loneliness, brought on by the all-consuming fatigue which made me housebound most of the time, and the constant feeling of hunger which never went away. In the later months, the sickness brought on a whole new dimension. Being sick when your baby is kicking you is a weird experience and I can only imagine what it must be like for the baby; being on an enclosed bouncy castle comes to mind.

The good news was that it did stop, our babies were born, and we welcomed parenthood and the next part of our journey, but the parental guilt was still lingering.

This was sometimes magnified by the additional needs our child was displaying, and I felt incredibly guilty that my body, and their time in uterine, had made some contribution to this, regardless of whether there was a direct link or not. Sometimes I feel as if I am in a guilt mire. After all, it is my fault, isn't it? My body let me down, let my children down. Their brains work in a different way because my feeble mother body failed them. That's what it feels like. Every time there is an issue. My husband has never blamed me. He is so brilliant and supportive. But sometimes, I wonder if he wishes he had had children with someone else.

Acceptance is key, and it's not that easily achievable. However, with time and therapy – in particular, 'Havening' was effective to my personal experience – I learned to overcome the guilt and, most importantly, embrace our children's unique qualities, celebrate their achievements and support them to navigate their path in life.

For my own children, as they have grown and become parents them-selves, they have had their own struggles with guilt. They worry if they are 'good enough' parents and if they will make the same mistake as their birth parents. Sometimes adults who were traumatized as children struggle with overcoming some of the demons they face. Sarah Dillon describes it like this:

I am a birth parent. I feel guilt beyond description.

I was a traumatized child; this affected my parenting ability. It *did not* affect my love for my children. My desperate need to be loved was a constant and powerful driver in my life. At times, I made decisions that weren't in the best interests of my children. But I didn't abandon them. They *never* went without food. I entered into unhealthy relationships with others because I was desperate for a loving family. These were the wrong people for myself and my children. I couldn't trust or get close to a partner. Eventually, I realized that this was significantly affecting my children.

I moved home far too often, trying to restart my life, to give us a fresh start. I was conditioned to keep moving due to my own history. I still told them I loved them *every* day; I kissed them at night and tucked them in (when they let me). I screamed and shouted far too much, I struggled to cope.

I knew they were affected by my own history of trauma, my inadequate parenting, mistakes, bad decisions and wrong relationships with ex-partners.

I remembered the therapeutic parenting I'd received from my foster mum, so I researched everything I could at the library, I read as many books as I could get my hands on. I entered into therapy for four years; I faced many of my demons and admitted my mistakes. I cried for my children and the child I was, I grieved for lost years. I chose to be single until my youngest child reached 18 years old. I sat my boys down and told them I was truly sorry. I couldn't promise them I would be perfect overnight. I learned how to become my children's 'rock' as a parent, and I became the best I could be at everything I did. I was determined to make a difference!

Yet *nothing, but nothing* could take away the horrific guilt I felt about my own now adult sons. I carried it around like a dirty secret in a worn carrier bag! The *only* person I could point the finger at was *me*!

Now those days are behind us and we can enjoy the successes of secure relationships, but I will always feel guilt and regret for those lost years.

Adopters and foster parents sometimes have very high expectations of themselves. It can come as a huge shock when we find that we might not like the children or connect to them very well. Sometimes we may find we are spending years trying to attach to the child. This can make us feel so guilty and that the child would have been better off with a different or 'more nurturing' parent. Someone better than us. Betty, an adoptive mum, describes it like this:

> It was easy to talk about Mark not being attached to us. I could give lots of examples of that. It was much harder to admit I wasn't bonding to him. Most of the time I didn't like him, let alone love him. I just wasn't feeling it. With David, I felt I loved him from day one and that love was quickly reciprocated. From those first few weeks with Mark, when I didn't get any reaction back, after spending hours each day trying to engage, I had become quickly deflated. I felt so awful as a human being about it that I couldn't tell anyone, not even my husband. I felt as if I was providing physical care to a robot, devoid of any humanity, and I couldn't help thinking what a horrible, self-centred bitch I must be, that I demanded to be loved in order to bond with him.

If you are feeling guilty for some, or many, of the reasons outlined above, know that this is normal. You are your own harshest judge. Guilt is debilitating and tiring. Guilt spreads out into little gaps of hope and positivity, leaving us constantly questioning our own worth as parents. This is not a good use of our emotional energy, but it is understandable. The strategies relating to this section reveal some tips on how you can live alongside, and gradually vanquish, the gluttonous grief.

See strategies: Cake, Chocolate, Empathic Listening, Essential Maintenance, Forgiving Yourself, Havening, One Step at a Time

H

☼ HAIR

When the children were young, I used to cut my hair with nail scissors. This is fine as long as you have a good selection of hats and hairbands. When Ray joined our family, he quickly decided to shave his head bald and keep it that way. Much quicker. Fast appearing grey hairs became less obvious.

If, however, you have learned the art of 'putting yourself on the important list' you will be visiting the hairdressers or barbers.

It's ideal if you can actually *go* to the hairdressers or barbers, rather than relying on home visits. You don't want to risk traumatizing the hairdresser, plus, if you get your hair done at home, you are still immersed in a tricky environment with children escalating due to you being unavailable to leap up and meet their demands. Far better to go to a nice salon, possibly including a silent drive there and back. There will be magazines to read, and you can even ask the hairdresser not to talk.

I know this means a bit of organization to make sure the children are kept in their routine (and it *did* take me three years to achieve), but trust me, it's worth it.

Feeling that we have nice hair gives us a bit of a boost and does a little filling of our cup.

See strategies: Brain Breaks, Essential Maintenance

 **HAVENING**

What *is* Havening?

First of all, you can easily find videos on the internet if you do a search on 'What is Havening?' to see what it looks like, and how it works, which will save me pages of complex descriptions!

What I found reassuring was that all the research and techniques associated with Havening are based in neuroscience. In fact, although at first glance it looks as if it cannot work and it must 'all be in the mind', it is actually a logical/neurological process, and it doesn't matter *one bit* if the participant thinks it will work or not!

Havening is a straightforward touch-based therapy which produces delta waves in the brain. It is a technique developed by Dr Steven and Dr Ronald Ruden.

Dr Steven Ruden explains:

> The Havening Techniques are a rapid, gentle and effective approach for helping people overcome anxiety-based problems. Distressing feelings such as intermittent panic, stress from trauma, chronic pain, fears, depression, addictions and other related issues are amenable to Havening... The brain is an electro-chemical-magnetic organ. Pharmaceuticals address the chemical imbalance and as long as the drug is in the system its effects are present. Havening harnesses the electrical side (electroceutical), and through a simple protocol introduces delta waves into the mind/body system.

When something traumatic happens to us physically, there are lots of changes in the body and some of the things we're likely to do include:

- wringing our hands
- touching our face with both hands
- hugging ourselves.

Havening uses these same instinctive actions and builds on them to increase delta waves in the brain. Therefore, if you saw me applying a Havening touch, you would see me touching the face, shoulders and hands of the client. Dr Steven Ruden describes it like this:

> Delta waves are very special in that they are normally absent during the awake hours and are primarily present during sleep when thoughts are stored. The mind/body holds memories. Sometimes these memories create symptoms and the use of an electroceutical (something that causes an effect due to an electrical wave) is able to alter those encoded ideas and remove their effect from our system. This removal changes both the underlying stressor and the individual's response.

The *real* beauty of Havening, however, is that the touch can be applied by the person needing help using 'Self-Havening'. This was a real lifesaver during the Covid lockdowns, and when many parents were struggling, we were able to deliver sessions remotely via the internet.

Sometimes, one session is all that is necessary, and we've certainly had some great results within an hour, where there has been one distinct event which needed to have the emotional, traumatic content removed. With more complex work, this would need to be undertaken by a therapist or psychotherapist with other related qualifications and a background in trauma. Although Havening *looks* remarkably simple and straightforward, it's not something that can be undertaken by an amateur with no thorough therapeutic grounding in the field.

Havening in therapeutic parenting

You know how when something really dramatic happens, you remember where you were and what you were doing at the time? Well, I remember exactly where I was, and what I was doing, when I first heard about Havening.

How I *wish* Havening had been invented when my children were young. Not only could I have used it to help them in a practical way, but also I could have used it to help me. I have seen miraculous transformations happen in very short timescales in situations where it appeared all hope was lost, when Havening Techniques™ are applied correctly.

When I learned what Havening *did* and how it worked, I was of course sceptical, but I also thought that even if *half* of this was true, it would completely change the face of child trauma. Since that day, I have made it my business to thoroughly research Havening and, also, with the team at The Haven Parenting and Wellbeing Centre (part of the Centre of Excellence in Child Trauma), to develop programmes which use Havening and include other psychosensory strategies, such as mindfulness, visualization and meditation, for maximum benefit, to help to interrupt trauma. Our 3 Steps to Connect – 3SC™ programme has produced dramatic results and works in a similar way to Havening, but combines all these methods together, along with empathic listening.

It's been an interesting journey. When I told my colleague Sarah Dillon about Havening, she decided to try it out in her psychotherapy practice, so she went and did the training, becoming an accredited Havening practitioner. She reported that the results she saw with the young people and families she worked with were incredible. I then also became trained in Havening and developed an interest in using this intervention to help therapeutic parents.

At our training, we began to speak to social workers and parents about Havening and also to point them in the direction to find out more, because we knew it would help so many families. We could almost see the delegates looking at each other in a bit of a quandary. I think they were thinking, 'The training has been going really well till now, and clearly they talk a lot of sense, but *what on earth* are they talking about now?' As we began to show them the effectiveness of Havening, and the way we combined this with the other psychosensory therapies, the sceptical stares changed to astonishment and hurried searches on the internet.

A lot of our direct work now at COECT is done with parents using these combined therapies to remove triggers and helping them to overcome traumatic events. There's not much I find more satisfying than having parents who were originally absolutely desperate, and feeling unable to go on, turn around, reconnect, rediscover their empathy and become a stable family unit again. The hope and joy we see on their faces is precious indeed.

For parents, the best thing is that they feel able to continue in a positive way. Maybe there had been a trigger that used to drive them away from the child. When that trigger is removed and they no longer have an emotional reaction to it, the chances for renewed connection increase.

Generally, at COECT we combine Havening and 3SC to:

- remove triggers for therapeutic parents
- remove the emotional content of traumatic events, making it much more manageable
- change a state of mind to a much more positive one.

Personally, I have also used Havening to help with weight loss, and for the first time in my life I've successfully lost a great deal of excess lard, without feeling like I was making an effort, or even feeling as if I was on a diet.

You can find out more about Havening from www.havening. org. For more information on our trauma interruption sessions, including our 3 Steps to Connect™ programme, visit the Centre of Excellence in Child Trauma at www.coect.co.uk and The Haven Parenting and Wellbeing Centre at www.thehavencentre.co.uk.

See strategies: Brain Breaks, Empathic Listening, One Step at a Time, Therapy (For Parents), Triggers (Managing), Views

 HOLIDAYS

In *The A–Z of Therapeutic Parenting*, I write about strategies for ensuring your holidays are easier and less triggering for children, like trying to go to the same places, keeping routines and so on. Yes, very dull for us I know. Here, I am trying to help you to not only *survive* the holiday, but actually have a nice time. Feels like an impossible dream, doesn't it? Well, it does for those of you who have already been scarred by the Disneyland or Center Parcs 'from dream to drama' experience.

The very first thing to consider is going on holiday alone. If you need to get away on your own, then go! I know it takes a bit of organizing, but oh my goodness, even a couple of days away gives us a whole new perspective on things, and it is the number one best way to get rid of compassion fatigue. The way I managed to escape alone sometimes was to get my friend to come to the house to look after the children. This kept them in their routine and ensured minimum disruption. It's true that my friend needed a fair bit of training up (and lots of bribing and favours returned), and we certainly needed preparation, but it was well worth it.

Going on holiday with our unique children is an adventure. It's also, often, bloody horrific. There are airports to manage, delays, different locations and self-sabotaging moments to overcome.

My worst holiday ever was when I was due to go to Greece with just one of my children when she was a teen. In the spirit of self-sabotage, she absented herself in a screeching rage, just as we had to leave for the airport. I went to the airport anyway and got on the plane. I was still furious on the plane, especially when a man put his sleeping daughter next to me so she 'could stretch out'. I was incandescent with rage. I had paid for that seat for my ungrateful, un-holidaying daughter. I did not want another child, *any child*, anywhere near me.

Yes, I *know* this was entirely unreasonable but, in my defence, I was in a rage for about ten hours. The rest of the holiday passed miserably. I checked up that my daughter was suitably dismayed at home, incredulous at the fact that I had gone ahead with the holiday in any case. I spent the whole week being alternately bored and furious. At least I had made the point that my plans would not be controlled by my daughter (and stuck to the therapeutic parenting train track), but I *did* get an early flight home.

In the section on 'Disappointment', I've already described some of our worst holiday fails. Here are my top tips and key information to make sure that you are mentally prepared and *your* holidays don't end up in a similar disaster.

Go on a cruise
Advantages:

- Hard for children to leave.
- Wall-to-wall kids' clubs.
- Soothing motion of the ocean.
- Can avoid airport horrors.
- All-you-can-eat buffets.
- You can hide.
- You can go on the exact same ship multiple times but go to different places.

Forget the concept of 'holiday'

- It's likely you need a break due to your children's behaviours. You won't get a break if your children are coming too, and they will be more dysregulated.
- You will have to plan every single tiny little detail.
- You will probably have to stay in a dull routine.
- Your children will still argue.
- Your children will still complain.
- You will still have to negotiate food.

It is unlikely you will be 'relaxing on the beach'. Instead, you will be:

- dealing with flies
- refereeing
- checking children have not drowned
- stopping children burying other children
- looking for lost children
- screeching at the children in the sea that they are going out too deep, while you are standing ankle deep in the surf, keenly aware that you are wearing shorts with pockets stuffed full of keys and phones, unable to actually wade out further, and trying to make your voice increasingly threatening in order to avoid having to go out deeper
- persuading children to wear sun cream
- watching children burn when they refuse to wear sun cream
- going back to the crowded beach trying to remember exactly where you had been sitting, to try to locate the pink sandals that the child only realized they didn't have when they discovered 'the pavement was hot'.

Take some essentials to try to make things nicer for you

- You will have to be an avid admirer of 'jumping in the pool' for the thousandth time, regardless of how interesting it is, so *dark glasses are a must*. Then they can't see whether your eyes are open or shut. Smiling and nodding looks the same.
- In order to drown out the screeches and arguing, take ear buds so that piercing shrieks can be heard but low-level arguing, bashing noises or demands for admiration are muffled.
- Make sure there is at least one other adult besides you and carve up the days without pity.
- Take a large bottle of gin.
- Take another holiday brochure for 'adults only' to book up for recovery on return, or to look at longingly and daydream.

Although it can be hard to relax on holiday with our children, due to their levels of anxieties or additional needs, it can still provide us with some great memories and fun times. Being on the beach might have been a bit full on, but it was also the place where my children were the most relaxed, especially with the regulating sounds of the sea. Provided I stayed switched on, and ensured I had good visibility, this gave them more freedom than normal. Just make sure you are within running distance of the tempting, dangerous cliff.

Since my children left home, I go wherever I bloody want to now. Sometimes, I even volunteer to take the grandchildren to a caravan. And do you know what? It's actually quite nice.

See strategy: Brain Breaks

 ## HOMEWORK (NOT DOING)

The advice I gave in my book *But He Looks So Normal* is still completely relevant, so I have revisited it here.

Breaking news: You do not *have* to do your child's homework! You do not have to sit down next to them for two hours out of your precious day to try to achieve an arduous 20 minutes of deep-pen-scouring 'work'. You don't have to keep trying to make it look as if they are more intelligent than they are, to get them put in a higher grade.

Step away. Stop. Do not do it.

When I realized that my children could not manage the transition of me changing from 'mummy' to 'teacher' and all the associated horrible behaviours that went with it, I simply stopped doing homework all together. My children did not die, and I did not go to prison.

Yes, alright, the school *was* quite cross with me and summoned me in. When I went in to see the headteacher about my 'total lack of conformity', he asked me why my children were not doing their homework. I replied that I had asked them to do their homework and I had created space and time for them to do it; however, unfortunately the children were too busy trying to make secure attachments or punching each other, and at the end of a long, hard school day they were unable to focus on yet more schoolwork. The headteacher retorted that I should 'support the school and enforce their boundaries at home'. I said, 'That is a brilliant idea! Can you please come round to my house at the weekend, tell the children to tidy their bedrooms and supervise them please? That will save me a load of work!'

The headteacher expressed some consternation. We came to a 'mutual understanding' – I would not be a teacher and he would not be a therapeutic parent.

As I suspected, my children all caught up later on, once their heads were less busy and the arguing, punching and noise had diminished somewhat.

See strategies: School Strategies, Useful Phrases

HONESTY

Also see Asking for Help, Birth Family Issues, Conflicted Feelings, Grief, Guilt

There are two aspects relating to honesty that come up time after time. The first is about the feelings provoked by the need to be honest *with children* and how that feels for *us*. The second concerns how we feel when people have been dishonest with us or missed out vital information, and the frustration that causes.

Honesty with children

There is a real difficulty here because we often know in our hearts what we *should* be saying, but we struggle with the *way* to say it. This is further exacerbated by conflicting advice from well-meaning others. The well-meaning others often want us to water down the much-needed, honest explanations with platitudes that they mistakenly believe will make the children feel better. In my book *The A–Z of Therapeutic Parenting*, I explain about this issue in relation to our children and provide strategies for sharing difficult truths.

For us, we can agonize over the smallest details. In our hearts (usually), we know that our children deserve the truth. It might be unpleasant, it might be difficult to say, it might break our own hearts as we tell our children these difficult truths, but we know there has to be at least one person our children can count on. If you are feeling it is safer or better for you to withhold these difficult truths, you do need to be honest with yourself at least, and acknowledge that you are most certainly storing up a whole load of heartache for later on.

Often, therapeutic parents will tell me horrendous stories about their children's pasts and explain why they can't share this with them. They ask me how on earth they could tell the children this terrible, tragic story. My answer is always the same. 'Your children already know this and if you fudge it they will know you are lying. They may not know it in the memory part of their brain, but their body remembers.' Not only that, but the very second they get on the internet and social media, they will find out anyway. I think this helps us to be brave and take that extra step to give our children the explanations they deserve. For us, it means that we don't have to live with two levels of knowledge. We don't have to promote a victim state of mind either. There are uncomfortable truths in our children's lives that we have to learn to live alongside. Far better to live alongside these now than to wait for them to burst out of their pit in all their desperate glory in years to come – unexpected, uninvited and full of renewed trauma.

Make sure that you give a great deal of thought to how you are going to share difficult histories with the children. It might be that you will do it in a natural, 'drip drip' way in response to questions. Whatever you decide, it is likely that you will struggle as much, if not more, with the telling, as you will with understanding the full implications of what you need to share. It's vital to ensure you have support in place for yourself, so that you can offload afterwards.

Honesty from others

Within our training and support services, we have noticed that many new foster parents and adopters have become frustrated, feeling that often they have not been adequately prepared for the task. For this reason, at the Centre of Excellence in Child Trauma, we have completely rewritten the whole assessment process, so it now includes all the fundamental foundation training in therapeutic parenting, and, crucially, ensures that the applicants really understand what lies ahead!

There's nothing more disheartening than starting out on your journey as a therapeutic parent, only to find that you have not been given the correct tools in your bag. You thought you were going to someone's house to paint their living room. On the course you went on, they explained all about painting and what sorts of brushes and paint to use. You've been assessed, you've passed the test, now you are feeling very confident for your first painting job. Unfortunately, not only have they forgotten to give you the address, but when you *do* eventually find the property, you find that there are no walls. In fact, the house is derelict. You're going to have to learn to put in foundations, be a bricklayer, build the walls and plaster them, before you can ever get to do the painting. This is very disheartening. It's more disheartening when the person who delivered the painting course, and sent you to this very house, claims that 'you should have known'.

Therapeutic parents are a pretty resilient bunch. I've seen so many people faced with impossible tasks step up to the plate, deal with it and get on with their lives. All we really want is a bit of honesty. If someone had told us that the house was derelict and taught us how to do the foundations in the first place, we would have learned. It would have been better to have had a bit of knowledge beforehand, rather than try to learn on the job. After all, we could always put a caravan in the garden while we build the house. 😉

See strategies: Brain Breaks, Empathic Listening, Essential Maintenance, Forgiving Yourself, Havening, Managing Visits (Contact), One Step at a Time, Protecting Self, Therapy (For Parents), Understanding, Useful Phrases, Walking

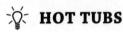 **HOT TUBS**

Hot tubs are absolutely great for so many things:

- They can help to regulate your child and get them clean at the same time.
- They can help *you* to calm down.
- They can make you temporarily unavailable.
- The bubbles make it difficult to hear any nonsense chatter or cries of 'Mummy/Daddy, watch me!'
- They can make you feel as if you are on a spa break, while still in your own back garden.

Hot tubs are only relaxing if you have them to yourself. Sitting in a large jacuzzi on holiday with disgruntled others, while your child does snorkelling in the jacuzzi to look at their pants, is not relaxing.

Word of warning, if you have an inflatable hot tub, make sure the children have not been able to sneak sharp objects in. Lesson learned.

See strategies: Brain Breaks, Co-Regulation, Timesavers

HUMOUR

Also see Resilience

I was very relieved to find that it wasn't just me who found things funny that many people thought inappropriate. As our resilience (and intolerance) grows, apparently our sense of humour warps and alters into a different, darker shape. I know this also happens in frontline emergency services, possibly due to the fluctuating levels of cortisol… Well, that will be us too then.

I've often laughed inappropriately. I can't really feel bad about this anymore because it kept me sane. Better to laugh than to cry, I think. As our resilience grows, we just find things funny that other people don't. That's their problem, not ours. Okay, the social worker might have raised her eyebrows a little bit when I burst out laughing after being told that one of my children had put paint stripper in the teacher's coffee…and yes, with hindsight, laughing was *not* the correct response. But to be fair, she had it coming, and I *had* warned her.

One of the best ways we have of protecting ourselves is to see the funny side. If you notice people looking at you in horror because you have decided that your child letting the goats out so they can do trampolining with them is actually quite amusing, this is their issue. Okay, the goats' horns *were* a bit pointy, but everyone seemed to be enjoying themselves. You just have to cope the best way you can.

Very often now, I go to the National Association of Therapeutic Parents' listening circles and hear evidence of this humour. Oh, how we laughed recently at the funny story that a parent shared with us about the armed police arriving to remove the AK47 their foster child pretended to have stuffed in their bedroom. The funniest bit of the story was the foster parent telling the policeman not to sit on the arms of the sofa: 'You wouldn't do that in your house, would you? Don't do it in mine!'

I used to make a note of some of the funny things that happened, and these notes have now become the source for many of my stories, talks and publications. I might have forgotten a lot of these things, if I hadn't written them down. Some, of course, are etched on my memory forever.

Therapeutic parents also become skilled in being able to see the funny side of the literalness of our children. Life would be very dull if we did not have some fun with this, not in an unkind way. I have taught my children to immediately start laughing if people around them start laughing at something they have said, or a question they have asked. They now pretend they have made a funny joke, then they ask me afterwards what was so funny.

When I recount the story of two of my children being put in a police cell at Orlando International Airport, people *do* laugh. At the time, I did *not* laugh. But guess what? One hour later we were *all* laughing about it and it got us safely through the journey home.

Here are some humorous moments from our lives and the lives of some other therapeutic parents to lighten *your* day:

- Denise's daughter smuggling an entire live lamb into the bathroom in her school bag, and then into the bath with her.

- Me giving Charley such a bad emergency haircut she earned the nickname 'Cabbage' for the rest of her junior school days.
- My three-year-old grandchild opening the door of the toilet wide and walking out, straight into full view of a garden centre, while I was on the actual toilet.
- Helen's foster son telling security at the airport that she was not his mother and had a gun up her jumper. When they asked her what relationship she was, she panicked and said 'none'.
- Bazza's first Mother's Day gift: 'poo in the bath'.
- On the way to visit the Dead Sea, me explaining to Charley it was 400m below sea level: 'Well, I'm not jumping in that then! That's way too high!'
- My girls all deciding to weigh themselves.
Rosie: Go and jump on my scales upstairs.
Crashing noise
Sophie: The scales are broken.
Rosie: What did you do?
Sophie: I jumped on them, like you said.
Laughing noises
Sophie: What? Why are you laughing?

And some of the questions/statements...

- Does fake tan work in England?
- At a girly spa party, 'Why do they make so much face cream when you don't have enough face?'
- What even *is* Nasty Sister Disorder? (narcissistic personality disorder)
- What's the queen got to do with the monarchy? That's where monks live, isn't it?
- I do believe in God, it's just that I don't really think he's any better than anyone else really.

- Does dog shampoo make your hands hairy? (Sophie, aged 22, and a qualified dog groomer.)
- Oranges are basically beige.
- I don't want a soft pillow, because I might fall into it.
- Are we in the swimming pool? (While standing together waist deep in the swimming pool.)
- Me: 'I used to work in the field of social work.' Charlotte: 'Why did you work in the field? I thought you worked with children.'
- Helping Sophie choose a new bed and discussing whether to stick with a single or go to double.
  Me: There's a 4-foot one.
  Sophie: But I'm 5 feet 2 inches.
- What's the difference between a hard-boiled egg and a soft-boiled egg? (Serious question, not a joke.)
- I can't get a car from Wales because it will have a Welsh number plate.
- Apparently, if you put yogurts down the toilet, it's really economical. I asked why, she didn't know, but had been tipping yogurts down the toilet anyway.
- Is the sauna hot?

See strategies: Laughter, Protecting Self, Sarcasm

 HYSTERICAL PLAYFULNESS

Therapeutic parents use 'playfulness' to help diffuse a tricky, tense situation. As we get into the swing of it a bit more, the 'playfulness' can become slightly hysterical, and may even become fun!

At the very time when it starts to be entertaining for *us*, it usually becomes 'embarrassing' to the children. It's not intentional. It's just one of the casualties of our parenting style. Oh well.

When Katie, aged 15, screamed at me that I was 'a fucking

moron' and engaged in an out-of-control smashing session, I thoughtfully went and put on my favourite neon orange wellies and my rescued purple pac-a-mac. I then presented myself before her with a flourish as a fashionista. Smashing noises stopped and were replaced with incredulous muttered gasps of 'What the hell are you doing now?'

'Well, I thought about what you said Katie, about me being "a fucking moron". I think you may have a point!' She tried very hard not to smile but failed. Once everything had calmed down, really, I should have just gone and got changed. But no. By then I was having such a thoroughly enjoyable time that I decided to do an entire fashion show, mixing together my favourite neons and pouting on an imaginary catwalk. The children gazed on mutely, not daring to say anything else in case I escalated. I think they were using 'child presence' to try to regulate me.

When Ray returned home, he took in the trashed room, glazed looks of boredom on the children's faces, and me, dressed up in un-matching neons, strutting up and down the lounge to Madonna's 'Vogue', and quickly put the kettle on. He had learned by then not to try to solve the problems nor enquire how my day had been.

A month later, William made the terrible error of saying something similar to me. I wore the same outfit to collect him from school. He never said it again. This was disappointing as I had enjoyed myself immensely (especially as the school-gate parents drew away in horror).

The children also learned very quickly not to call me a 'fat cow', as 'fat cows' have a tendency to drag themselves about on the floor, mooing loudly. This could be embarrassing if they had friends round.

See strategies: Dancing (Mad Dancing), Jolliness/Jauntiness (Fake)

I

 ## ICE CREAM

Ice cream is very satisfying as a treat. For a start, it takes you longer to eat it, so your treat lasts longer, and also it's easier to hide. Our children are unlikely to go searching underneath the healthy vegetables in the freezer. Don't fall into the trap of getting the ice cream out in anticipation of being able to eat it. This is a flawed plan. Once the children are settled, take the ice-cream tub out of the fridge and keep it near you. If you are called off to deal with a bedroom incident, put the ice cream back in the freezer, otherwise it is likely you will end up with a thick ice-cream milkshake. Just not the same thing to be honest.

See strategies: Alcohol, Cake, Coffee, Krispy Kreme Donuts, Tea (Cups of, Cream)

INADEQUACY (FEELINGS OF)

Also see Compassion Fatigue, Conflicted Feelings, Doubt, Guilt, Overwhelm, Valuing

I remember the day when I put my youngest child in the clothes I had bought for her, placed her in her new pushchair and took her for her first walk along the sea front. All the way along the promenade, I expected the police to come and arrest me, and ask me why I had stolen the baby. You see, I felt as if I was pretending to be a mum. I felt like this for a long time; when the children called me 'Mummy' and other parents looked at me sideways, this only heightened that feeling.

I never thought I would feel that way. In fact, I was ready to embrace adoption and parenting and looked forward to all that it would entail. I didn't expect to feel like a fraud.

After a couple of months, I did start feeling like 'the mum', and I was certainly experiencing it with the amount of washing I was doing. But this impostor syndrome niggled away in the background. As the children's difficulties became more obvious, and I became less clear about what I was doing, I began to feel that social services might have overestimated my capabilities. I began to feel inadequate and to panic that I might not be up to the task. The more the level of the children's trauma and associated difficulties became apparent, the more inadequate I felt.

I was suddenly jettisoned into the cosy world of nurseries and schools. Along with the fully formed cobweb of intricate relationships, developed through years of pregnancy, childbirth and toddler tantrums, I had missed everything, from rejoicing at the blue line on the pregnancy testing kit, to the first days at nursery, and even, for two of my children, first days at school. All of that, of course, was an integral part for the mums and dads gathering outside to meet their children. Many people assumed that I had moved to the area, but when they realized I hadn't, there was confusion and suspicion. I wasn't a real parent after all, was I? I was a pretend parent. This wasn't helped by parents even saying that kind of thing, albeit in a slightly kinder way. They couldn't help being nosey. I soon learned to grow a thick skin and to develop my own responses to these clumsy questions. It didn't help me to stop feeling deficient though. It didn't stop the judgement in the eyes of others.

I think I was so lucky that I had worked in social work in children and families, fostering and adoption. I honestly don't know how I would have managed to navigate my way around the plethora of assessments, meetings and chaos that surrounds children with additional needs, and their movement from family to family. People accepted me in meetings and welcomed my opinion due to the fact that I was a social worker! I found myself falling back on this professional qualification in order to justify my knowledge of my own children! The irony was, of course, that my professional qualifications and experience had no bearing whatsoever on what I learned about trauma *from* my children.

I was also lucky because I had spent many years working as a nanny. I understood what I needed to carry in my bag in case of explosive diarrhoea accidents in the soft play. Most adopters who have not had children do *not* know this and there isn't really a lot of training for it. Unfortunately, when you come up against your first difficult incident and find that you don't have the right equipment, this only reinforces your feelings of inadequacy.

We can also feel as if we aren't enough when those instant feelings of love don't pop up as expected. It's unrealistic to expect this to happen, but pressure is put on parents to have that instant bond. This contributes to feelings of failure. If that's where *you* are at the moment, just step back and let that go; it will come to you, but it won't come if you keep staring at it.

See strategies: Brain Breaks, Empathic Listening, Essential Maintenance, Forgiving Yourself, Havening, Jolliness/Jauntiness (Fake), One Step at a Time, Protecting Self, Self-Regulation, Space, Therapy (For Parents)

ISOLATION

Also see Anti-Socialism, Blame, Criticism, Family,
Friendships, Perfect Parents, Top Trump Parenting

There is such a pattern of isolation affecting therapeutic parents. It is this which drives everything we do at the Centre of Excellence in Child Trauma.

It is one thing to be struggling with a problem: it is quite another to feel not only utterly alone with that problem, but also blamed and judged for how you are trying to *handle* the problem.

I started feeling isolated about six months after my children came home to me. It took me a while to notice that this was indeed the case, maybe because I was just so busy. But gradually, I realized that other parents had 'slidey eyes' when talking to me. They didn't seem too keen on chatting at the school gates; they just weren't comfortable. One parent even said to me once, 'Don't you feel bad taking other people's children?'

It's not only difficulties in making and keeping friends, but also just the day-to-day interactions. Nowadays, I am frequently walking my five dogs. We make quite a spectacle. Very often, people will stop and chat and smile. They will pet the dogs and say things like, 'You've got your hands full, haven't you?' Not once did this happen *ever* with my five children. Then, people crossed the road to avoid us. Walking into a restaurant meant people huffed and sighed, anticipating a horrible rowdy bunch. (They weren't. They were always great, as long as food kept arriving.)

Now, when I look back, I feel desperately sad for the old me. The one who thought that her friends would remain friends. The one who anticipated exciting new friendships with other parents, play dates and cosy coffees. More and more we were on the side-lines. More and more I found myself on the defensive, explaining why my children behaved the way they did, how I was trying to help them. But then, finally, I stopped. I could not be bothered to keep justifying myself to everyone constantly. I no longer felt like explaining away my children's behaviours to ignorant parents who only wanted to indulge in a bit of one-upmanship parenting or blame and judgement. Even, to some extent, family fell away. They didn't want the turmoil that went with the busy visits and full-on tantrums. I didn't even blame them really.

But I *did* get lonely. I have never felt more alone than when I was desperately struggling and no one at all was there to even listen, let alone help. Before I became anti-social, I did really want to be part of the gang. But when the gang rejects us, we reject them back. Before we know it, we are caught in a cycle of withdrawal, sadness and loneliness, determined not to take any risks with new friendships, that seems to work like this:

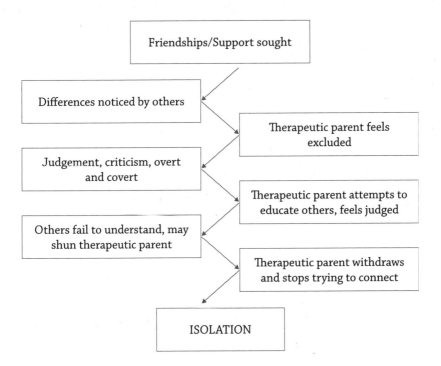

At the National Association of Therapeutic Parents, people tell us that the feeling of isolation is the most debilitating problem they face. This is why we started to hold listening circles and link parents up together. The only real antidote to isolation is to connect with people on the same page as you – someone who does not need a two-day explanation about what a 'bad day' means. I am so happy that today I know that no parent of birth children with additional needs, or foster parent, adopter or special guardian, or any other type of therapeutic parent, needs to be isolated because of differences in parenting. No one else will ever need to scream alone in an empty house... Although, of course, that can still be quite cathartic at times.

See strategies: Babysitters, Dogs, Empathic Listening, Essential Maintenance, Protecting Self

J

JEALOUSY

Also see Conflicted Feelings, Guilt, Perfect Parents, Relationship Problems

Jealousy is normal. Guess what? Even people who are not therapeutic parents get jealous. Not of us, obviously, as their lives are so bloody perfect with their pristine furniture, un-bogied cars, and polite, helpful children who come top in maths while running local volunteer projects.

Jealous, me? No. My life has been more 'interesting'. I've learned a lot. All the perfect families had were children coming top in maths. They never learned how to stop children trying to jump out of moving vehicles, *and* they have zero skills in pointy-eyebrow death stares at teachers.

Okay, maybe they did have a few things I might have liked:

- Occasional quiet evenings.
- The opportunity to watch an entire film with children, without remote controls being used as weapons.
- Chocolate that actually stayed in the cupboard.
- Fewer children.
- Friendships with other parents who did not feel the need to put in caveats around their requirements for a visit.
- Holidays where people seemed to have a nice time.
- Less loneliness.

Sometimes, we know we have to keep quiet about things that ignite jealousy. For example, our children get an awful lot of time, attention, therapy and input. That's completely right; they are entitled to that. There are endless meetings, assessments and sessions we attend. In every session, in every meeting, we talk about the child – how they're feeling, what we need to do to help them to improve, but we have this sneaky resentment sometimes. That devious, quiet, little voice saying, 'What about me?' Now, we might think that's jealousy, and it *feels* like jealousy, but actually it's just a leftover fear from our sense of isolation and of our feelings being ignored.

Very often, at COECT, we get asked for help by parents who are struggling with their *own* relationship. The arrival of the children has awakened feelings of jealousy. Sometimes, the couple relationship has suffered. An adopter once said to me, 'I feel like I've lost him [husband]. I've lost my relationship with him and the children have taken it. I don't want to feel this way, but I do. So, then I feel like a bad person, small minded, nasty, guilty. Where does it end?'

It is very true that 'the grass is always greener'. We don't need to spend hours feeling envious of all the happy family photos on Fakebook.

At Rosie's wedding, a friend with securely attached birth children said to me, 'I have always envied you, your life and your family.' I was astonished!

'Why?' I asked.

'Well,' she replied, 'life has never been dull. You are such a strong and resilient family...so bonded!'

I smiled a little smile to myself. Yes, it's quite true. Our lives have never been dull.

See strategies: Empathic Listening, Essential Maintenance, Havening, One Step at a Time, Protecting Self

JOLLINESS/JAUNTINESS (FAKE)

What with all our pausing, mad dancing, distracting playfulness and general hysteria, it's no wonder that we may gain a little edginess to our pseudo jaunty act. Everything is fine here! Nothing to see! All is well! What a *jolly* time we are all having!

Fake jauntiness is used in the following situations:

- When your child is about to start a full-scale tantrum and needs fast distraction.
- When you are forced to take part in the parents' race at the school sports day. (I would saunter to the finish line, waving and smiling happily, making no effort to actually run.)
- When the teacher is heading towards you with an angry face and a sulky child. ('Oh hello! How lovely to have time for a little chat!')
- When the police arrive at your house with your child, after the latest shoplifting event. (NB: Too much jauntiness can be dangerous here.)
- When you are trying to get through customs and your child is trying to shout that you 'make bombs'. ('La, la la...it's his new song at school! What *do* they teach them these days?')
- When your child has just punched Mickey Mouse in Disneyland because he 'doesn't like people in costumes'. ('Oh, deary me, what *is* he like? Hahaha...sorry...')
- When you have just been told by the lifeguard that you are not allowed in the pool because 'you have too many children', after spending an hour getting them all changed. ('Come along everyone! I've just had a *much* better idea about what we can do... No William, don't worry about the poo you've accidentally left in the swimming pool, I'm sure the nice lifeguard will have a lovely time playing "Hunt the poo"!')
- Getting a phone call from the headteacher asking why your

child has said you are 'putting her back into care'. ('Goodness me! *What* an imagination, bless her!')

- When the social worker tells you to start using a reward chart. ('Oh, you are *so* funny! You *do* make me laugh!')

See strategies: Dancing, Hysterical Playfulness, Useful Phrases

K

KINDNESS

Also see Acceptance, Asking for Help

People describe me (sometimes) as a kind person. I can accept that in relation to thinking about nice treats for others. I can accept it regarding my devotion to animals and my drive to rescue them. I cannot accept it when people say I am 'good' or 'kind' for having adopted my five children.

That does not fit, and it does not feel right.

The parents of unique children either through birth or adoption and fostering can find it difficult when others decide we are somehow saviours. I adopted my children for selfish reasons. I wanted to be a mum. At no point did I think, 'I am going to save the world and be really good and holy and adopt five needy little waifs and strays who are starving outside my house.' I think there's a bit of a Victorian ideology around adoption and fostering. While it's true that you certainly *do* need to have a slightly altruistic outlook, and also be very tolerant, primarily we do what we do because we *want* to. Gone are the days when children went up chimneys and were rescued by charitable institutions. I am not a charitable institution, and although I *do* have a chimney, my children have never been up it. (Well, not to my knowledge anyway, but anything remains possible.)

It's not quite the same when a birth parent has a child with a disability or additional needs. I don't hear many people telling *them* that they are 'good and kind' because they kept the child. It is just expected. This can breed resentment. Yet there is plenty of criticism for those parents who struggle day in day out, with little or no support, and are just expected to cope *because* the child is their birth child. They are castigated and blamed if they even *suggest* they may not be able to cope.

The truth of it is, most therapeutic parents are kind people; they may not have started out that way, but life has dealt them that hand. That kindness comes out in our children, and later in life we usually see that kindness coming back to us. I would say that some of the most caring people I know are my children. My second youngest daughter has such empathy and kindness for animals; the child who was scared of dogs when I met her is now devoted to them.

For this reason, I think kindness gives us hope for the future. If we accept it from others, we can pass it on more easily to our children. That can be a real challenge though, and accepting kindness from others may feel the same as accepting help. Sometimes this makes us feel as if we are exposing ourselves and somehow being weak. This is not the case. You are entitled to receive kindness. You show your children kindness every day, so allow some to come back to you.

See strategies: Empathic Listening, Essential Maintenance, Protecting Self, Useful Phrases

 KITTENS

I am allowing kittens to have their own section, distinct from cats, because kittens are seriously cute. They definitely have a feelgood factor and stimulate the production of happy hormones.

Word of warning: if you get yourself a lovely cute kitten to make yourself feel better, it will grow up into a cat that will treat you with contempt.

See strategies: Cats, Dogs

KRISPY KREME DONUTS

Any kind of cake is going to make you feel better, but Krispy Kreme Donuts are basically the King of Donuts. If you want a really lovely treat, make sure you have a whole box. Even our children are unlikely to be able to stuff the whole box. (NB: This is not guaranteed.) Make sure you hide at least one for yourself and eat it the day you buy it, otherwise it won't taste very nice.

In order to remind myself of the happiness I've had while donut eating, I've nicknamed my dog Duncan, Dunky Donuts. This way I get a little happy burst every time I call his name.

See strategies: Cake, Coffee, Ice Cream, Tea (Cups of, Cream), Vanishing Treats

L

 LAUGHTER

I found a really great strategy was 'laughter imprints'. What I mean by this is when you're having a great time and laughing with your children, put down a 'marker'. When I was having a snowball fight with my children on a skiing holiday, everyone was laughing hysterically, falling over in the snow and generally being pretty dysregulated to be honest. Everyone was giggling so much, so I said, 'This is great fun, isn't it? I'm always going to remember this snowball fight.'

Because I put down that laughter imprint, I could reference it in the future and get us all back there pretty quickly. We would always smile when we remembered that time. It can just lift the mood. Going back into a happy memory, when we were all glad to be delighting in each other's company, can distract from whatever the tricky thing is we're trying not to look at, at the moment.

See strategies: Hysterical Playfulness, Sarcasm, Valuing

LETTING GO

*Also see Adult Children, Conflicted Feelings, Drained (Feeling),
Exhaustion, Fear (of Child), Grief, Guilt, Overwhelm*

There is no harder decision, no more desperate circumstance, than when you find yourself thinking you cannot go on. Sometimes we feel we have reached the end of the road because we are exhausted. Or it may be that the impact on others is too great. The price is too high to pay.

It might be that our partner or family is advising that 'it has to end'. Perhaps there is anger, rejection and violence. Your child may be taking risks that are simply too dangerous to tolerate. Maybe there are mental health issues which have made a difficult situation impossible. We may feel we are being pulled in every direction. And almost always, we still desperately, painfully, love this child.

Sometimes it is not our choice, not one little bit. Our children vote with their feet. They shake off the bonds of attachment, reject any links to past trauma, any association, and reinvent themselves.

And we sit by and watch. We try everything. We use all our strategies. And at night we are torn apart by conflicting guilt, relief and terror.

And onlookers judge... 'She gave up on him and he'd already been through so much', or: 'He turned his back on her and she hadn't even *done* anything.'

Well, they don't know. They can never know our pain, our trials, our sadness and devastation.

When we let go, it can feel permanent. It can really feel like forever, a visceral rejection, 'after everything we've done'. Hold tight, wait. It might be a long wait, but letting go is *not* the same as giving up. I never gave up, although there were days when I thought I had. I only realized later that the light was still shining. Those relationships had changed forever, and for one of my children I needed to change for them. Be someone different. Be a patient person. We can all learn to change; our children teach us that.

See strategies: Empathic Listening, Essential Maintenance, Havening, One Step at a Time, Picking Your Battles, Protecting Self

 ## LOOKING GOOD

Looking good can be difficult to achieve when you are forced into cutting your own hair with nail scissors.

I remember once a social worker advising me to 'give myself a treat' and go to the hairdressers. I nearly collapsed laughing. The idea of sitting in the hairdressers for about two hours, with no interruptions, no worries about where my children were and what they were doing, evidenced to me how completely out of touch she was with our lives. I knew that if I had the audacity to go to the hairdressers, I would certainly end up running down the High Street with tin foil in my hair. When I told the social worker this, she said, 'But surely with three weeks' notice, you could sort something out?' I asked if she was volunteering. She wasn't.

The thing is, when we look like shit, we feel like shit. I might as well have worn a bin bag a lot of the time. I tended to circulate three different tracksuits with varying patterns on them to conceal the detritus of the day, which seemed to glue itself to my body. I got to the point of avoiding looking in the mirror because it was too depressing.

However, when I started working at a college I realized that my detritus tracksuit look wasn't going to cut it. My hair was so appalling I wore a wig to teach one day. I then immediately decided never to do this again as three of the students asked me if I was wearing a wig. I thought it was really subtle and no one could possibly guess.

I realized that I needed to make a slight effort. I started by updating my tracksuit wardrobe. By adding in some colourful tops which were still comfy over some leggings, I immediately looked as if I'd made a slight effort. The effect on me was instantaneous. Because I stopped looking like a bag lady, I felt like making more effort from the neck up. This didn't mean I instantly ran off to the hairdressers but I *did* find a hairdresser who was hard to traumatize and always visited when the children were at school. Most importantly, I did learn over time how to effectively tap in to support to actually physically leave the house and go to the hairdressers, eventually. This took about three years to achieve, rather than three weeks.

When we make a slight effort with our own appearance the knock-on effect can be really positive. Yes, I know it can feel like another job to do. But if you have to go to a meeting and you are sitting there looking like something the cat dragged in, people will not listen to you or take you seriously. They will make pitying judgements. It is an uncomfortable reality that in order to be taken seriously by professionals, we need to look like a professional, even when really we are just a Warrior Parent in disguise.

Here are my top tips for shortcuts to looking good (or at least not pitiful):

- Sort your clothes out the night before, no matter how tired you are. This will stop you putting bin bags back on in a rush, when there is a new emergency.
- Get a hairdresser/barber who will do home visits during school hours.
- Make sure your wardrobe is full of comfortable clothes which match, no matter what order you put them on. No, this does not mean everything has to be black.
- Once a month, schedule in an uninterrupted bath and apply fake tan afterwards. This will at least make you *look* rested and healthy.
- If the chocolate and wine have added a few pounds, invest in flowing tops or shirts. Life is too stressful for weight loss sometimes.
- Wear bright colours. My neons tricked people into thinking I was more confident than I felt.

See strategies: Badminton, Essential Maintenance, Hair, Holidays, Running, Smile, Timesavers

 LOSING THINGS

For a start, it's not our fault that we lose things. Sometimes things aren't lost, they are stolen by our children. But our children are so convincing and so good at making us think that we have lost the item, sometimes we believe them.

The other reason we might lose things is because our brain is simply too full of important things. I mean obviously it's essential to know where you put the car keys, but that does pale into insignificance when you're trying to coax your child away from the fourth storey window.

Here are my top tips for looking a bit more organized and making sure you don't lose really crucial items:

- Make wearing a bum bag part of your 'getting dressed' routine. In the bum bag you need to make sure you have at least your car keys, credit cards, house keys and phone. It's a really good idea to keep any cash here as well.
- If a bum bag is too difficult, then get zip-up jumpers/hoodies with interior pockets. These are great to put on first thing, along with all the essentials for any running away episodes, stashed safely within them.
- Sort out the children's clothes and shoes the night before. Hide them if necessary.
- Get a safe. You can put the really important things in there like birth certificates, passports and essential documents, so that they're easy to put your hands on when you need them. We tend to need to access these more often for our children than other families, so it makes sense to keep them accessible and separate.

- Stop caring about matching socks. It doesn't matter, life's too short.
- Start saying out loud where you have put things. This really helps later on when you know for sure that you put the item in that place, but your child is looking at you with wide innocent eyes, explaining that they never saw it and weren't even there. When you have spoken out loud, you remember saying it. This can make you much more certain in your therapeutic parenting responses, and handily reassures you that you are not losing your mind, along with everything else.
- Losing children is a bit careless. Luckily, nowadays there are all sorts of handy trackers you can use in the form of bracelets, watches or apps on their phone. Just put trackers on them, it's not difficult. Oh, and if the Patronizing Ignorant Expert (PIE) tells you that you are invading their privacy, ask them to do a risk assessment, assuring you that they will take responsibility should anything happen to your child when they are missing.

See strategies: Timesavers, Useful Phrases, X-ing Out (Crossing Out)

LOSS OF IDENTITY

> *Also see Adult Children, Drained (Feeling), Empty Nest, Forgotten, Friendships, Humour, Perfect Parents, Relationship Problems, Unappreciated*

There's not much more boring than a parent who goes on endlessly about their child. There, I've said it. As my friends began to have children and wittered on endlessly about playgroups, the content of nappies and the best type of sugar-free juice, I often yawned loudly and excused myself. Before my very eyes, I saw formerly interesting people become dullards... And then I became a parent.

I was as guilty of this as anybody. It was the way I coped. I was struggling and I needed help, so I used to talk to anyone who might look like they could listen a tiny bit or help in any way. This made me very dull. I failed to notice my friends' eyes glazing over, sometimes rolling into the back of their heads. I became consumed by my children's needs. Over the course of two years, I changed from a vibrant, spontaneous, lively person into a dull, grey blob, who only obsessed about schools, how to get the bogies off the sofa, and how I could face the next day.

It's very easy to lose our identity and to reinvent ourselves as 'the parent of unique children'. Our children *do* take up a lot of our time, thoughts and energy. I eventually learned that it did *not* mean I had to lose my personality.

How do you know if you have lost *your* identity? Well, what does your social media photo look like? If it's a picture of your child, change it. Now. This is how the merging starts, and it's bloody annoying. Your child is not you. You are not your child.

When apathy strikes, we feel that it's too difficult to do anything for ourselves and this contributes to our loss of identity. It was only when I began to take brain breaks (taking advantage of any little bits of help that were offered to me to make sure that I could escape, even for a few minutes) that I started getting the *real* me back.

You will need the *real* you for when your children leave home. Otherwise, the grey, dull blob will simply sink into a heap of nothingness. This is very unattractive. I know it seems impossible, but one day your children won't need you as much. We must keep a bit of ourselves back. For me this was taking up a new hobby. At times, it was very difficult to drag myself out of the door to go to my weekly singing lesson. Now, looking back I am so glad that I kept a tiny two-hour section just for me, once a week. It is this tiny two-hour section that gradually swelled and became me-shaped again. It is *this* me who now sings, walks in the woods, laughs with my adult children, and is spontaneous and joyful.

It is *this* me who could let my children leave, assert themselves as adults, rejoice with them in their newfound freedoms, and commiserate with them in their life lessons. I could do this because although I am still 100 per cent their parent, and fully committed to them, I can *only* be that parent because I am me first.

See strategies: Babysitters, Brain Breaks, Dancing (Mad Dancing), Dogs, Essential Maintenance, Hair, Looking Good, Music, Protecting Self, Singing, Walking

M

 MANAGING VISITS (CONTACT)

The way you manage visits between your unique child and their birth family depends on a couple of things. If you are not clear about the set-up, or expectations of you, then it's worth asking, or researching to clarify the answers. Establish the following:

- The legal requirements. (Is the child obliged to go legally?)
- The nature of the relationship between the parents and the child. (Is it positive or abusive?)
- Who is expected to transport the child to and from the visit?
- The status of the relationship between you and the birth parents. (Are they related to you?)
- Your professional status. (Are you a therapeutic foster parent or an adopter?)
- Geography.
- The nature of the visit. (Is it expected to be in a park, family centre, or your home, for example?)
- How frequent are the visits meant to be and how long will they last?
- What support is available. (Is there a contact supervisor or social worker involved?)
- The actual place where the visit takes place.

Often when we are thrust into a situation which feels as if it's beyond our control, the best we can do is manage our own responses and feelings in that situation. I know that many therapeutic parents are forced to take children on visits that they do not agree with and do not want, but unless you are quite happy to break the law or run away to another country with the child, your options are limited.

What *can* we do?

- Be clear with all parties in advance about what you will, and will not, accept.
- Make sure you do this in writing. Where there is a telephone call, follow it up in writing afterwards and expect acknowledgement.
- Find out what behaviours from any party would necessitate an immediate end to the visit.
- Establish what support you, and the child, would get in the event of an unplanned ending to a visit.
- Find out if the birth parents are expected to travel to the visit too. (It's important to establish a culture where the child is not expected to travel long distances frequently.)
- Decide if you are comfortable taking a child to visit a birth parent where there has been abuse. Most therapeutic parents are not, as this can be damaging to the relationship between the child and the therapeutic parent. Where there is not a legal choice about the child going to the visit, seek reassurances that a supporting professional will transport the child and stay with them.
- If there is contact via video calls and the relationship is abusive/traumatic ensure that this also takes place outside your home. This will help you to keep cortisol levels lower in the home, including yours!
- Manage your own feelings – use some of the strategies around anxiety and anger to help you to manage your own feelings. (See strategies listed below.)

- Keep comprehensive behaviour diaries to clearly demonstrate patterns in behaviour, and send these diaries to relevant parties.
- Become an award-winning actor. Many birth parents also need therapeutic parenting. We can use therapeutic parenting responses to avoid argument, tension and heated debate.

You can get specific advice and signposting from the National Association of Therapeutic Parents (www.naotp.com).

Independent legal advice can be obtained from Child Law Advice, a registered charity offering legal advice on all matters relating to children, including contact (https://childlawadvice.org.uk).

For special guardians and kinship carers, check if your local authority has signed up to provide you with independent support through Family Action (www.family-action.org.uk).

See strategies: Brain Breaks, Empathic Listening, Havening, Jolliness/Jauntiness (Fake), One Step at a Time, Pausing, Picking Your Battles, Therapy (For Parents), Trailblazing, Training, Triggers (Managing), Understanding, Useful Phrases

☼ MORE

When you find yourself catapulted into an even more dire situation than the one you were expecting, there is only one strategy:

- More cake
- More chocolate
- More cups of tea
- More coffee
- More wine.

MOTHER'S DAY

Also see Disappointment, Forgotten, Unappreciated

Best not. That is my only advice really. Think about how you manage birthdays and apply the same strategies and planning.

You might be one of those really lucky parents who feels appreciated and has wonderful Mother's Days. Good for you. We really do not want to hear about it.

To be fair, my Mother's Days are *great* now. But I have been very patient...

The same applies to Father's Day, birthdays, wedding days... I could go on...

See strategies: Alcohol, Birthdays, Cake, Celebrating, Chocolate, Christmas Survival (and Other Celebrations), Essential Maintenance, Expectations (Managing), Protecting Self

MOTIVATION

Also see Conflicted Feelings, Doubt, Drained (Feeling), Eeyore Parenting, Exhaustion, Letting Go, Overwhelm, Valuing

Some days it is hard to feel motivated. We are motivated by success, reward and breakthroughs. Where we are experiencing a relentless tedium of unreciprocated care and effort, our motivation may pack a bag and go, leaving us with only drudgery as our faithful friend.

One of the hardest times to rediscover that motivation is when we feel we have gone two steps backwards. Suddenly the ground we thought we had made up has disappeared beneath our feet, leaving us 'back at square one'. These are dark days indeed.

I remember once standing in a room with a social worker. I was right on the edge of giving up on one of my children. I really felt that I could not go on any longer. Then she said the best thing she could possibly have said to me: 'I think you have to accept that "this placement" has disrupted, and they will have to move.' Referring to my child in this clinical, depersonalizing way as a 'placement' was all the fire I needed. 'It's not over until the fat lady sings,' I replied, 'and I'm not singing.'

This seemingly insignificant exchange reminded me of why I was doing what I was doing, and how far we had come as a family. It gave me a glimpse into the future, a future where my child would become a transient, easily discarded 'placement', a life where all the good we had done would unravel before our very eyes.

It's not always as simple as this. Sometimes it's *much* harder to rediscover our motivation. Even a glimpse into the future may not be enough to help us feel motivated enough to carry on. Occasionally, we might lapse into a kind of exhausted, negative Eeyore-parenting frame of mind.

Know that it's okay to feel this way and that it *will* pass. Everything changes constantly, even though it doesn't feel like that sometimes. Along with those changes are differences in circumstances, feelings and situations.

Sometimes, after a particularly negative bout of 'I can't do this anymore', I would make a deal with myself to see if I still felt the same in one week's time, or even 24 hours' time, then re-evaluate. We have to take care of ourselves when we have lost our mojo. Extra treats, reflecting on past successes, built-in breaks and just little light-hearted moments are what is needed to tempt motivation back through the door.

See strategies: Essential Maintenance, Faith, Havening, One Step at a Time, Reflecting, Therapy (For Parents)

 # MUSIC

Music can completely change the sentiment and energy in a heartbeat. It's such a valuable strategy. You already know that if you are feeling a bit sad or miserable, and a depressing piece of music comes on, it can tip you over. In the same way, a conscious decision to stop the wallowing, or lance the tension, with upbeat music can shift momentum rapidly.

You can easily create a 'happy music list' on your phone or home entertainment system like Alexa. Just say 'create playlist', then give it a name. In the mornings, I say, 'Alexa, play my happy morning playlist.' This means there are no adverts and no risk that there is suddenly going to be a triggering piece of music, linking back to a sad memory.

Another good use of music is to develop some 'theme tunes'. These can inspire, comfort and motivate you – and keep you going. While my children were growing up, some of my theme tunes were:

- 'The Show Must Go On' (Queen)
- 'I'm Still Standing' (Elton John/Bernie Taupin)
- 'I Want to Break Free' (Queen/John Deacon)
- 'Rabbit' (Chas and Dave)
- 'I Won't Back Down' (Jeff Lynne/Tom Petty)
- 'When You Walk Through a Storm' (Rodgers and Hammer-stein, *Carousel*)
- 'Smile' (Charlie Chaplin/Nat King Cole).

I would sing 'Rabbit' happily as my daughter nonsense chattered at a million miles an hour. This kept me smiling. There are lots of compliments in the song, along with an expressed exasperation for the amount of talking. Very cathartic.

I've reproduced some of the lyrics of some of the other songs here, so you can see when I used them. Often this would be in my car, windows down, screeching the words at the top of my voice. Or allowing a little Eeyore-parenting self-pity moment (with tears on my face when the children were absent).

I'm Still Standing *(Elton John/Bernie Taupin 1983)*

You know I'm still standing better than I ever did
Looking like a true survivor, feeling like a little kid
I'm still standing after all this time
Picking up the pieces of my life without you on my mind

Rabbit *(Chas and Dave 1981)*

Now I don't mind havin' a chat,
But you have to keep givin' it that.

No, you won't stop talkin',
Why don't you give it a rest?
You got more rabbit than Sainsbury's,
It's time you got it off your chest.

When You Walk Through a Storm
(Rodgers and Hammerstein 1945, Carousel)

When you walk, through a storm,
Hold your head up high,
And don't be afraid of the dark,
At the end of day there's a golden sky,
And the sweet silver song of the lark
Walk on through the rain, walk on through the wind,
Though your dreams be tossed and blown,
Walk on, walk on, with hope in your heart,
And you'll never walk alone,
You'll never walk alone.

*See strategies: **Audio Books, Hysterical Playfulness, Podcasts, Reading***

N

 NATURAL CONSEQUENCES (ALLOWING)

Yes I know, it's very difficult as caring parents to stand to one side and allow a mistake your child has made come to its natural conclusion. It feels very conflicting. Look, in order for a natural consequence to work, you have to *let it bloody happen*!

There, got that off my chest.

When my daughter stole the laxative chocolate, I did not intervene. She did not do it again. It was quite a big bar. 😌

Daily, our team at the Centre for Excellence in Child Trauma is inundated with parents asking, 'What is the natural consequence for...?' Well, the clue is in the title. Natural. A *natural* consequence happens when you don't intervene. You have to be a pretty strong parent to stand by and make a conscious decision not to intervene and to let the consequences occur. But the thing is, if you ever want your children to appreciate you (and others for that matter), you do *need* to stop saving everyone from the consequences of their own actions. We have to help our children to link cause and effect, and, luckily, that means less work for us if we stick to a non-intervention policy.

Not intervening is a positive decision and a really effective strategy. While we understand the benefits for our children, there are benefits for us too.

When we are able to allow natural consequences to happen it's usually the case that we understand what we are doing, and we have a plan. Our plan may be undermined by well-intentioned (and by that I mean patronizing/ignorant) others. (See 'Useful Phrases'.) It's difficult when others are judging us as 'harsh' because we are not replacing the 24th 'accidentally' broken phone or have chosen to allow the child to be late to where they need to get to. Well, we know best, and they can basically jog on. We are brain surgeons building synapses, they aren't. In *The A–Z of Therapeutic Parenting*, I explain the natural consequences for over a hundred different behaviours and situations.

There are occasions when obviously you might *need* to intervene, so for the avoidance of doubt I've provided a handy reference chart below.

Action	Natural consequence	Intervene (yes/no)
Child breaks own phone	Phone is broken. (No more running off for liaisons with drug dealers or unsuitable others, less worry for you.)	No.
Child is nasty to another child	Child does not want to play with them anymore. (Less hassle for you regarding play dates, etc.)	No.
Child breaks TV	TV is broken. (No more fighting over the remote control and arguing about programmes.)	No.
Child trying to run into busy main road	Child would likely get run over.	Yes, obviously. I mean, seriously?
Child hurts pet	Pet avoids child.	Yes. For your pet's sake.
Child moving slowly, will be late for school	Child is late for school. (Time for an extra cup of tea for you.)	No, but you could drop a line to the school just so they don't make a fuss.

See strategies: Brain Breaks, Essential Maintenance, Jolliness/ Jauntiness (Fake), Homework (Not Doing), Reflecting, Training, Useful Phrases

NEIGHBOURS

Also see Anti-Socialism, Asking for Help, Criticism, Friendships, Isolation, Perfect Parents

Maybe you are very lucky and you have neighbours who are supportive, interested and helpful. I found I had to move to more and more isolated places. For some reason, they took offence when one of my children would try to sleep in the shed. They also didn't like it when another took up burglary as a part-time activity. They were just so intolerant...

The problem with neighbours is that you never know when you're going to *need* them. If you're home alone and you end up with a 'blue light Saturday' (like we used to most Saturdays), you do sometimes need someone very close by to come and look after the other children while you rush/saunter off down to the hospital/police station.

We had one brilliant neighbour once. On the day that Ray and I had got married she offered to look after the children for the evening so we could go out. She ended up calling the police because she couldn't manage. At least she tried. So that was a nice wedding night...

The other problem with neighbours is that they do silent, judgy staring. If you're screeching in the back garden like a banshee because you just lost it, you can be sure that raised eyebrows will appear over the garden fence.

The other issue I used to have with neighbours was when they would drop in unannounced. Luckily, this stopped really quickly because my children would either immediately limpet onto them and adopt them as their new favourite surrogate parent, or try to steal their purse, depending on what their frame of mind was.

I would put in quite a lot of security so that I was aware when children left the building without my knowledge, and this doubled up nicely to give me an early warning system for an approaching neighbour. If it looked as if a complaint was coming, I would then grab my bag and say we were just leaving. This did cause problems sometimes, when the children would contradict me and say we were just about to have dinner.

Some of the worst neighbours I ever had to deal with were when I was running groups of children's homes. The children were really pretty good. You wouldn't normally have known there was a children's home in the street, except it was just busier. One day, however, there was a fire in the home. Almost immediately all the neighbours were up in arms, complaining that they 'could all have died'. The houses were all detached, the children's home observed fire drills, and everyone got out safely. Had it been a normal home, it was more likely the house would have burnt down, and no one would have woken up. The neighbours weren't interested in this. They wanted to continue the dramatic dialogue about how they 'almost died' because there was a children's home in the street. It was more exciting. Their amygdalas (survival brains) were well and truly activated and it was all so exciting. It was even in the local newspaper. I asked them where they thought children who could not live at home should live. I suggested they might prefer it if the children lived in the woods, or an adjacent field.

This is what we're up against, but it's just fear and ignorance. We went round and educated the neighbours about trauma. We explained to them how our children often overreact or act through fear. We found that taking this approach brought the neighbours much more on side. Some of them even made us cakes! We do have to balance this with the amount of information we give neighbours. Personally, I found I could identify one or two neighbours who had a clue and were more tolerant than others. These are the neighbours that I could rush off to.

It's worth putting in some effort and fighting down our natural resistance to taking the risk. We don't want the neighbours phoning the police every time they see the children... So, a bit of education goes a long way. Nowadays, I have no neighbours. We live in the middle of the woods with our dogs. On Sundays, I get very angry and resentful when walkers come past the house. That's how bad it's got.

See strategies: Paddington Hard-Stare, Pointy-Eyebrow Death Stare, Smug Smile, Training, Useful Phrases

 ## NONSENSE CHATTER (SURVIVAL OF)

Unfortunately, it is not just the odd question we get, it is an endless, streaming bombardment of total nonsense assaulting ears and brain. I used to feel as if my brain was actually frying in my head. It took me a while to realize that I did not *have to* answer this stupid nonsense. Yes, this is true. You do not have to answer nonsense questions. In fact, if you do not answer them, you can even use some of our strategies to help your child grow new synapses in their brain. What great parenting!

I made up happy little songs in my head or, in more desperate times, used headphones or earbuds. I would tell my children I was learning a new song, swiftly put my headphones on playing loud opera music, and start screaming along with it, thereby killing two birds with one stone, by lowering my own cortisol levels.

Although it's not actually a therapeutic parenting strategy, I know that occasionally we may walk away quickly to get some relief, or even say (quite loudly), 'Just be quiet for five bloody minutes. Please!' Understandable and human after all.

Here are some other things you can do:

- Tell the nonsense chatterer that your ears are full up, but that you will have capacity to listen to them at exactly...

(convenient time). Give them tea and cake or something very chewy that makes it tricky for the child to talk too much.

- Tell the nonsense chatterer you don't want to miss anything, so can they please go into the next room and record it all into this handy recording device. (NB: Do not give them your phone as they may use up the entire memory.)
- Tell the child it's 'very interesting' and you are sure that Granny/Grandad/Aunty Julie would love to hear about it. This is very useful where Granny/Grandad/Aunty Julie has been criticizing you for being too impatient.
- Say, 'That's very interesting, why don't you ask Alexa?' This saves *hours*.

Specific behaviour management strategies for this can be found in *The A–Z of Therapeutic Parenting*.

See strategies: Brain Breaks, Essential Maintenance, Music, Protecting Self, Useful Phrases

O

 ONE STEP AT A TIME

There are so many issues and feelings we experience that need strategies for breaking down into a 'one step at a time' approach that I have separated them out for you here.

Pointless worrying

When you don't know what to do, it is a complete and absolute waste of time to put loads of energy into worrying. What if this happens? What will I do?

If the answer is not clear, and you do not know what to do, do nothing. We use up so much energy worrying, and our mental stress increases. Make sure you choose a distracting activity to push the pointless worrying to the side a bit. The answer you need will become clear in five minutes or five days, usually when you are not using the worrying part of your brain. There is nearly always time for a cup of tea and quiet reflection. I really like the saying, 'It will be okay in the end, and if it's not okay, it's not the end' (Fernando Sabino).

Catastrophic thinking management

When we are overwhelmed by the latest catastrophe, or are feeling completely hopeless about the future, it can feel as if a huge wall of insurmountable bleakness is towering over us. It's all too tempting to look at this wall and think 'I can't' or 'I don't know where to start'.

Sometimes we are just utterly beaten, that yet again something as devastating as this has happened to us. How much more can we take?

At these times, we must take a step back. Turn away from the wall and ignore it for a short tea-break or walk. The wall will still be there after the cup of tea, or the walk in the woods, but you will at least have had some respite from its shadow.

Normally, in therapeutic parenting, we are looking ahead with hope to when the days will be easier and we will have achieved our goal, but where the 'Bleakness Wall' is in the way, we need to find a foothold first, or a way round it.

Once you have had a little break, stop, prepare, and look at the wall. Look at it carefully. There will be footholds, it's all about finding them. Have a little picnic or two while you try to find your way. Treats are needed for Bleakness Wall climbing.

Sometimes our catastrophic thinking has got in the way and we are simply standing under the shadow of this mighty wall, gazing at the top where it blocks out the sun and thinking all those worrying, catastrophic thoughts. By looking nearer the ground, looking *carefully*, we are only searching for the next step.

In practice, this is what it looks like. Take an average overwhelming/catastrophic thought process such as:

1. She is being rude to the teachers
2. Therefore, she will be excluded
3. Therefore, I won't be able to manage anymore
4. Therefore, she will have to move
5. Therefore, she will unravel
6. Therefore, I will never forgive myself
7. Therefore, my life is over.

Our wall of bleakness starts around 5, 'Therefore, she will unravel'. So, back pedal. Practise 'rewind > logic > reframe > reset', which looks like this:

- Overwhelming thought: 'Therefore, she will unravel.'
- Rewind thought: 'What started this thought?'
- Logical thought: 'She was rude to the teachers, and I am worried she will be excluded.'
- Reframe: 'What made her be rude?'
- Reset thought: 'How can I help to calm this situation?'

Then, if it does seem as if we are able to progress through to 2, 'Therefore, she will be excluded', we apply a logical reset to get through the exclusion and reframe to look only at that particular problem *right now*. What can I do to make the exclusion work? How can I help to prevent this happening again? Do I need to think about alternative education? And so on.

Overwhelming reality

Where a tragedy or dreadful incident has already happened, or is *definitely* going to happen, so it is more than just a dread that it might, we still need to apply 'one step at a time' thinking. You may be in a situation where:

- someone has died
- someone is going to die
- someone has committed a crime
- a significant relationship has ended
- there is an unexpected, unplanned pregnancy/end of pregnancy
- someone has been seriously injured
- your child is missing outside any usual timescales or patterns
- anything else is happening which is creating overwhelming grief/dread/fear/anxiety.

As I write this section, our own family is facing a certain and dreadful tragedy in the near future. It is of no use or help to look too far ahead with thoughts of 'How will we get through this?' or

'Will they be able to survive this?' It's easier (and less frightening) to concentrate on *the next thing*. Currently, we are looking at the next appointment and making no plans beyond that, holding no discussions about 'what-ifs' and 'maybes'. We will do the next thing, pause, look at what we have now and make the next decision. We will also use 'pre-event Havening' to help us all manage (see 'Havening').

Where someone has died, we may find ourselves catapulted forwards into the future with a visceral fear about all the things we now need to face without this person. Life looks different. It has changed forever. Therapeutic parents have additional worries about how they will keep the children stable throughout these times. How will we get us (and them) through the funeral? What about changes to finances? Again, stop, *tell yourself* to stop and look at *just* the next thing. This might be an appointment with the undertaker, for example. Plan this. Think about what you want to say, things that were important to the person. Focus on this and this alone. We need quite high levels of mental discipline to do this, so one of the exercises I used when I lost my dad was what I nicknamed 'mental swap'. If I was thinking a particularly sad thought, with some fear for the future thrown in, I would replace this thought immediately with a positive, strong mental image of my dad in good times. This became so automatic that, over time, I could no longer access traumatic last life events which had haunted me. I did also use Havening to help with this too, and found it to be very effective.

I have also found herbal remedies such as St John's Wort to be really helpful at very difficult times in my life, and when the children were older I also sometimes took herbal sleeping remedies. This meant I did not need to seek medical help from my doctor, but if there had been no improvement, I would have done. There is no shame in saying, 'Life is too difficult at the moment. Please help me.' I know it's really hard at these times to think about getting medical help, but if you are depressed, the doctor *will* help.

Delegation and instruction

Where you are facing an overwhelming situation, like an unplanned ending and a child suddenly moving – delegate. You do not want or need to impart the same dreadful news a hundred times. So, tell one person. Ask them to let key people know and also give them instructions for how you would like those people to respond to you. For example, you may not wish anyone to contact you, or you might want to do something different and be seeking distraction. You may want the school or extended family to be informed. Don't be afraid to state clearly what you need, and what you need *as a family*, right now. It's also really useful for those around you to be told the information and also to be given instructions about what actions and response you and your family would like (or do not want) from them.

Changing perspective – zooming out

When we are facing difficult times, a change of perspective, or 'zooming out', can be really helpful. We know that if we are standing close to a picture – very close – we cannot see it all. It's maybe just dots. But as we take a step back, and then more steps back, the picture becomes clearer and clearer until we have an overview.

In the same way, when we are mulling over a difficult event which is likely to happen, we can become so focused on that event and the people directly concerned, we forget to think about how others might be affected. We also need to think about:

- how it happened
- how it started
- whether it can be prevented from happening again.

All these thoughts can only gain traction when we 'zoom out' and stop ourselves focusing on the one significant event.

Carrying on

We may hit our own Bleakness Wall and feel that there is no *particular* causative significant event – life may be just too overwhelming. We sometimes feel as if we cannot go on. And yet we do.

One of the easiest ways to lose motivation is when we tell ourselves we can't do something. It's an easy trap to fall into, especially with the difficulties we often face. When we are overwhelmed or feeling that everything is too much, we find ourselves thinking, 'I can't do this.' Changing that simple statement into a positive, 'I *can* do this. I've done this before, I know *how to* do this', alters our attitude and increases our prospects of success.

Sometimes, when my children were teenagers and we were in very difficult times, I used to wake up in the morning and think, 'I cannot go on.' I would make a deal with myself and think about what I *could* do. 'Well, I *can* get out of bed! What I will do is get out of bed and see how I am feeling when upright.' Then I would gradually move to each next step, culminating with an early morning cup of tea, before the children woke up, sitting in the garden. And then of course, I had started...

See strategies: Brain Breaks, Essential Maintenance, Havening, Picking Your Battles, Protecting Self, Switching Off

OVEREATING

Also see Catastrophic Thinking, Compassion Fatigue, Drained (Feeling), Exhaustion, Relationship Problems, Sleep Problems

Sometimes we overeat to overcompensate. Well actually, most of the time I overate to fill the gnawing void of dread.

When we're not having our own emotional needs met, or we're feeling anxious, we have high levels of cortisol, so we reach for food. That's basically all the time, then. It is hoped that the food we reach for might be a lovely, healthy stew or salad... Sorry, I had to wipe the laughter tears away just then. Never in times of stress did I *ever* reach for a healthy diet bar, let alone a salad.

Most of us overeat on unhealthy stuff. Oh well, if that's what it takes.

This is not the book that is going to take 'over snacking' away from you.

A top tip I *can* offer is to try and have your main meal at a weird time of day. For me, it worked really well to have it about 2:30 in the afternoon. This meant that during the merry-go-round mad meltdown between end of school and dinner, I had enough in my stomach to keep me going and stop me reaching for the cake.

I carried a lot of excess weight during the time I was raising my children. That's all the more astonishing considering that I virtually never stopped moving, apart from when I was asleep. I think it was a bit like a conveyor belt of constant snacks. The fat I held onto fondly was obviously due to the constant stress overload, driving me to seek sugar (much like our children do).

You may be pleased to know that since my children left home, I have lost three and a half stone.

If excess weight is worrying or depressing you, that's a separate matter. We know feeling rubbish and weight gain are inextricably linked, so first of all we have to feel better in order to be able to lose the snacks. I found Havening was absolutely brilliant for this, as I easily began to rethink my lifestyle and replaced snacks with other treats; without even caring!

See strategies: Cake, Essential Maintenance, Gardening, Havening, Krispy Kreme Donuts, Looking Good, Running, Walking, Yoga

OVERWHELM

*Also see Acceptance, Catastrophic Thinking,
Compassion Fatigue, Conflicted Feelings, Drained
(Feeling), Exhaustion, Letting Go, Motivation*

If your children have a very high level of need and are nearly always with you, you may feel suffocated, overwhelmed and resentful. That is allowed! It's what we do with those feelings that counts.

The scale of the task before us can leave us feeling disempowered and frightened. We can find ourselves overwhelmed when we are looking too far ahead. We might start expecting failure, then we feel fearful of failure, and become almost emotionally paralysed, trapped in a self-perpetuating, doom-laden cycle.

There are days when we feel fearful and hopeless. The hopelessness overwhelms us. There are days when the endless meetings, decisions we have to make, the lack of progress and the constant day-to-day drudgery is truly paralysing.

At these times, we may question if we've done the right thing. We might sometimes think that if we *could* make changes, we would make them. We go back in time in our heads and imagine a different life, *anything* other than this life we are living now. We often don't see the differences we are making, or we stop caring about that. What can change?

There is no light at the end of the tunnel, it has gone out. The path we are walking is truly hidden with fog or brambles. We may feel as if we are insignificant and invisible.

Know that you are not alone with these feelings. Many therapeutic parents have been there and will be again. The strategies linked to this section should give you some reassuring advice to help you to find your way through to the other side.

See strategies: Brain Breaks, Celebrating, Empathic Listening, Havening, One Step at a Time, Protecting Self, Space, Therapy (For Parents)

P

 PADDINGTON HARD-STARE

For those of you who have watched Paddington, either when you were young or with your children, you will be aware that when Paddington does his hard stare, his face doesn't change. It can't, can it, after all? The Paddington Hard-Stare is demonstrated simply by maintaining eye contact and sticking your chin out. It's really useful to use this in difficult meetings or when someone is talking utter crap at you. A bit of silence, teamed up with a Paddington Hard-Stare, can work wonders.

The Paddington Hard-Stare can also be combined with the 'Stop-it-now' face to manage children at a distance with maximum effect.

See strategies: Pointy-Eyebrow Death Stare, Smug Smile, Useful Phrases

 **PAUSING**

Pausing is my number one most effective therapeutic parenting strategy. It keeps us sane and stops us from making terrible errors (most of the time). Resilience and pausing go hand in hand, because as you learn to take a breath and evaluate the situation, your strength in meeting this new, unexpected excitement grows. I say 'excitement', but what I really mean is 'horror' at yet another shocking incident. It's more fun to call it 'excitement', more positive.

I knew that I had reached the pinnacle of positive pausing recently when my ceiling fell down. I had renovated my office with new desks, chair, carpet and so on, so that I could write and do all my other work in semi-comfortable surroundings. A few days later, I went to the shops, and when I came back with all the heavy bags, out of the corner of my eye I saw that 'something had happened' in the office. Instinctively I knew it was not a good 'something', so I did what any self-respecting therapeutic parent would do. I closed the door, so I didn't have to see it. Then I went into the kitchen, humming to myself, unpacking the shopping and idly wondering what might have happened in the office. Once I had unpacked the shopping, I felt brave enough to go and look at what had happened. As I opened the office door, I realized the extent of the damage. Most of the ceiling had fallen in on top of my work, my desks, my laptop, and ruined the new carpet too. My overriding thought was, 'Thank goodness the dogs weren't asleep in there!' (When I am working, they normally hem me in on all sides, making it impossible to move, once I am sitting at my desk.)

As (now at least) I am a good pauser, instead of rushing about shrieking and phoning people up for sympathy and no help, I carefully closed the door again and went and made myself a cup of tea and a snack. Now, I can assure you that this is by far the *most* positive way to pause if ever you get the opportunity. Bring in snacks, doughnuts, cups of tea, coffee, anything really. Pause-enhancement is delivered by beverages and little treats. The great thing about that is it makes us more likely to pause again in the future, because there's a little benefit in there for us.

Once I had finished my snack and sat in the garden contemplating the view for a few minutes, I sighed and prepared myself for the big clean-up. I did this quite cheerfully, knowing that this was an incident which was just 'one of those things' and would be sorted out. Furthermore, while I was clearing it up, I knew that no children would burst in demanding my full attention immediately, and I could choose whether or not to answer the phone.

We already know that pausing means we are less likely to say or do something we might regret, and that therefore the interactions are more meaningful, empathic and therapeutic for our children. But there are huge benefits to our own mental health when we practise deliberate pausing:

- We think more clearly.
- We feel less guilty.
- We feel more successful as parents.
- We get better results.
- We feel less stressed.
- We laugh more.

Sometimes the pauses are much harder to grab with children in full flow; however, every time I used deliberate pausing with my children (even if it was just for a couple of seconds), the outcome was better. Pausing is definitely a skill which gets easier as you practise it.

Occasionally, it can feel really counter-intuitive to pause, and obviously there are times when you cannot, and you just have to head straight in. When immediate action is needed for safety reasons, pausing is a *very bad plan*, and frankly just an attempt to avoid the inevitable.

Here are some really handy ways to grab a pause and stop your-self from launching straight into screeching attack mode:

- Focus on something just outside the room.
- Look out of the window and take a deep breath.
- Pretend to look at your phone 'for information'.
- Pretend you have to rush to the toilet. Lock the door.
- Say you have forgotten something, rush out of the room and run up/down the stairs. This also lowers your cortisol and helps you think straight (see 'Self-Regulation').

- Go on a two-week cruise with no phone or wi-fi. (Okay, I did have to wait a few years for that one...)

See strategies: Brain Breaks, Essential Maintenance, FFS, Havening, Picking Your Battles, Protecting Self, Self-Regulation, Space, Useful Phrases, Zones

PERFECT PARENTS

Also see Anti-Socialism, Boundaries, Criticism,
Friendships, Isolation, Jealousy, PIEs

When we talk about Perfect Parents, we know that, often, they will have little competitions about how much better, or easier, their child is than yours. The implication here is that you are failing as a parent, and they are the winners! Oh, how wonderful they are! Let us all revel and rejoice in their achievements. Let us celebrate their cello playing, hot-housed little angels. Well, they can rejoice if they want to. I will sit at the sidelines and eat cake, swapping horror stories with other therapeutic parents, and pretending not to be bitter about how annoying they are.

You see, they started from further forwards than we did. We had a lot of ground to make up in the first place, just to *get* to the same starting place. The things that we celebrate and rejoice in are different from their celebrations. Also, we don't rely on our children to boost our ego and donate some reflected glory. Lucky really.

It is Perfect Parents who obsess with microscopic, irrelevant nonsenses. I remember one day sitting with a Perfect Parent (ex) friend, and she was *seriously* trying to have a conversation with me regarding why I had not been careful about the type of cotton in my sons' underpants. Now, I'm not being funny, but on a scale of 'things I had to worry' about, the cotton content of my sons' under-pants was less than minus 10,000. I was much more concerned with the poo content. However, this really did seem to worry this person, and I had this ice-cold waterfall moment of clarity, when I realized that our brains simply did not meet anymore. Her worries were not mine. Her utterances were not *completely* boring but were taking up valuable 'emergency planning' space in my head.

It wasn't her fault, it's just the way it was. Perfect Parents don't *mean* to be terribly annoying, pond-life fixated, competitive, dull, sources of irritation, it's just that they don't have a lot more to think about. I mean they can't do, can they? It's a bit like if you have your leg amputated, you don't really worry about the cut on the other knee. It becomes a bit immaterial.

So, if you are always worrying about how your children are going to survive, and how you're going to actually live through the next week, the content of underpants (other than when they're full of poo) becomes a bit irrelevant.

This is why Perfect Parents are extremely annoying. We may even be jealous of the fact that they still have available brain space to think about these types of things. We find ourselves increasingly stunned and amazed at the depth and breadth of nonsense topics and competitions that Perfect Parents can have. And it makes us feel bad. It makes us feel bad because we don't have that time to put into those types of topics and maybe part of us wishes that we *did* have that. Oh, the luxury of being able to wonder about whether or not your child should have a part in the school play, and then make a plan to lobby the teacher to make sure they do, while many therapeutic parents are crossing their fingers and hoping to God that their child is off sick in 'school play' week.

Perfect Parents can also be quite hurtful. They get a bit scared and worried when our children behave differently, loudly or worryingly. Fear drives their withdrawal. Gradually, Perfect Parents hurry their children away from ours. Sleepovers and playdates dry up. You have become 'that family'. Oh well. Guess what? We *are* 'that family' and there are bloody thousands of 'those families' just like us. *They* won't mind if our children shit the bed and pull the heads off their flowers. They will probably just roll their eyes and be a bit relieved they are going home soon.

About four or five years in, I definitely stopped feeling regret at missing out on being part of the Perfect Parent brigade. I started looking at them with something akin to pity, thinking how dull their lives were. Not for them the exciting challenges of never knowing what the day would bring, the terrific highs of breakthroughs, the lows of exclusions and eating problems. No, their lives were one long dullness of cakes, fetes, PTAs, compliant children and fun family days out.

Now the children have grown up it is a bit different. I think that the balance has changed somewhat. My children have overcome a great deal (despite all the negative doom-mongering from others in the early years). People with perfect children, who believe they are Perfect Parents, expect to have perfect young adults and often this is not the case. I never expected to have perfect young adults (luckily), so I'm not disappointed. My children are colourful, interesting, resilient young people. Okay, they might swear a lot, but *c'est la vie*. Perfect Parents, however, who thought their children would go to university and probably become the next Prime Minister, are now floundering in horror that their children have decided to experiment with alcohol or answer back. This can be a very hard experience for Perfect Parents. Ironically, they now ask *my* advice, although they don't want to hear it. This is very weird. I think it's because they haven't yet accepted the difficulties they are facing. They want me to tell them it will all be fine and that they have been brilliant parents. They want me to tell them that their child is not rebelling because they inflicted a punishing schedule of hot-housing over-achievement on them. Well, I am not saying that because it would be a lie. They have not allowed their children to be children, so they're jolly well making up for it now!

Strangely, they also no longer want to talk about the importance of cotton underpants, when little Johnny is smashed out of his face and in a police cell.

The next time a Perfect Parent is sitting opposite you, telling you how bloody great their child is, how they have found the answer to global warming because they are soooo kind and intelligent, and how they can 'hardly fit in' all the swimming, Taekwondo and ice-skating lessons, fast forward a few years in your head and smile to yourself. Just think, 'One day they'll be asking my advice, and maybe I'll give it…and maybe I won't.'

See strategies: Paddington Hard-Stare, Pointy-Eyebrow Death Stare, Protecting Self, Sarcasm, Smug Smile, Useful Phrases, Vanishing Helpers

 ## PICKING YOUR BATTLES

When I came home from work one day to find that the goats were on the dining room table with goat poo all over the lounge, it was not the right time to ask who had let the goats out. It was never the right time to ask why everyone had ignored the goats on the dining room table, as the answer may have traumatized me. The important thing was to get the goats back into their pen.

This is a good example of how we choose our battles. I could equally have chosen to have a full-blown inquest into goat-gate afterwards. Fortunately, I had dinner to make, cups of calming tea to drink, and five children to get to bed. I never felt there was the time to stop and do a post-mortem of events, which wasn't going to change anything anyway.

Winning

Some parents really struggle with this and get trapped in a cycle of needing to 'win'.

Because we often feel tired and frustrated, the arguing can spill over to us too. We join in the sniping and fall into the 'we *will* be victorious' trap. Well, you can either win the argument (and let's face it, you *can* win because you're probably right), or you can win by having an easier life.

Knowing that you're right needs to be enough, frankly. You can waste two hours of your life arguing about who stole the £5, and proving *beyond doubt* using CCTV who it was, or you can decide that you know who took it, put in the consequences and get on with your life instead. Yes, I know it's frustrating when you know you are being told a ridiculous lie and you can prove them wrong, but you will live a longer, happier life, if you are able to smile cheerfully and look mysterious while stepping away. You can also add in little phrases such as:

- That's an interesting point of view!
- Well! I never did!
- Who'd have thought?
- Yes, we all have our different ways, don't we?

These kinds of phrases are also useful to use where there is contention and stress around birth family visits or extended family time. It means you are freed from the need to correct or battle constantly during what is already a stressful time.

If the person is very annoying indeed, and you really *do* feel the need to at least *look as if* you have won, while stepping away, simply use those phrases but add in a mysterious little smug smile. This gives the *impression* that you are the winner anyway.

Refereeing

When we are placed in the position of referee (or clumsily assign that role to ourselves), the best way to get relief is to *stop* refereeing. Now obviously, if there is punching, you do have to intervene, but I found it was better to be a bit non-committal and not have 'seen anything' or not 'be there'. Sometimes I would conceal myself to see how a situation would play out if the children thought I was absent. This usually gave me the courage to take a bit more time before I intervened the next time or to stop refereeing for that particular set of circumstances, altogether.

Here are some useful phrases to help you avoid refereeing:

- I don't know.
- What do you think should happen?
- That's not going to happen.
- That's an interesting idea.
- I've just remembered something urgent, hang on...
- I've decided...
- Yes, I appreciate you feel it is unfair, but I have decided this is the best/safest way (repeat *ad infinitum*).

If you frequently find that people are contacting you to 'put you in the picture' or let you know how poorly someone has behaved, tell them that you see what is happening. You are being given the unwanted role of referee. They want you to sort out their problem. They want you to take their side. In this case, I always say, 'Have you spoken to [person involved]?' I suggest you do that first. Sometimes I will even helpfully arrange a meeting... Works a treat.

Winning against PIEs

Similarly, we need to pick our battles with PIEs too. There is no point putting tons of effort into fighting for a tiny little victory that is unlikely to have any impact on your child's life, especially when there are bigger battles to fight.

Where you have someone arguing with you about why reward charts work, it is exhausting. Yes, I know it's tempting to wrap the reward chart around their head, so they get a really good close-up view. This will only cause trouble for you. There are more positive ways of winning an argument than violence or actual arguing! And yes, of course you can print out tons of resources and have meetings proving you are right, but sometimes it is simply a matter of agreeing, then getting on with what *you know* is right. This results in much joyful smug smiling at a later date, when it transpires that you ignored the 'advice' and that the positive outcome is a direct result of what you said needed doing in the first place.

Evaluating battles

In order to evaluate what battles are worth fighting and what we can put off to another day, look at what we can and cannot change. We can save ourselves hours of heartache and stress by simply doing a stocktake and asking ourselves the following questions:

- Can I change this today?
- Am I likely to be able to change this anytime in the near future?
- If I manage to change it, will the difference be significant?
- If I manage to change it, might something worse happen instead?
- Can I take a step back and see what happens?
- What's the worst that could happen?
- What can I put in place to mitigate that?

Remember that the *real* win is keeping your cool and living to parent another day. This saves our mental health and enables us to keep our strength for the important battles which inevitably arrive.

See strategies: Essential Maintenance, One Step at a Time, Useful Phrases

PIES (PATRONIZING IGNORANT EXPERTS)

Also see Allegations/False Allegations, Blame, Criticism, Disempowerment, Family, Friendships, Schools, Support

This section is longer, because when I asked therapeutic parents for subjects they wanted covered in this book, this topic was overwhelmingly the most popular!

People who are Patronizing Ignorant Experts don't mean to be that way. I know because I was one.

When I qualified as a social worker, I'd also worked for years as a nursery nurse. What *I* didn't know about behaviour charts wasn't worth knowing, frankly. I'd spent an enjoyable couple of years patronizing lots of lovely foster parents and adopters, telling them how they were doing it all wrong. (They weren't. I was talking out of my arse.) I didn't *mean* to be patronizing and I didn't *mean* to act like an expert, it's just that it had been kind of implied that I *was* during my training.

Luckily, my children taught me that I was in fact a complete idiot, who knew nothing whatsoever about how to respond to children with trauma. It was a bit of a shock to be honest, and I now unreservedly apologize to all the people I patronized and railroaded into stupid decisions in the past.

It's really hard when you have a PIE who:

- doesn't *know* they are
- won't accept that you might have a relevant point of view which is actually right

- continues making damaging decisions for your children which you know are going to cause you all loads of stress and heartache
- continues to quote, as if still factually accurate, from outdated, discredited models of behaviour management.

I have seen before my very eyes many PIEs change into well-informed, compassionate, genuine experts, who really *do* understand what they're talking about. I'm lucky enough to know many social workers and therapists who have gone the extra mile, done the extra training and truly 'get' developmental trauma and therapeutic parenting. These supporting professionals are like gold dust, and are highly valued by adopters, foster parents and other therapeutic parents.

Sadly, PIEs still remain. Many...

There are two types of PIEs: the 'very annoying' ones, who generally have qualifications and have studied a lot and therefore do believe they are experts, and then the 'less annoying' ones who have no qualifications whatsoever but just *think* they know everything. For ease of identification, I have inserted them into the table below.

Very annoying	Less annoying
Therapists	Your parents
Educational psychologist	The lady in the café who has had lots of children
Teachers and teaching assistants	The checkout operator in Sainsbury's who knows exactly what you need to do
Social workers	Your sister-in-law who already has a five-month-old and is therefore an expert
Child psychiatrists	The parents at the school gate
Paediatricians	Your partner
Doctors	The receptionist at the doctor's surgery

Play therapists	The receptionist at the leisure centre (who is apparently an expert about trauma-related swimwear)
Other general therapists (occupational, etc.)	The receptionist at the dentist's surgery who finds your children very annoying and rude
Police officers	Your former best friend
Youth offending team	Your MP when you ask him to help you lobby for resources and he doesn't understand. After all, what did you expect?
School counsellor	The elderly person in the supermarket who has a 'sucking lemons face' while watching your child have a tantrum
Managers of any of the above	The man who has come to lay tiles on your bathroom floor and advises you to 'give your child a slap'
Anyone else who is inserted into your child's life, who believes they are an expert	Your ex-partner, who buggered off because it was so hard, and now wants to tell you what you are doing wrong

Basically, in the 'less annoying' category, they can either be tackled under the 'Family' and 'Friendships' sections in this book, or they can just be disregarded with contempt. We don't need to worry about the majority of them. Also, luckily, we can usually swear at this category without fear of reprisals.

The PIEs in the 'very annoying' category usually have some really interesting 'talents':

- A degree in 'interested yet disappointed' face.
- An ability to hear what you say, ignore it, discount it, then later pass it off as their own discovery.
- Making you feel like a victim.
- Telling you that you need a break, but then doing nothing whatsoever to make sure that happens.

- Moving children without thought or concern for the impact on that child, the important issue being to prove they were right.
- Failing to plan, then blaming everyone else that no plan was made.
- Gaslighting (see 'Disempowerment').
- Using demeaning language like 'placement' to depersonalize a child or your home.
- Talking about their own, securely attached child as if their issues are in any way comparable.
- Disagreeing with each other and having 'most important PIE competitions' in critical meetings, where (unbelievably) their ego is *not* actually the main issue at stake.
- Giving us conflicting 'advice', then separately demanding we carry out their different instructions.
- Mistaking 'support' for 'what I've decided you need, regardless of your view'.
- Confidently talking about future possibilities as if they *actually know* impossible things are fact – 'They will grow out of it' or 'They won't remember anything'.
- Writing 'assessments' which draw no conclusions and help no one, but probably imply, whatever is wrong, it is your fault, or that you have to sort it out.
- Believing literally everything that comes out of our children's mouths, regardless of whether it is even *possible* it could be true.

With the majority of PIEs I have encountered over the years, I have mainly felt infuriated, disempowered and heartbroken for my children, or the children I have been working with. When they made yet another catastrophic decision, I didn't exactly want to stab them (I am not a violent person), but I wouldn't have been sad if they had accidentally fallen onto sharp objects, necessitating a long break from work, giving time for a non-PIE to take up the slack. Every time a social worker chose to move a child in an unplanned, chaotic way in the fostering teams I was involved with, my heart broke for the child, while the PIE social worker just seemed to believe that somehow the child 'would be fine'. Well, they were not fine. Some of them have never recovered.

By far my most astonishing experience with a PIE was when I had a stroke while she was doing an assessment on my son. She didn't notice I had lost the power of speech and had suddenly started slurring and making no sense. When she discovered what had happened, she phoned me in hospital three days later to tell me she 'felt bad for not noticing' that I had had a stroke. I didn't reply. Even this did not stop her completing an assessment which offered no meaningful support or help whatsoever, and generally just speculated on why my son was 'naughty'.

Betty, an adoptive mum, writes:

> Being a therapeutic parent often feels like going into battle, every day, all day, for as far as you can see into the future. That battle seems immense, relentless and fraught with pain and suffering. It often feels like your adversary is the child, and also a raft of well-meaning but ignorant professionals, family members and friends who feel it is their duty to undermine you, by giving you the benefit of their 'wisdom'.

I have a lot to thank PIEs for. They made me absolutely *determined* to change things. So, the last bit has been going quite well. Many of them have read our books and come to our training. Many of them are no longer PIEs. They are ex-PIEs. It's so important to stay vigilant though – they walk among us.

See strategies: Essential Maintenance, Paddington Hard-Stare, Picking Your Battles, Pointy-Eyebrow Death Stare, Protecting Self, Responding to Allegations, Sarcasm, Smug Smile, Training, Understanding, Useful Phrases

PITY

*Also see Compassion Fatigue, Disappointment,
Eeyore Parenting, Empathy, Forgotten, Motivation,
Overwhelm, Unappreciated, Valuing*

Self-pity

It's okay to have pity days. I would have a little pity party for one. It usually consisted of tissues, tears, chocolate and wine. Things were always better the next day.

We are entitled to a bit of self-pity, and we all have those days. It becomes a problem when the pity day becomes pity weeks, months or years. This is not okay. We can't put *too* much effort into self-pity, because other people will draw away from us, fast. Then, not only do we feel sorry for ourselves, but we're lonelier too. And let's face it, no one wants a long pity party with only a loyal dog and stuffed animals for company.

Having compassion for yourself is different from holding a little pity party. With compassion, you are forgiving yourself, making allowances and giving yourself a little treat to make up for it. That's healthy, and it's a way of being that helps us to grow as parents. Pity is 'My life is dreadful. Everything bad always happens to me. I need chocolate. Someone's stolen my chocolate.' So that's okay for the short term, but it's pretty easy to get stuck in an unfulfilling rut if we overindulge. Self-pity is unattractive and usually messy: compassion for self is a sign of insight and strength.

Pity from others

What I found much more difficult to manage was when *other people* would give me pity that I had not sought or indeed expected. It's very annoying when people who have no concept of the challenges of our lives make patronizing, sympathetic faces and offer us treacly sympathy. Sometimes, a person would do a pity face at me for an issue that I hadn't thought was in the least bit challenging or difficult. I found this could sometimes really distract me and put me off my stride. It would make me take a step back and think, 'Oh is this difficult? Should I be feeling sadder or be more affected? What is wrong with me?'

The thing I learned was that people judge your life on what *they* can cope with. So, therefore, if they struggle with your challenges, then they will give you pity. They can't imagine what it would be like to face the challenges we have. Sometimes, their lives have been more limited, and they have never had to cope with very difficult events.

When we're going through difficult times (so most days then), we often just want to be able to get on with it, so unless people are going to actually *help* us, we need them to shut up and go away. Doing a pity face at us is unhelpful and undermining. I don't need your pity; I don't want it. Take your pity and shove it up your arse.

Now, I know that sounds a bit rude and ungrateful, but pity is quite debilitating and very different from kindness and empathy. When people were being kind to me and trying to help me, that felt very distinct from somebody saying, 'Oh poor you! I don't know how you manage!' It's those people who never help us anyway, so we can do without them, thank you.

See strategies: Alcohol, Brain Breaks, Cake, Chocolate, One Step at a Time, Protecting Self, Useful Phrases, Vanishing Helpers

 ## PODCASTS

Using podcasts is a brilliant way of switching off or getting information you need in bitesize sections. I struggled to access podcasts initially because I didn't understand how they worked. I thought they were locked in cyberspace somewhere and you needed a special key. Now I know I can simply ask Alexa or any other smart speaker, life has got much easier!

At the Centre of Excellence in Child Trauma we record our own free podcast series (The Therapeutic Parenting Podcast), covering a whole range of topics from behaviours, child trauma and the system to feelings of isolation. They are about 20 minutes long and you can listen to them on headphones to block out nonsense chatter, or in the car while your children are listening to the Baby Shark song for the 58th time on full volume.

Sometimes, I also use podcasts to help me relax. This is particularly handy after a stressful day. Picking your favourite comedian or just searching for comedy podcasts will give you a quick burst of happiness. If you combine this with walking as well, so much the better.

If you worry that your brain might be dying and you need to build some new synapses (so your brain has a change from endless, repetitive dullness), try listening to some podcasts on learning new languages. This will grow lots of lovely new synapses in your brain and increase your problem-solving abilities.

See strategies: Audio Books, Laughter, Reading, Switching Off, Training

 POINTY-EYEBROW DEATH STARE

The Pointy-Eyebrow Death Stare combines the use of raised eyebrows with maintained eye contact. It is more forceful than the Paddington Hard-Stare. This one gives the impression of being surprised or astonished while not backing down. I used to find this quite useful with teachers when they were talking shite about my child's position on their reward chart and my child was standing next to me. They tended to dry up pretty fast.

See strategies: Paddington Hard-Stare, Smug Smile, Useful Phrases

PROTECTING SELF

Protecting ourselves from child to parent violence

Occasionally, I see a post on our Facebook group from a parent saying something like, 'I can't do therapeutic parenting, because I can't keep sitting here while they hit me.' I always say, 'Good, because that's not therapeutic parenting.' In my book *The A–Z of Therapeutic Parenting*, I offer lots of strategies around managing violence and aggression.

In order to help you with the feelings that this invokes in *you*, you need to ensure that you are connecting to the right people. You need to be speaking to someone who understands, and who's been through a similar experience. You may connect to others through the organization I run, the Centre of Excellence in Child Trauma (COECT), by going along to one of the National Association of Therapeutic Parenting's (NATP) specialist listening circles or another support service offering expert help in child to parent violence, such as PAC-UK (www.pac-uk.org).

It's vitally important to access relevant training in managing violent behaviour in order to make sure you are able to protect yourself physically when needed. A good place we recommend to start is Dynamis Training, which offers online and face-to-face courses worldwide. COECT has worked closely with Dynamis to develop a specialized approach that does not conflict with therapeutic parenting, preserves the child's dignity and relationship with you, while keeping everyone physically safe (www.dynamis.training/parents).

Protecting ourselves by saying 'no'

One of the main ways we can protect ourselves is by saying 'no' when people's expectations are unreasonable. If your life is full of people thinking it's okay if they just descend on you at a moment's notice, or that your children must simply 'learn to cope' with social situations that are not yet possible, we have to decline. Learn to say 'no'. Literally practise it.

You can say 'no' in the following ways:

- 'I'm sorry, we'd love to have you over for lunch but unfortunately I can't guarantee your food wouldn't be poisoned.'
- 'It's such a shame we can't meet up for coffee, today is completely impossible. (Give no reason.) Next Tuesday, however...' (this gives you time to think of a better excuse).
- 'I'd *love* to help out at the school fete. Who can look after the children for me that day?'
- Cultivate a public personality of forgetfulness and then simply choose not to turn up at events, or to be out when people call. By nurturing your famous, absent-minded persona, you can fall back on this whenever you need to with 'I'm so sorry...you know what I'm like', eye roll.
- Be really straight with people and just say, 'No, I'm sorry, my commitments don't allow that unfortunately.' Then, when they argue and tell you to 'lighten up' or 'give yourself a break', just repeat, 'As I say, I'd love to, but my commitments don't allow for this.' By not giving an excuse (such as 'I have to get their tea by 5pm'), you make it much harder for them to argue against.

Protecting ourselves from sexualized behaviour

First of all, we need to tackle sexualized behaviour head on and be very clear about what is happening, because if you're targeted or you *feel* targeted, then it invokes shame in you. By being very open and honest about what's going on, you remove the shame and demystify it. When you are very clear with the child, and with others around you, about what is and is not acceptable, you will start feeling more in control. Practical arrangements such as ensuring a second person is around as a witness at vulnerable times can also be effective.

In the moment, if you are feeling cornered, a pretend urgent telephone call can allow you to exit without showing fear and give you time to think.

You must ensure that you record everything in writing (or verbally with written follow-up), and pass it on to a supporting professional or another independent person. This protects you from allegations.

Don't hesitate to put a lock on your own bedroom door if you feel threatened. You need to be able to sleep at night!

In *The A–Z of Therapeutic Parenting*, I cover lots of strategies for managing sexualized behaviour in children and ensuring we do not invoke shame. It's important that for our own mental well-being, we also employ strategies of effective support.

Protecting ourselves from embarrassment

Practise, practise, practise!

If you are naturally a shrinking violet who regularly wishes the ground would open up and swallow you whole, it can be really tricky to merrily shrug off the latest public shaming episode. We really do need to cultivate our Teflon coating, so embarrassment does not permeate. It can take a long time to achieve this, but luckily, every time there is an incident, the Teflon grows a little tougher and more resilient. You don't become *more* sensitive and *more* embarrassed with each incident, it just kind of starts to fade. I think it's practice and exposure to these situations that helps.

The first time my children had a joint-party-melt-down-fest in a supermarket, I certainly tried urgent whisperings and bribes to stop the outraged stares of the judgey others. After a few times, I just stopped feeling embarrassed and developed my Paddington Hard-Stare for the onlookers. Five years later, in Birmingham Airport's departure lounge, the children renewed their efforts, so I just lay down on the floor and counted the ceiling tiles. The noise soon stopped. I did not feel any embarrassment at all. It had just kind of worn off by then.

Protecting ourselves from disappointing birthdays

I found it useful to reallocate my birthday (like the Queen). I had my *actual* birthday and my *pretend* birthday. For seven years, my children celebrated what they thought was my birthday, when actually it was the following day. On my *actual* birthday, I would go off shopping and have lunch out with a friend and it was lovely. On the pretend birthday, there was much tension and stress, culminating in a party-tea-food-fight-competition-with-arguing, but I was able to deal with it completely fine, because after all it wasn't my birthday.

Protecting ourselves from the unreasonable demands of adult children

Once our children grow up and leave home, it can be really difficult knowing where to draw the line with support. Naturally, we want to support them as much as we can and help them transition to adulthood. There comes a time, however, when deep down we *know* we should be withdrawing that support, and the additional help we are giving them is actually curtailing their independence. It can feel really counter-intuitive to say 'no' and very difficult emotionally in these circumstances.

I think it's really important to be completely straight with our adult children and tell them exactly what we're doing. It's fine to say, 'I would love to help you but it's not good for your personal growth if I do, and I know you might be angry with that. Because I've helped you lots of times, this hasn't helped you to learn to be independent, so now I'm going to help you to be independent.'

Here's what my adult children taught me:

- Never take out a phone contract for them in your name.
- Never offer to be the guarantor without first testing the reality of their capacity to meet their obligations.
- Don't give them money – give them food, clothing, furniture and anything else they need, but not money, as it will just go to McDonald's or the friendly neighbourhood cocaine dealer.

- Allow natural consequences to occur, even if this means a period of uncomfortableness.
- Avoid chasing after them; allow them to come to you.
- Put in boundaries about your availability. (This may mean gradually not answering the phone on the first ring.)
- Take off any trackers you have on their phones! If they have moved out, it will only worry you to death.
- Don't take everything at face value.
- Don't worry if their new best friends are completely unsuitable. They are likely to change in six months.
- Stop accepting the blame for everything that has gone wrong in their lives.

Protecting ourselves from criticism and blame

Where you have ignorant others constantly criticizing or patronizing you, it can be really wearing. We do need to make sure our Teflon coating is securely in place to deal with this (see 'Useful Phrases'), but we also need some strategies to directly challenge it.

There are plenty of quick-read resources, publications and books available now which explain the basics of child trauma and therapeutic parenting. At COECT, some of these resources are written for therapeutic parents to give to teachers, social workers, friends and family to explain the impact of trauma, brain development and why our children need different parenting. If you are constantly up against ignorant others, give them one of these resources (like my books *Therapeutic Parenting in a Nutshell* and *The Quick Guide to Therapeutic Parenting* or the fact sheets from NATP), and say you will be happy to discuss this with them when they have looked at it. Have a look in the 'Training' section of this book for other easy access ideas on this.

We need to add another layer for our Teflon coat for this, and I certainly used to put on my special overcoat with the blame-repellent lining when I knew I had a visit from a 'blamer' due. I found it useful to remember that just because a person was choosing to blame or criticize, it did not mean I had to accept it. I soon learned that people blamed the most when they felt out of control or ill-equipped themselves. Sometimes it was really useful to confront that head on:

Blamer: You should make him behave better!

Me: Oh, I see, this behaviour makes you feel uncomfortable. I wonder why that is?

Blamer: Because he is so naughty! He is out of control!

Me: Yes, sometimes people can get very anxious when they don't understand where this comes from.

Protecting ourselves from running on empty

We know that often our children are not able to give back until later. So where else can we look to get our hearts replenished?

- Dogs, and other reciprocating pets (not goats – lesson learned).
- Our partner, parent or close friend.
- Another therapeutic parent.
- Date nights or one special evening or lunch held regularly no matter what.
- NATP listening circles.
- Brain breaks.
- Treats and quiet time.

Protecting our couple relationship

First, remember to get a good babysitter and organize breaks! (See 'Babysitters' and 'Brain Breaks'.)

To make our lives easier, there are some simple agreements couples can make together. We need to:

- be kind to one another
- step away from tiredness competitions
- learn about and employ empathic listening strategies.

Just these three simple things can help partnerships to stay strong.

It may feel impossible to put on a united front when you are being sabotaged, but our children *really* need us to be able to do this. Keeping our children emotionally secure means that our lives become easier.

Agreements need to be made that if there are differences of opinion they will be addressed out of the earshot of the children. If you are in a relationship where your partner constantly undermines you, and you are worried that damage is being done to your child, you have four questions to ask yourself:

1. Am I being reasonable?
2. What are the risks to the child?
3. Is one or both of us suffering from compassion fatigue?
4. Can we get our parenting on the same page, or at least in the same chapter?

Once you have the answers to these questions, take the most appropriate action relating to that answer. For example, if you think one or both of you may be suffering from compassion fatigue, look at our suggestions for strategies relating to this, such as Havening.

It's also important that we value and respect each other's needs for time alone, just to be able to process our lives. This can be built in on the way to or from work, shopping or just a coffee in the garden. Mutual consent is advisable, with key phrases to alert the other person that you are going for some time out!

Be open and honest with each other about the impact on your relationship, without blame. Giving one another compliments, and noticing what has gone well, pays dividends. 'I know you are great with...but I struggle when...' is much easier to hear than a sulky accusation.

Protecting ourselves from unpreparedness

I advise all new adopters who have not had children to get themselves a basic parenting manual. Don't bother with all the stuff around traditional parenting and discipline (because none of that is applicable to your children), but just get a grip on changing nappies, the contents of nappy bags, the kinds of basic routines that children need. Social services expect us to get this by osmosis and that's not very fair, because having a child come to live with you who has suffered trauma is a big job in itself. The scaffolding of everyday needs, physical routines and so on needs to be embedded so we can at least *look* confident.

There is nothing worse than feeling inept because you genuinely thought your one-year-old could use a knife and fork, only to be met with the amused glances of others. Yes, this did happen, but luckily not to me. So, for those of you who have children coming to live with you, but have no childcare experience, this little list is for you:

- Get a rucksack type of bag so your hands are free.
- No matter what age your children are, always carry wet wipes and a plastic bag. This deals with most incidents.
- Keep a change of clothes nearby, either in a bag or in the boot of the car.
- Keep essentials like phone, keys, tissues, money in a bum bag so you aren't rooting through the massive 'needs of child' bag for personal essentials.
- Carry pain relief for you and your child.
- Carry drinks with sippy straws which seal themselves and also feel nurturing for the child to drink, no matter what age.
- Carry bananas. These are great for filling snacks and melatonin. (NB: Make sure you check the bag for dead bananas as this can get very nasty very quickly (see 'Disorganized'.)

- Carry cream for bites and stings. This is also good if the child has imaginary illness or pain, so you can put in a bit of quick nurture and nip an escalating incident in the bud.
- Wear comfortable shoes that you can run in.
- Wear a top that hides sick stains.

See strategies: Brain Breaks, Empathic Listening, Essential Maintenance, One Step at a Time, Paddington Hard-Stare, Pausing, Pointy-Eyebrow Death Stare, Responding to Allegations, Space, Switching Off, Training, Useful Phrases, Zones

Q

QUEUING

If you have managed to weave in a joyful trip to the supermarket alone, make sure you choose the longest queue for checkout. Conversely, obviously, if you have to shop with children, it's pack as you go, self-scan and get out as fast as you can.

If ever you are foolish enough to take the children to Disneyland, trust me the Fast Pass (queue jumper) is worth its weight in gold several times over. We do not want to queue with children. Ever.

R

 READING

Reading takes us into a different world. It unlocks the mysteries of child trauma and therapeutic parenting. Even now, you might be curled up with a lovely drink, enjoying a little smile at this book and wallowing in the relief that there are indeed other parents just like you. And they are still alive.

When we cannot actually physically escape, reading (or audio books) takes us elsewhere. I spent many nights in my children's rooms helping them to settle (or stopping them from killing each other), just by sitting there. But 'sitting there' is a bit dull, so a good book can help us to stay put longer, and is more relaxing than looking at our phones, then seeing the latest horror email arrive from the school.

I also read about people in worse situations than me, which oddly makes me feel better. So, when I was feeling trapped in lockdown, I read lots of books about people's experiences in France under Nazi occupation. Well, that certainly made me feel luckier...

See strategies: Audio Books, Brain Breaks, Podcasts, Switching Off

REFEREEING

Also see Arguing, Conflicted Feelings,
Family, Relationship Problems

I never wanted to be a referee but for some reason people decided I should be one. This meant that suddenly I had to decide who was right and who was wrong, when often I couldn't possibly know. If I just wanted to play football, I'd play football and I would pick a side; I wouldn't have been the referee who has an impossible job and is always wrong for at least 50 per cent of the people.

Sometimes, when I was cast as referee, the expectations and boundaries were completely different. For example, with securely attached stepchildren at war with my 'fighting to death for last banana' unique children. Not only were they on opposing teams, but they were also not even in the same league. In fact, looking back now, I am pretty sure that some were playing football, and some were playing ice hockey on the grass.

Refereeing in these circumstances is doomed to failure, and, yet, increasingly we find ourselves in that position. The difficulty is that the more we do it, the more we are *expected* to do it.

More complex is when we find ourselves refereeing when adults are involved. This might be between:

- our partner and our children
- stepchildren and partner/ex-partner
- supporting professionals who are not in agreement with a plan
- extended family, where there are special guardianships and kinship care issues
- extended family with differing/opposing views to others regarding our parenting.

This can be a very lonely place. Let's face it, on the football pitch we don't see the referee surrounded by his or her mates. There's a reason for that, they are standing on the sidelines, waiting to see who the crowd picks as the winner.

See strategies: One Step at a Time, Picking Your Battles, Protecting Self, Reflecting, Triggers (Managing), Understanding

REFLECTING

I find it very easy to reflect on my time as a therapeutic parent, when I am sitting on a cruise ship, watching the sunset. At these times, the warm glow of the sunset extends its tendrils to my mind and rosily tints the memories of the past.

Then I wake up and remember it was more like a fire than a sunset.

Reflection is really useful when it helps us to change our course or to find a solution to a worrying problem. Although my reflections nowadays, luckily, tend to be at a slower pace, we still have our fair share of issues that we need to think about.

You can't reflect in the moment when it's all happening – you do need some space. A brain break, a walk, a holiday or just a cup of tea in a quiet room will help. These moments of reflection allow us to play back whatever it was that happened, like a tape in our head, and to look at it as if we were a bystander. We can then think about what happened, the impact on us and others, and how we might do things differently in the future.

Sometimes, I would leave my phone on voice record during a difficult incident or conversation. Later on, I could play that back and think about things I might have missed at the time due to a high emotional state or whatever. It's amazing how many little things our children say that we can miss in the moment. It's also great to be able to replay something when we're calm and our logical brain is fully online!

In a couple relationship, joint reflection can really help open up communication. By taking a curious approach and removing blame, it's possible to strengthen your bond and ensure that your boundaries are even more secure. Here are some useful statements or questions to use in joint reflection:

- I'm not sure what happened earlier. What's your view?
- I feel as if that all went a bit pear-shaped. What do you think?
- Well, we need to make a plan for how we're going to tackle that in future.
- We have a couple of hours before they come home. Let's make a plan.

It's this reflection that helps us to grow, not only as a therapeutic parent, but as a person. There is no shame in making a mistake, the problem is making the same mistakes over and over again, learning nothing from it while clinging desperately to the belief that if we keep repeating the same action, somehow the outcome will be different. When we are stuck in a cycle of blame > useless strategy > unwanted action > blame, then we need to change *our* action in order to change the actions of others. Active reflection helps us to identify what it is we need to change.

See strategies: Celebrating, Empathic Listening, Essential Maintenance, Forgiving Yourself, Protecting Self, Tea (Cups of, Cream), Understanding, Useful Phrases, Vanishing Treats

REJECTION

Also see Adult Children, Empty Nest, Letting Go, Valuing

When Rosie came to live with me, she was eight years old. She did not need another mother; she did not want another mother and she certainly was not going to allow anyone else to look after her. This meant that I was rejected as a parent for about nine years.

The feeling of not being needed by your children can be lonely and devastating. Some of us may have longed to be parents for many years, and when we are rejected, or we feel as if we are not needed by our children, it can indeed be a dreadful blow. Sometimes we can feel as if there's no point in keeping on giving, and we draw back from the child. At other times, we may try too hard, driving the child away.

Some of us are parenting children who are on the autism spectrum and struggle to demonstrate reciprocal feelings, or even experience them. There can be no more lonely experience than watching your child respond to an upsetting event in a way that is devoid of emotion. We are left alone with the sadness of the event, and the fear for our child's emotional development.

In my training, I often talk about 'hugging a carrot'. Recently, Rosie and I were having a laugh as she explained to somebody that she 'carroted Mum'. This is what it felt like when I would hug her (and some of the other children too). Sometimes, they would go all stiff and lean away. That kind of rejection is instinctive on behalf of the children, but nonetheless hurtful towards us. We keep trying and they keep 'carroting'!

It can be helpful to remember that, almost always, no matter what the children are saying, they do *want* us to keep trying to connect to them. Rosie says now that she never wanted me to stop trying, and even though she would snap at me or be angry and rejecting, deep down she was glad that I kept trying to connect.

We make critical errors where we look to our children to fill *our* emotional needs. Our children cannot meet those needs and we must not look to them to do so, not yet at least. We have to accept that sometimes we will feel rejected, sad and lonely but that this will almost certainly change.

Now I find it difficult to remember those years when Rosie was distant and rejecting. On the other hand, other newer rejections remain fresh and raw.

Rejection by adult children can be particularly hard to bear. We might be mindful that they have rejected us to work through their own trauma, or perhaps they have connected to people whom we do not approve of, and they cannot mesh their two worlds together. Whatever the reason, this rejection, after years of thoughtful, empathic parenting, can be a sledgehammer to the heart. It is hard to 'wait and see', almost impossible to give them the space they need to work things out and then return to us. Sometimes, we have hard decisions to make. Should we 'let go'? We have to grieve that loss and hope for the best. If we have done everything we can, relentlessly pursuing an adult child who is desperately seeking distance from us can push them even further away.

I experienced distance from a close family member for nearly 40 years. This relationship was healed in the most unexpected way, and now it feels as if that gap never happened. Never say never...

See strategies: Dogs, Empathic Listening, Essential Maintenance, Expectations (Managing), One Step at a Time, Protecting Self, Training, Understanding

RELATIONSHIP PROBLEMS

Also see Anger, Asking for Help, Compassion Fatigue, Empathy, Family, Fear (of Child), Overeating, Refereeing, Single Parenting

My practice husband was unable to let go of traditional parenting models, so I let go of him. I didn't have a choice as the 'traditional parenting' included allowing the children to cross busy roads when they were unable to judge the speed of traffic, due to the fact that 'they should be able to'. I did actually put him up for sale on eBay as a broken 'action man' and sold him for 3p with no returns. Now, this is not a good solution, and I am not advising it as a strategy. I think I was suffering from compassion fatigue at the time. To be fair to my practice husband, I believe that he also had compassion fatigue at the time, but in those days, I had no clue what I was doing, and just getting through the day was a major achievement.

Communicating

For many years, my (real) husband Ray would come home and find me either:

- mentally absent
- being fake jaunty/hysterical, wearing a rictus smile
- trying not to cry
- furious and slamming things about.

In the early years, he made the fatal error of asking how my day had been.

If you return fresh from your adult-filled, lunch break, coffee-machined world and ask the stay-at-home therapeutic parent how their day has been, it will not go well. It is better to make a cup of tea, nod sympathetically at the torrent of mania, and do some active empathic listening (see 'Empathic listening').

Different experiences

There are few situations more frustrating than trying to parent children with additional needs when your partner is not on the same page, and they have also lost the ability to read. This makes putting on a 'united front' really tricky.

At our training, we speak to many parents who feel frustrated with their partners. Different ideals of parenting are highlighted when we are parenting children with unique needs. Although the odd bad day is manageable, we can't fudge it in the long term. We can't make the best of it and hope it will be okay in the end. Even small errors can have quite catastrophic effects, leaving one of the parents to pick up the pieces. This breeds resentment.

It's not a surprise that some marriages and partnerships breakdown under the additional stress. We know that our children are built for survival, and part of this means that different parents will see a different side of the child. For example, in a male/female couple relationship a child may be targeting the female in the relationship and be much more careful with the male where there has been previous abuse from a man. This leads to situations where Mum will be really struggling but Dad doesn't see it and decides Mum is over-exaggerating, blaming the child or being unnecessarily harsh. This scenario can also be reversed. Naturally, this leads to feelings of resentment and isolation. It's a good idea to seek external help and support to get a more objective viewpoint in these situations.

Different people have different triggers. It's essential we notice our triggers and take action to support partners in dealing with theirs (see 'Triggers (Managing)').

Unrealistic expectations

Another issue that causes a problem is if one of the parents feels that the child should be able to do more than they can. They may be unable to accept the limitations that are placed on the child due to development delay, for example. My practice husband would expect the children to be able to do things that were simply impossible for them, and then he would become frustrated and angry when the children were unable to do these things. When that marriage ended, ironically life got easier. Although I was busier and I had a lot more to do, managing the children was easier.

I'm not saying that the answer to relationship issues is to split up and become a single parent, but you *do* need to both get on the same page, fast!

When one or both parents also have children from previous relationships, problems may be heightened. I remember a very tense conversation about why some (securely attached) children could not help themselves to food when they were at our house!

Compassion fatigue and coping

One of the major problems I see in couple relationships with thera-peutic parents arises from the high levels of tiredness and compas-sion fatigue. This leads to couples having tiredness competitions. It can be really difficult to cope with a partner coming home from a day's work claiming to be tired, if you have been at home with the children all day dealing with very difficult behaviours. Very quickly, we get into a little bit of a competition to prove who is the most tired. This takes away our last vestiges of tolerance and patience, and before we know it, we are embroiled in tense arguments and slamming things about.

Ray joined our family at what was probably our most difficult time. The key to this relationship working was simply to be kind to each other, even when we were feeling exhausted, and to use active empathic listening. I got in the habit of making *him* a coffee when *I* was feeling crap. That little kindness made sure that he was kind back to me so we both felt better for it. I was also lucky that Ray was open to learning and let me take the lead in parenting. Agreeing this between you is useful. There has to be an agreement from the outset that if you are parenting children with developmental trauma or with additional needs the parenting must be different. We need to throw away our ideals of traditional parenting.

See strategies: Babysitters, Brain Breaks, Empathic Listening, Essential Maintenance, Pausing, Protecting Self ('Protecting our couple relationship'), Reflecting, Training, Understanding

RESILIENCE

Also see Bad Days, Boundaries, Humour, Rejection

Happy news! During the first year, quite a few things may happen that will leave you stunned. This wears off very quickly and, soon, nothing fazes you. Events which used to be truly shocking, with lots of associated deep thinking, analysis and wakeful nights, now merely raise an eyebrow and elicit a sigh.

Nowadays, I mainly float through life in an unoffended fog, marvelling at the outrage that people express over the tiniest things. Where do they find the energy? Years ago, I would have been one of the outraged people. Now I save my fury for things that *require* outrage, such as when schools fail children.

I don't feel I *need* to be outraged about the fact that a local road has closed and I might have to go round the long way for a couple of weeks. I mean, who actually cares? I don't get it anymore, but I *used* to get it. I *used* to be really good at being angry about *everything*.

Growing resilience is one of the big benefits of having constant hassle in our lives. As our children and PIEs test and try us, our fuses become longer, and our inner strength grows too. Therapeutic parents are some of the most laidback people I know, and yet their lives work like clockwork. Any little inconvenience that pops in their way (like losing a child in an international airport, for example) is usually met with controlled concern and positive action. If this does not sound like you, and you are still rushing about screeching and panicking, you're probably very early on in your therapeutic parenting journey.

How do you build resilience? The sad news is that it happens automatically. You just can't sustain that level of outrage, fear and anxiety for very long, to be honest. I'll give you an example. The first time one of my children was excluded from school it was a massive deal. Oh, the shame. Apart from 'the incident' and associated meetings, what on earth was I going to do with them? How was I going to organize work?

The second time it happened I'd begun to realize that the school were being a bit stupid, so my overriding feeling was one of anger towards the school. The 15th time it happened, we had everything sorted out within five minutes, I knew how to handle my child and I knew how to handle the school. It was just part of the routine really. But for other people, their child being excluded would still be a major event.

How proud we should be that our resilience grows, enabling us to deal competently with all kinds of things like:

- shoplifting
- school exclusions
- burglary
- absconding
- PIEs talking shite at us
- child to parent violence
- screeching tantrums in supermarkets
- extended family giving us irrelevant advice
- children hiding in the garden (to avoid haircuts)
- child protection case conferences following false allegations.

The list is endless! How lucky are we? How resilient are we?

How tired are we?

Later on, as the children get older, you retain this resilience, and you can use it and apply it in almost any situation. When the Covid crisis happened, many therapeutic parents managed much better than others. They were used to taking difficult days in their stride, and the lack of cortisol-fuelled transitions made some households a lot calmer.

Nowadays, I cherish my resilience. It has helped me to overcome health issues and ensures that I can continue to meet my adult children's needs. Even if I do that sometimes from a cruise ship... by email...once during the week.

See strategies: Brain Breaks, Essential Maintenance, Holidays, Laughter, Pausing, Protecting Self, Sarcasm, Self-Regulation

 RESPONDING TO ALLEGATIONS

If you are facing an allegation, the first thing you need to do is contact the National Association of Therapeutic Parents (NAOTP) to get a copy of The Allegations Support Pack (ASP). This is free of charge, kept up to date, and can be downloaded or accessed from the NAOTP website at www.naotp.com/theasp.

The ASP gives you invaluable advice about:

- why allegations happen
- staying connected with your child
- what you can expect
- getting help with your own mental health issues
- accessing immediate and effective support.

One area that is often overlooked during allegations is the impact on *your* mental health. That is why we produced the ASP.

It's really important to take one day at a time during an

allegation, as it can be too tempting to fast forward and indulge in a bit of catastrophic thinking. Also, you need to be aware of your rights, as quite often, the investigation side can drag on too long and information may not be shared appropriately with you.

Accessing the correct level of support is essential. This is something you're *entitled* to and you may need to be proactive about. You're not alone in this. Remember, many therapeutic parents have faced allegations in the past and many will again in the future.

There are differences in legislation and regulations depending on whether you are a birth parent, foster parent, special guardian or adopter and also the nature of the allegation. The ASP will direct you to the correct resources.

See strategies: Empathic Listening, Essential Maintenance, One Step at a Time, Picking Your Battles, Protecting Self

 ## ROUTINE

We know that if we don't have a routine for the children, we'll probably die quite soon. Although it's really dull, we quickly (normally) get into a regular routine just so that everyone stays sane.

It's also important, however, that we have our own little routine for us. This might be something as simple as a little self-care routine around skin care, taking off make-up, brushing hair, showering and so on.

One of the best ways to ensure that your routine helps to look after *you* is to get up *before* the children. I know it can be tempting to spend those extra few minutes of comfort and denial snuggled down between the duvet and sheets, pretending that life won't happen today, but, trust me, it's much easier to start the day from an alert perspective!

If you set your alarm half an hour early, not only can you get up, have your shower and get a cup of tea, you can also find all the lost shoes and get the breakfast on the table before anything bad happens. This ensures that everyone starts the day in a much calmer place and you're not dragging yourself about feeling half dead, because you've already had a bit of caffeine.

See strategies: Dogs, Essential Maintenance, Looking Good, Losing Things, Protecting Self, Timesavers

 RUNNING

No thank you. Too many wobbly bits...

And running away from the children does not count as a therapeutic parenting strategy, although it *will* lower your cortisol.

See strategies: Self-Regulation, Yoga

S

💡 SARCASM

I have heard it said that sarcasm is the lowest form of wit. I disagree. Well, I would, wouldn't I? Being quite a sarcastic person.

We can use sarcasm as a good defence strategy. But it's never a good idea to pretend that you were being empathic and nurturing with a child, when really you were being sarcastic. They will know. It will backfire.

The best use of sarcasm is with idiots who have no clue and who patronize you. If you are quick, they are never sure if you really meant it or not and assume they must have misunderstood:

Unaware other: Mrs Naish, could you bring in some cakes for the school fete?

Me: Yes, of course! I just love baking; it fills up all my spare time when I am just sitting there twiddling my thumbs!

When the cakes didn't arrive, they realized I was being sarcastic, but by then it was too late.

See strategies: Humour, Protecting Self, Useful Phrases

SCHOOLS

Also see Criticism, Disempowerment,
Drained (Feeling), Frustration, PIEs

As a therapeutic parent of five, I needed a break. School was the only break for a long time, but unfortunately school mainly behaved ridiculously and became the source of torture for the majority of my children's childhood. I think this was because we had different expectations. I expected school to just keep my children there and let me have a little bit of recovery time; school expected them to learn something.

Once or twice, we were lucky and had a brilliant school that really got it (or if they didn't get it they allowed me to go in and deliver training to receptive teachers). I cannot tell you (but I'm sure you can imagine) the enormous difference this made to our lives. Most of the time, I was dealing with ridiculous suggestions like putting all five children in five separate schools so that they (the children) could manage better, when in reality it was about the teachers being able to cope. No help obviously around picking them up or getting them to school – that would just happen by my magic flying carpet, presumably.

To be honest, I am a bit spoilt for choice to describe all the annoying things that happen relating to school, so I've just included a selection here:

- The receptionist phoning you up because they've been tricked yet again by your child into believing they are genuinely ill. It doesn't matter that you're 50 miles away, about to finish a very important meeting, or in the adjacent school at yet another behaviour management meeting about a different child. It's 'very sad' that they're not allowed to give the child any medication on health and safety grounds. And it doesn't even matter that this is the 45th time your child has pulled this particular stunt. You are a terrible parent if you don't drop what you're doing right now and go and sort your child out. Naturally, when you arrive at the school, the child is miraculously 'better now' due to the fact that PE has finished. The receptionist still insists on you taking the child home to stop them cluttering up their tidy reception. This is despite the fact that you have to return in half an hour anyway, to collect the other children.

- A fixation with unrelated, clumsy, behaviour-based reward systems, catapulting children into toxic shame on a daily basis.
- Saying really stupid things like, 'But he looks so normal... who would think...?'
- Constant patronizing reminders about 'how to do a healthy packed lunch' whenever lunch boxes were raided prior to lunch time without the teaching staff noticing, leaving staff to draw their own (incorrect) assumptions at lunchtime when my child opened their sparse lunch box, yet again.
- Completely unrealistic expectations about what the children could and could not manage, with the infuriating fuckwit response of 'But they have to learn to fit in' whenever I challenged the discrimination dished out on a weekly basis.
- Irrelevant 'letters home' (otherwise known as purveyors of stress), which were supposedly transferred via the child, thereby ensuring that I was never informed of important events like parents' evenings and detentions, but always received 'reminder' letters about the exciting school trip, happening tomorrow, with payment due of £3.74p in exact money, no change given.
- Non-school uniform days for yet another charity. So I had to pay for my children to go to school and have a really horrible day, due to dysregulation and hypervigilance issues.

Our unique children are often very gifted in eliciting sympathetic responses and additional protection from teachers, assistants and (crucially) catering staff at school. Even when there was no risk, and nothing bad had happened, my children were brilliant at ensuring they got the teachers on their side or the extra cake. Sometimes this even followed situations where the event that happened was definitely my child's fault, but somehow they managed to convince everyone that they were the innocent party. In *But He Looks So Normal*, I described how Charley had done just this:

> Charley was particularly gifted at this. I was almost proud of her ingenuity. One day I had a call from the school (the Head no less) to say that he was very sorry to tell me, but Charley had been punching a 13-year-old girl and was in serious trouble. By now I had learnt the hard way not to get too involved, so I made suitable 'oh dear' noises and, 'Do what you think is best,' etc.
>
> When Charley returned I merely stated that I knew something had happened. (By now you will notice I had become a bit more expert with therapeutic parenting and my bad-temperedness was squashed down inside and hidden from view a bit more.)
>
> Naturally, Charley did lots of huffing, sighing and stamping about, saying how innocent she was, they always picked on her etc. By now, however, I knew that the school would do what the school wanted to do regardless of my input.
>
> I had also realized that Charley was expert at manipulating people and getting the solution that she wanted. After all, this was the child who had manipulated a whole swathe of teachers into letting her off homework because they believed I was terminally ill.
>
> I didn't feel inclined to have a conversation with the school yet again reminding them of this. I thought I would just sit back and enjoy the show preparing to pick up the pieces; whoever they might belong to. (My money was on the Head frankly.) Sure enough, the next day the Head phoned me and his first words were: 'Mrs Naish, I have to congratulate you on what a well-brought-up child Charley is! I have spoken to her about what happened yesterday, and she has explained everything to me in a very mature fashion.'

At this point I put my phone on speakerphone, mouthing at Patient Husband, 'You have GOT to hear this; it's going to be a classic!'

The Head went on to say that having listened to Charley's 'very compelling and grown-up' response he realized that in fact he had been slightly responsible for the incident that had happened the previous day, and as a result, there would be no consequences for Charley because she had been so apologetic and managed to explain to him how he had contributed to the incident.

I was going to ask him how he thought he had been responsible for a 16-year-old punching a 13-year-old at the opposite end of the building to him but thought it best to leave it there. By now I was crying with silent laughter, so I ended the call and thanked him for his time. Patient Husband shook his head in silent wonder and asked, 'How does she do it?'

When Charley came home I looked at her, smiled, and offered my congratulations. With her big innocent eyes in her wide, lying face she said, 'What?'

I answered, 'You pulled a blinder there, didn't you?'

As she sashayed away, I swear I saw a little triumphant smug smile beginning to form on her lips.

The hardest thing about managing schools is finding our way through the jungle of the ever-changing special educational needs provision. It can be a full-time, frustrating job where the goal posts seem to move regularly. In the 'School Strategies' section of this book, I provide you with links for up-to-date road maps for a way through the complex system in the UK.

At the Centre of Excellence in Child Trauma, we know that there needs to be a huge change in the school system to properly support children who have experienced trauma and/or have additional needs. We spend a great deal of our time providing resources and training for schools and gradually we are seeing a shift in some areas of the country. In 2021, the very first 'Trauma School' to be fully recognized by the Centre of Excellence in Child Trauma opened in Gloucestershire, UK, and the team involved with that school provide resources and publications for schools, teachers and parents.

See strategies: Essential Maintenance, FFS, Homework (Not Doing), Jolliness/Jauntiness (Fake), Losing Things, Natural Consequences (Allowing), One Step at a Time, Pointy-Eyebrow Death Stare, Protecting Self, Routine, School Strategies, Self-Regulation, Training, Vanishing Helpers, X-ing Out (Crossing Out)

SCHOOL STRATEGIES

Educating school

There are some really great schools out there who have ensured that staff are 'attachment aware' and 'trauma trained'. Sometimes this training hasn't managed to transmogrify into *actual* strategies. As therapeutic parents, it often falls to us to become the 'trailblazers' (occasionally referred to as 'rude, stroppy parents' by school). The National Association of Therapeutic Parents already has quite a few schools that are members, and there are resources written specifically to be given to schools by therapeutic parents.

Another great place to go to for free, trauma-informed resources is Beacon House (www.beaconhouse.org.uk).

If you are struggling to get your child's school to understand what the differences are for our children and the best way to ensure that they can stay in school, it's worthwhile signposting the school to these resources. Let them know that they can also access training via the Centre of Excellence in Child Trauma, including short, online video-based courses. There really is no excuse anymore for schools *not* to get up to speed with the differences that must be made in schools.

Some parents find it useful to print out our 'letter to schools' and other resources explaining neural development following trauma, and give it to the school, asking for a meeting to discuss adaptations which need to be made.

Find the right school

It is worth uprooting your lives and moving many miles if you are 100 per cent confident that you have found the right school for your child. For my children, it meant moving 125 miles to a school where they had the same teacher for three years, were in a class of 20, allowed to see their siblings whenever they needed to, with a headteacher who was open to learning about development trauma. It did also mean walking through a field of cows to get to the school, which was a little cortisol-inducing but never mind…

When looking for an appropriate school for my children, I was not always looking at government ratings, as the government's view on the education my children needed differed significantly from mine. Nowadays, I would always be looking at farm schools or forest schools first, where children spend a majority of the time outside and there seems to be a much higher awareness around our children's needs and functioning. Here are the kinds of questions I would ask a school:

- How many fostered/adopted children and/or children with special needs do you have in the school? (If they don't know, then don't bother with any further questions.)
- What behaviour management systems do you use? (If they are reward based, test how open the school is to an alternative view.)
- Do you have any memberships to professional bodies or organizations that offer support to education regarding trauma insight, attachment awareness and so on? (For example, both Adoption UK and the National Association of Therapeutic Parents run school support and education programmes.)
- What courses have the staff done around attachment and

trauma, and/or teaching children with additional needs in the last two years? What was learned and how has this been implemented?

- Are you open to your staff receiving training in trauma-aware teaching?

School stays at school

The quickest route to despair is trying to enmesh your child's school into your home. In *The A–Z of Therapeutic Parenting*, I give you strategies around this in the section on 'Schools'. For you as the parent, it is imperative for your own mental health that instead of trying to enforce ludicrous school consequences, which have no meaning, you distance yourself from this. If you do not agree with what the school are doing, you are not obliged to join in. That's not to say that you actively undermine the school, it just means it's unrealistic of the school to expect you to support them in a behaviour management strategy that you know does not work.

You can take alternative actions instead – such as have a cup of tea and commiserate with the child, while sending yet another photocopy of the handout to the school, explaining why this strategy doesn't work. (Also see the 'Useful Phrases' section for ideas about what to say regarding this.)

Home schooling and home education

If I had had to home-school my children, I think they may have left home a lot earlier, but some therapeutic parents become so disillusioned and exhausted with the school system that they make the sensible and equally brave decision to educate their children at home or in a less formal setting. Nowadays, there are a lot of resources and support systems available to parents who decide they can no longer face the daily battles.

Alternative schools

If there had been a few more farm schools and forest schools about when my children were young, they would definitely have all been enrolled and spent the majority of their school days there.

The feedback we get from parents whose unique children have switched to a farm or forest school is very positive. If your child struggles with staying indoors and just keeping still, one of these different types of school, even for just a few hours a week, will take a lot of pressure off you. It's worth researching if you have any in your area.

Research local alternative education provisions for your child, other than school. In the UK, this is called 'EOTAS' (education otherwise than at school) and local authorities have to offer this if school isn't a suitable place.

Getting the right support for your child before you actually go mad

I usually find that every time I recommend a particular strategy or process to follow to a parent stuck in the education mire, the process has changed before the words have finished leaving my mouth.

For this reason, I am listing here the websites which we refer to (in the UK), to ensure we are giving up-to-date advice and support to therapeutic parents. There are some really great resources out there. Many charities and 'not for profits' are being run by people who have walked a mile in your shoes and would like to spare you more pain.

Local support and information

For local resources and contacts relating to special educational needs (SEN) provision, type in the website below, then add your county at the end of the URL: www.senschoolsguide.com/local-SEN-services/NAME OF YOUR COUNTY

Free, independent SEN advice and resources

IPSEA (Independent Provider of Special Education Advice) – Offers free, independent legally based information, advice and support regarding education for children and young people with all kinds of special educational needs and disabilities. Particularly useful for navigating the process to ensure your child has access to the correct plan and legal entitlements: www.ipsea.org.uk

SENDIAS (Special Educational Needs and Disabilities Information Advice and Support Services) – Offers information, advice and support for parents and carers of children and young people with special educational needs and disabilities (SEND). This service is also offered directly to young people. Free, independent and confidential service: www.kids.org.uk/sendiass

SOS/SEN – Great for immediate advice on the phone to chat things through, and there are also walk-in SEN advice centres: www.sossen.org.uk

The Special Needs Jungle – Great for lots of resources and also for a step-by-step guide with flow charts for getting the right assessment completed for your child: www.specialneedsjungle.com/get-prepared

Home and alternative education

Cambridge Home School Online – Great website giving an overview of the legalities around home schooling, getting started and important resources: www.home-education.org.uk

Educational Freedom – Provides valuable guidance, template letters and contact with local groups: https://educationalfreedom.org.uk/contact-us

Education Otherwise – A very useful organization offering support to parents who have decided to look at alternative education outside the mainstream system. It also offers templates of letters to send to schools and local authorities, which is a real timesaver for therapeutic parents: www.educationotherwise.org

Legal advice

Independent legal advice can be obtained from Child Law Advice, a registered charity offering legal advice on all matters relating to children, including school provision and SEN: https://childlawadvice.org.uk

See strategies: Homework (Not Doing), One Step at a Time, Protecting Self, Useful Phrases

 # SCREAMING

Have you ever felt like walking up to the top of a very steep hill and screaming at the top of your lungs at the summit? Alternatively, you may have felt like marching down to the beach and screeching at the sea? Sometimes you might not have made it out of the house and there might have been lots of screaming indoors. This can be very loud and make your ears shake. It's also really cathartic.

It's a good idea, if possible, to disguise your screaming as singing. You can do this by pretending to be learning opera singing and then any noise that comes out of your mouth (even a full-on scream) you can claim is actually singing. Who would know?

The benefits of having a massive scream cannot be overestimated. Here are some of the things that I had a good scream about:

- The latest idiotic 'Have you tried talking to him?' event.
- Finding that my child had been excluded from school yet

again, handily clashing with a very important meeting I had to attend the following day.

- Finding that my child had gone missing just before another vital meeting, which he needed to come to, in an effort to convince everyone that he didn't abscond anymore.

- Seeing my child running away up the hill two minutes before we were due to leave to go on holiday.

- Suffering four hours and thirty-seven minutes of uninterrupted nonsense questions, in stereo, at full volume, while on holiday as a single parent, lost and driving.

The happy news is that it is *official* that screaming is cathartic. There is even a therapy called 'primal screaming'. So, next time you are screaming your head off, letting all that frustration out, and someone asks if you're okay, just turn and smile sweetly at them and say, 'Yes it's a new therapy, didn't you know?'

NB: It is *not* a good idea to do loud, sudden screaming in the car when your children are with you. Lesson learned. (Having said that, screaming in the car on the motorway is a pretty good place to choose because no one else really hears it, and it looks like singing if you do a bit of a smiley face at the same time.)

Screaming at Adult Children

Yes, I know, in therapeutic parenting you are not allowed to scream at your children. It is not a strategy. However, when the children are adults, a lovely ranting scream at them, telling them exactly how disappointed/ hurt you are can be truly liberating. I know. I've tried it. Sorry not sorry.

See strategies: Essential Maintenance, Protecting Self, Self-Regulation, Singing

 # SELF-REGULATION

It is true that we have to be able to calm our brains to access our strategies, and frankly you're not going to do that if you're rushing about shrieking and panicking. Moreover, your children will rush about shrieking, panicking, pooing and breaking things at the same time. It is a lose–lose situation.

Self-regulation, otherwise known as 'calming oneself down', is an essential – and tricky – skill to learn. If I'm angry, upset or just a bit irritated and someone tells me to 'calm down', I don't *actually* punch them, but I metaphorically do. There's no point in someone telling you to calm down, because you're either beyond that anyway, or you *are* calm. It's the most irrelevant phrase ever invented.

There are a few ways that you can calm yourself. If we discount the ones that involve alcohol (messy and too much payback), then we are left with cortisol-lowering strategies. This might be eating something sweet (cake), eating something else sweet (chocolate), drinking something sweet (cup of tea with sugar in, hot chocolate) or just moving about (less fun but useful).

We know that movement lowers cortisol for children, but it does for us too, of course. So, when I'm in a difficult situation, I walk. I walk when I'm on the phone; I walk when I'm trying to think straight for writing. When someone's made me very angry, I run up and down the stairs. If you're in a situation with a child and you can feel your blood boiling, say you've forgotten something and just rush off to 'get it'. Hurry up the stairs or do pretend searching. Lots of cortisol-lowering is happening as you move heavy furniture to look behind it for an imaginary lost thing. Sometimes I used the 'rushing to the toilet with pretend diarrhoea' strategy in order to spend a few minutes in the loo gathering my composure. I could easily have spent a week in there at times.

When dealing with my adult children, who were not at home and could not see what I was doing when I was on the phone, I would make sure I had a clear walkway with a cup of tea at the end. This way I could stay regulated by walking up and down when having a tricky conversation with one of my children. My husband also used to give me extra challenges if it was a particularly difficult conversation. He would slide me a piece of paper with words written on like 'unicorn' which I then had to try to insert into the conversation. This was a great way of staying regulated and light-hearted.

Some parents find that raising their adrenaline levels through high-risk activities is a good way to manage their stress hormones. Having done a parachute jump myself and feeling bad-tempered all the way down for some weird reason, I can't really speak from first-hand experience. Having five unique children was high-risk enough for me most days.

I also notice parents who use 'excessive busyness' to distract themselves from whatever it is they are avoiding looking at or dealing with. Although this strategy *does* keep your cortisol levels low, the thing you are avoiding will still be staring at you afterwards, so it is best to deal with it.

We also need to find ways to calm ourselves down after a difficult or traumatic event. We can be left stunned and amazed at the ways our children seemingly revert back to normal after what would have been a life-changing incident for most people. Some take bereavements in their stride and shrug off major injuries. This can leave us reeling. A difficult day with lots of high tension and drama can leave us reaching for the gin bottle and seriously considering taking up smoking. The important strategy here is getting perspective, and fast. If you can get away from the site of the drama and take in a different view, then use some of the strategies around mini brain breaks and lowering your cortisol levels; this will help enormously.

You can also predict times when it's likely there will be a heightening of stress. In the middle of difficult meetings, for example, don't hesitate to excuse yourself, go to the toilet and do a few star jumps to get your cortisol levels down. Okay, the person who has come to find you may be a bit perplexed to see your head bobbing up and down with heavy breathing and jumping noises, but needs must.

See strategies: Brain Breaks, Breathing, Co-Regulation, Havening, Pausing, Reflecting, Switching Off, Therapy (For Parents)

SEXUALIZED BEHAVIOUR (IMPACT OF)

Also see Conflicted Feelings, Embarrassment, Fear (of Child), Guilt, Letting Go

It can be really uncomfortable having a child who appears to be flirting with you. Sometimes it takes a while to notice it or be sure it is happening. I remember one of my very first foster children sitting on my practice husband's lap and squirming about. Of course, I look back at that now and realize that this was just a learned behaviour that she had, but back then it was very difficult for us both to try and manage.

We may feel:

- shame (self)
- ashamed (of child)
- embarrassed (by the behaviour)
- de-skilled (don't know what to do)
- blindsided (this is a new behaviour, out of the blue)
- shocked (this is so inappropriate)
- horrified (expected reciprocation)
- hunted/stalked (if the child is targeting you with sexualized behaviour)
- uncomfortable (there are uneasy undercurrents that are hard to tackle).

Although we can use our therapeutic parenting strategies to manage this behaviour, we are often left with these uncomfortable feelings. Seeing a child behaving in a sexualized way *is* uncomfortable.

By changing our mindset and reframing this as socially unacceptable, like picking your nose in public, it helps us to think in a more matter of fact way and deal with it in a similar fashion.

In my book *The A–Z of Therapeutic Parenting*, I give you lots of behaviour management strategies for this particular behaviour. This is one of those issues where you do need to be proactive. In the section 'Protecting Self' in this book, I give you some ideas for this.

See strategies: Empathic Listening, Protecting Self, Responding to Allegations, Space

SHOPPING

Basically, there are two types of shopping: the stressful type and the healing type. In order to help you to differentiate so that you can choose the right type, I've created a handy reference list for you.

Stressful shopping (to be avoided)

- When the children have to come.
- When there is a rush.
- When you have to find a specific item.
- Combining any of the above into one expedition. (Truly horrendous. Why do you think online shopping was invented?)

Relaxing shopping

- Alone or with a friend who moves at the same pace.
- Building in plenty of time for cake and coffee or other refreshments.
- When really you should be at home cooking tea.
- When buying treats for oneself.
- Online meandering, when the children are in bed and you can arrange for it to be delivered when they are at school so you can safely stash all the treats away.

See strategies: Brain Breaks, Queuing, Tea (Cups of, Cream)

SINGING

Singing was the first thing I ever did which made me feel sane once the children had moved in. Once a week I'd go off and do 'opera singing' (#controlledscreaming). I'd come home feeling much better. Singing helps us to lower our cortisol and adrenaline levels, keeping us healthier and drowning out the bashing noises.

I also used to sing difficult statements or instructions to stop them sounding angry. It's quite hard to sing a song about 'who left this enormous poo in the toilet, please flush the chain', but you can get quite creative.

My children did not like me singing and it didn't take long for me to learn that this was a handy behaviour management strategy. When we were all out shopping together (yes, I know, it didn't happen often, but I didn't always have a choice), I could stop a little fight in its tracks, simply by starting a threatening little hum.

Now I didn't *intend* the hum to sound threatening, but to the children, it *was* threatening. The threat was not 'Mum might be angry'. The threat was 'Mum might sing'. The children learned to distract me fast, thereby averting their argument and me singing loudly in the store.

*See strategies: **Brain Breaks, Dancing, Essential Maintenance, Music, Screaming***

SINGLE PARENTING

Also see Anti-Socialism, Asking for Help, Boundaries, Disorganization, Isolation, Relationship Problems, Support

Let's be honest, it's not all bad, is it?

Having been a single parent to my five children for the middle years, I can honestly say there were some big advantages compared to the time when I was with my former, utterly useless, lump of a practice husband. Now, obviously, I am with a wonderful man who actually *helps* me. But when I was with my practice husband, I really believed I would be better off on my own, and this proved to be the case.

It can be simultaneously overwhelming and reassuring to know that *you* are the person who has to sort everything out. This is much better than believing that your other half:

- has prepared the sandwiches, only to discover at one minute to school-leaving time that this is not the case
- is definitely going to be home when you need to go to the important meeting, only to discover that they are down the pub with their phone switched off
- is going to be a therapeutic parent, when they cling on desperately to traditional parenting methods, thereby undoing every bit of progress you ever make
- will stay sober at your children's birthday party, only to find them in a cupboard with their best friend Jack Daniels, and a stupid grin
- will contribute positively to the professionals' meeting about your child's care plan, only to see them blatantly playing Candy Crush on their phone throughout the entire meeting
- will look after the children so you can go out one evening, only to discover that they put the clocks forwards one hour to make the children go to bed early, thereby guaranteeing a very early start with grumpy children the next morning.

With this kind of 'support' I decided I would be better off on my own. Okay, some bits were difficult, but to be honest I had already got used to taking all the children everywhere with me anyway, as I just couldn't trust my practice husband. When you know it's all down to you, you have to be super organized and plan a lot in advance. It can also get really lonely, so you *must* be proactive about getting that support network in place. Just because you are single does not mean you have to be alone.

Often when I speak about getting a break, therapeutic parents will say to me, 'It's impossible, I am a single parent.' Um, no. It is *not* impossible, it is actually even more essential. It does take a bit of organizing, but once it is in place you can get brain breaks left, right and centre. Once you have your breaks sorted out, you can enjoy some of the benefits of being a single parent:

- Your rules are the only set.
- There will be no heightening of anxiety/dysregulation caused by a partner coming home from work.
- There is less competition from the children as they know they have your attention.
- If you decide not to do something, you won't be undermined.
- You get all the chocolate.
- You don't need to hide your snacks from at least one person.
- You choose where you go on holiday.
- You get the remote control.

I must admit, however, that I will never forget the day that I was just loading all the kids in the car to take them to the supermarket and my newly acquired, wonderful, non-practice husband said, 'Why are you taking them all? Leave them here with me.' It was a truly liberating moment. I skipped down the aisles at Tesco's and did not care one jot about the worried glances.

*See strategies: **Brain Breaks, Empathic Listening, Essential Maintenance, Holidays, Protecting Self, Shopping, Timesavers***

SLEEP PROBLEMS

Also see Anxiety, Catastrophic Thinking, Drained (Feeling), Exhaustion, Fear (of Child), Overwhelm

Although I sometimes struggle to sleep a bit now, I must be honest and say this is only because I insist on my lovely dog having the right to sleep on our bed. Naturally, he regards our bed as his personal kingdom, and expects us to move during the night in order that he can relax. I fully accept that this particular sleep problem is entirely my own natural consequence, and I am prepared to live with that. Sometimes, Ray sleeps in the spare room. He says it's due to his 'early work start' but I'm not so sure... On those nights, Cuthbert (the dog) stretches out, revelling in the luxury of his righteous, Ray-less space.

It's normal, of course, to experience times in our lives when sleep doesn't come or doesn't come very easily. Sleep issues in therapeutic parenting are unique in that the stresses we live under can go on for a very long time. This means we might get into very entrenched patterns of disturbed sleep or insomnia.

If you are woken up multiple times in the night, it becomes harder and harder to be able to switch off. This means that we are running on empty, or nearly empty, the following day.

An adopter told me recently how she woke up in the middle of the night to find her seven-year-old son standing and looking at her. He had his hand behind his back. She asked him what the matter was, and he said, 'Think of all the lovely things before I kill you.'

Luckily, as an experienced therapeutic parent, she was able to gather her thoughts and reply with, 'Okay, I'm just going to lie here and think about all the lovely things we've done.' She then started reciting a few happy memories. Luckily, the child only had his teddy behind his back. Most parents would not have been able to respond in this way. Normally, this would give parents a few sleepless nights thinking about a few catastrophes that could have happened or wondering where this particular behaviour had come from.

With very young children, we expect to have some nights of broken sleep. Early mornings are common too. The difficulty with parenting unique children is that not only may we have late nights and early mornings, but we might also have a few events during the night as well. This is particularly common where you have multiple children, or children with additional needs who need care and attention during the night.

We find ourselves 'sleeping on the edge', never really getting to that very deep sense of relaxation, and ready at a moment's notice to spring into action. Our cortisol and adrenaline levels can stay so high that we simply can't switch off and fall asleep in the first place (see 'Self-Regulation'). This creates difficulties in relationships as well, especially where your other half is sleeping peacefully and you want to punch them so that they wake up and join in in your worry or stress. (NB: This is not reasonable, but I understand the feeling.)

Here are some common sleep issues for therapeutic parents:

- Frequent night disturbances, noises, unsettled child and so on.
- Raised adrenaline and cortisol levels from a stressful day.
- Anxiety, stress and worry about the following day.
- Catastrophic thinking.
- An expectation that you will be woken up.
- Anger.
- Grief and/or bereavement.
- Guilt, where there has been a difficult day.
- A child sleeping in bed with you.
- Needing to sleep in child's room or stay with them.
- Feelings of disempowerment and worry around health, social care or the education system.
- A habit of being unable to sleep.

Long-term problems with sleep can be extremely debilitating. Our lives are difficult enough already. We have to be thinking clearly and able to access all our strategic planning just to get by day to day. When we are sleep deprived, we cannot be our best selves. It's hard to feel motivated, and instead we find ourselves trying to sneak in quick little naps during the day, if we can. This might include snoring in the car while waiting for the children to come out of school.

Frequently, we fall into a habit of expecting things to improve or 'be better tonight'. This means that we trick ourselves into believing that this is a short-term problem that will be resolved tomorrow. Because we know that a lack of sleep can be sorted out by simply having *one* good night's sleep, that's what we keep expecting and hoping for. Be honest with yourself though. Do you feel tired most of the time? Can you actually remember the last time you had a good night's sleep? If the answer to one of those questions is 'no' then you *do* have to take action. Sometimes, just a little bit of pro-active planning enables us to get that good sleep that we need. In the strategies for 'Switching Off' I share some of the things that worked for me.

See strategies: Audio Books, Babysitters, Brain Breaks, Breathing, Essential Maintenance, Holidays, Hot Tubs, Music, One Step at a Time, Protecting Self, Reading, Self-Regulation, Singing, Space, Switching Off, Tech Control, X-ing Out (Crossing Out)

 SMILE

Smiling at yourself in the mirror feels really weird, but actually it helps. Many a time I have caught a glimpse of my watery eyed trembly face, turned fully to the mirror, then had a word with myself and put on a big smile. The effect of seeing yourself smile usually makes you feel better very quickly.

If it makes you feel stupid (or more wobbly), you can console yourself with the fact that at least you tried and all that effort deserves a pretty massive cake.

See strategy: Cake

 **SMUG SMILE**

The Smug Smile can be used when proved right, without actually saying a word. Practise a closed mouth joyful smile for maximum effect. Sometimes, I would add a 'figure of 8' movement with my nose. Be warned, though. This is *very* annoying.

See strategies: Paddington Hard-Stare, Pointy-Eyebrow Death Stare, Useful Phrases

 SPACE

Sometimes, we might go a little bit too far to try and get some much-needed space, like the time when I falsified the date of birth on Charley's birth certificate, so she could get into nursery three months earlier. This went really well until I went to nursery one day and found them all singing Happy Birthday to her with Charley wearing a confused look, as her birthday was three months later. Bit awkward.

My bedroom was my sanctuary. If you feel overwhelmed by your children, it's really important that you have a place you can go to that's yours and yours alone. This may be your bedroom, or it might be a shed in the garden. It might even be a special chair outside, hidden away. For me, sometimes, it would be a bench on top of a certain hill. I used to sit on that bench and drink a flask of tea and this was my safe space.

Don't be afraid to use locking door handles to safeguard personal space. A locking door handle does not look terrible, and you can have some relaxation knowing that some valuables are safe. It's important not to be lulled into a false sense of security, however. As our children get bigger, older and cleverer they are very able to pick locks, or even crowbar open doors should the need arise, so remember to adapt your strategies as your children grow. Having a locking door handle does not necessarily mean everything is safe within, so think outside the box.

See strategies: Brain Breaks, Protecting Self, Switching Off, Zones

SUPPORT
Also see Diagnoses, Empathy, Family, Friendships, PIEs

How useful is scaffolding that looks really robust, but doesn't actually touch the house? You can't keep on pretending that your support is okay, just because supporting professionals have built lovely scaffolding. Scaffolding that doesn't actually *do* anything needs dismantling and taking away because otherwise it's just cluttering up what would be a lovely view.

Over the years, I have seen many well-intentioned attempts at 'support' that fall wide of the mark. This is usually because the people who are designing the 'support' are basing it on their own values and experiences, and not the experiences of therapeutic parents (see my story in 'Anger', for example).

Sometimes, I used to feel that people were firing random support missiles at a target. Unfortunately, they were blindfolded, facing the wrong way and had little chance of hitting their target. Meanwhile, I sat at the target site with the children, waiting for something positive to happen, and watching the missiles landing nearby, doing nothing but change the scenery around me. This wasn't helped by the arrival of supporting professionals looking very pleased with themselves and congratulating each other in meetings about what a great job they were doing, and how many support missiles they had fired today.

Here are some well-intentioned (but useless) ideas of support:

- Meetings which result in no action or useful strategy.

- A 'support' visit where the professional offloads to you about how difficult their life is.
- Assessments which only apportion blame.
- Therapy which you wait two years for, only to find it's completely unsuitable.
- Coffee mornings or 'support' groups arranged for foster parents or other therapeutic parents, where no one is allowed to talk about the children and mainly people resort to moaning about the staff or local authority.
- A conference where the speakers only know the theory and have no idea what they are actually talking about and how that relates to real life (see 'Training').

If you have a supporting professional who is currently offering you one of these strategies for support, they are probably a PIE, so please feel free to show them this section of the book.

Here is a list of support strategies that are actually *needed*, but rarely provided:

- Practical childcare at key times.
- Help with school issues, including transport.
- Someone listening without immediately jumping in with a solution.
- Advocacy in meetings from someone who truly understands child trauma and can explain it to others, including help to write education plans and so on.
- Training and conferences with speakers who have walked a mile in our shoes (like COECT).
- Cake.
- Informal meet-ups with other therapeutic parents, with no fixed agenda and not policed by social workers.
- Funding for key resources which are unexpectedly and urgently needed.

See strategies: Babysitters, Brain Breaks, Cake, Coffee, Empathic Listening, Protecting Self, Therapy, Training, Understanding, Useful Phrases

 SWITCHING OFF

I can't count the number of times I used to lie in bed wide awake, seething with fury or consumed with anxiety. Over the years, I learned some really good ways to switch my busy little brain off and get the sleep my body desperately craved:

- Changing your internal dialogue from 'I can't sleep' to 'I am going to sleep now. I know how to do this, I've done it lots of times, I'm going to sleep in a minute.' Telling your body that you *are* going to sleep is much more likely to enable you to sleep than lying there repeatedly saying in your brain frustratedly that you can't sleep!
- Increasing the delta waves (see 'Havening') in your brain to induce sleepiness. You can do this through Self-Havening. If you can't be bothered to look that up, just stroke your face from forehead to cheeks repeatedly with both hands. Do this for a minimum of seven minutes and you will notice that you feel calmer and sleepier.
- Pinching some of the strategies that work for your children – such as increasing intake of melatonin through eating bananas and drinking milk. We can also add in herbal remedies and supplements, taken with the milk. I found it was important to take these before I went to bed. I also discovered that the local supermarket brands were just as effective as the more famous brands.
- Getting control of your breathing. If you are lying there awake and you notice your breathing, it's likely that you will note that it is faster than normal. By taking a slow breath

in to a count of three, holding it for three seconds, then releasing it over five seconds, and repeating this cycle for five minutes, you get control of your breathing. The message to your brain is, 'Everything is under control, I can relax.' This helps us to fall asleep.

- Using Alexa or other home/phone app support to ask for a short sleep-inducing hypnosis or mindfulness/meditation programme. I found these really effective.
- Placing your phone out of reach and ensuring it is on 'do not disturb'. (See 'Tech Control'.)
- Making sure you don't actually get into bed if you can feel your cortisol levels are high and you are stressing out. Use some of the strategies in 'Self-Regulation' to help you calm first.
- Using some great strategies around sensory input. I used to use plug-ins that emitted different relaxing aromas, such as lavender. I also had a lavender pillow spray.
- Keeping a notebook next to the bed to make any notes you are scared you might forget about. (See 'X-ing Out (Crossing Out)'.)

See strategies: Brain Breaks, Breathing, Essential Maintenance, Havening, Self-Regulation, Tech Control, Therapy (For Parents), X-ing Out (Crossing Out)

T

 TEA (CUPS OF, CREAM)

In my books, I often refer to spending some time that *could* be stressful having a nice cup of tea instead. I used 'having a nice cup of tea' as a mental reward a lot of the time. During an abscondment or after a particularly vicious verbal attack from one of the children, a nice cup of tea seemed to make everything a bit better and forced me to pause and reflect. It's imperative that it is 'a *nice* cup of tea' rather than 'a cuppa'. Psychologically, there is a difference.

Handily, of course, tea also contains caffeine, which can rescue us from the debilitating tiredness we feel at times. A cup of tea quickly added to a thermos flask became a handy companion during the school run. A few quick swigs to get me going, followed by a relaxing five minutes finishing it up after the children had gone into school.

For those times when we need more than just a cup of tea, add in a cream tea for a lovely treat. These can be easier to arrange than an evening out with friends because you can often get them in garden centres and random cafes at two o'clock in the afternoon. This fits in better with school run time and also ensures that we're not picking the children up feeling hungry. I used to schedule in a cream tea about once a month. I actually managed to get to the cream tea every other month. Sometimes this was a hurried, dry scone after supermarket shopping, but it was the principle that counted.

At NATP, our listening circles will often include cream teas and a variety of cakes. Go on, you know you're worth it!

See strategies: Cake, Chocolate, Coffee, Krispy Kreme Donuts

 TECH CONTROL

Phones

I have taken part in many meetings and conversations with therapeutic parents when they constantly look at their phones and have everything pinging away. Some of them have even invested in watches which give them even higher levels of alerts. Why? I mean seriously...if your child goes missing at school they will ring you. They won't just send you a text message and hope for the best. Technology is there to *enhance* our lives, not to control them, but by allowing it to control *us*, it also elevates our stress levels.

By allocating set periods in the day when you read your emails and look at text messages, you are taking back control. I always have all my messaging systems on silent along with any other notifications, and I check them four times a day at a time that suits me. I can then include a cup of tea and chocolate as required, depending on the anticipated/actual content of the messages.

I know it may sound obvious, but if we constantly have our phones next to us at night, making weird noises, it *is* going to disturb our sleep. We need to activate the 'do not disturb' on the phone and just allow specific people to ring. For example, if you have a partner or child who may need your help *genuinely* in the middle of the night, then they would go on to your list of allowed calls. This stops the unnecessary regular 3am calls from drunk people, who are perfectly capable of making other arrangements. There's a natural consequence right there. I made a point of telling all my adult children that I had 'do not disturb' on my phone between 10pm and 7am, so therefore if they rang me at night I'd be unlikely to hear them. I then gave them alternative methods for contacting me in an emergency. (This included calling the police so that the police could come to my house!) Over time, I was able to refine this and add the children to the 'allowed list'. Now I know that if they *do* ring in the night, it is a genuine emergency.

My stress levels lowered considerably when I bought a second phone. Not an expensive one, it was just one for home use. My second phone or 'home phone' only has my home email on it and I have very few contacts. This has been a really good tactic to enable me to step away from work at weekends. If you run two phones, you can choose to keep all the stress-related (PIE) stuff on one phone, and the important (but hopefully not stressy) stuff on the second phone. This means that on holiday, for example, people can still contact you, but only those who really need to and are unlikely to cause undue stress.

Emails

When writing an email, it is a good idea to send the email to your-self first. Then walk away for a couple of hours. By going back and re-reading the email you can check that you really *did* mean to say that you are bringing all the children to the social services' office and leaving them there, before you actually send it.

Remember, though, that just because someone has sent you an annoying email, you are not obliged to reply. You might forget...for a long time. It might go into your junk file – accidentally.

Another really handy tip regarding emails is to schedule when they are sent and ask others to do the same. It is simply not fair to receive an email about a pending disaster at 11pm at night. While you really do need to develop the self-control to step away from your emails, you can also ask the sender to schedule them in future, so that they arrive at a time when you can actually do something about the issue and respond. Using this tactic for yourself, you can write a full, detailed email and get all your thoughts written down; then by choosing to send it the next day at 8:30am, you can manage to get it all off your chest without risking annoying someone at bedtime.

Tracking

These days I find it very interesting getting daily reports on how far my dog has walked and seeing his little routes. (Always much longer than my actual route. I have thought about getting a Fitbit and attaching it to his collar so it looks as if I've done 25,000 steps a day and can therefore eat as much as I want.) These trackers are handy as they do not rely on a phone, although for a decent one, you do need to pay a small monthly subscription.

The 'Find a friend' on iPhone and other tracking apps such as 'Life 360' are really useful. There are multiple free apps for tracking, depending on what you need them for.

I find that many children and young people quite like having this on their phone because they can see where *you* are as well. If children do not like having the app, they soon learn how to remove it! Top tip: learn how to 'pause' the app so you can arrive home unexpectedly sometimes. ('Oh sorry, I think the app must have frozen.')

If you are looking for ways to get control of your children's social media and technology, that is covered pretty comprehensively, with strategies, in *The A–Z of Therapeutic Parenting* under 'Social Media'.

See strategies: Losing Things, Protecting Self, Routine, Switching Off, Timesavers, X-ing Out (Crossing Out)

 THERAPY (FOR PARENTS)

We know that there is a great deal of therapy available for our children and we support them through it. However, I didn't find it useful when we attended family therapy, only to discover that, as the adults, our lives, issues and worries were irrelevant (obviously), as all the focus was on the children, who vacillated between eye rolling, bargaining hard for cakes, and walking out.

The irony, of course, is that we didn't *need* therapy before our children came to live with us. It's not their fault, but the behaviours and levels of stress with all the associated triggers often mean that therapeutic parents also need extra help and support. For example, before I adopted I was *not* hypervigilant and overreactive to sudden noise, but now I am.

When my children came to live with us, we had a very forward-thinking adoption social worker. She insisted that we had weekly meetings with an attachment therapist so we could talk about whatever we wanted. I remember laughing to myself and thinking I had nothing at all to say and trying to reassure the social worker that we wouldn't need it. Luckily, she held her ground, and I saw that therapist every week for the first two years my children were with me. My practice husband refused to see the therapist (presumably on the grounds that he 'already knew everything'), and he left the family home, unable to cope with the children's needs after 12 months.

Sometimes it is felt that the support of a social worker was a sufficient replacement for 'therapy', and indeed often that is the case, especially if you have a 'gold-dust' one who understands all about child trauma and knows you really well. If, however, you have a different social worker every five weeks and they haven't yet learned what *you* know, then you are just left in a lonely place, feeling inadequate.

Over the years, I have come to learn that the best therapy for me was any mixture of cake, coffee, cups of tea and a friend with a kind, listening ear. But what is the right kind of therapy for us when cake, chocolate and empathic listening don't cut it anymore? I've lost count of the number of parents who have contacted us over the years in despair, due to the fact that they have been sent for generic 'counselling' and have endured hours trying to explain the basics of trauma to a so-called counsellor who only wants to focus on topics the parent feels are irrelevant. The difficulty is that when you are raising a child from trauma, you become a bit of a trauma expert, and you need somebody who understands that too.

Some of the different types of therapy available are listed below with short explanations, so you can identify the best one for your needs. You do actually need to make time to go though!

Attachment therapy

If you have a lot of triggers and you want to de-link them, an attachment therapist can often help you to establish why a particular behaviour is triggering and where it comes from. This enables you to get a sense of perspective.

Cognitive behaviour therapy (CBT)

Although at the Centre of Excellence in Child Trauma we don't advocate CBT when working with children from trauma, it can be useful for therapeutic parents. Some parents find CBT very useful in helping them to change the way they think, particularly where they may be very anxious and fall into patterns of catastrophic thinking.

Counselling

If you just want a safe place where you can go back at regular intervals and have someone alongside you, helping to reflect, then counselling can be a very grounding and useful tool for growing your own insight and resilience. Some counsellors have different areas of specialism (like 'inner child' work), so it is worth researching which area you want to focus on.

Dyadic developmental psychotherapy (DDP)

Increasingly, we find that DDP therapists work much more with the parents than with the children and parents together. DDP is an ideal therapy for therapeutic parents and the environment is constructive and empathic. DDP can also be very useful where the parent also experienced trauma as a child and has issues to work through which are impacting on the relationship with their child.

Emotional freedom technique (EFT)
Also known as 'tapping therapy', this will often be sought to help lower cortisol and stress levels. Some parents have come across this therapy with their children, seen its effectiveness and then used it for themselves, with great success.

Eye movement desensitization and reprocessing (EMDR)
This is a relatively new therapy which uses eye movement to de-link the emotion associated with traumatic memories. Some parents experience its effectiveness with their children and then go on to choose to have some sessions for themselves. Some parents who have had a traumatic childhood find this particularly beneficial.

Havening and delta touch therapies
We have had exceptionally positive feedback about the impact of Havening. This is popular with therapeutic parents because it can produce dramatic results very quickly! (See 'Havening'.)

Hypnotherapy
Hypnosis can be a really helpful way to increase delta waves in the brain and to access ideas and thoughts that may have been hidden due to stress. Some parents have also used hypnotherapy to help them discover the source of a trigger that was puzzling them.

Meditation and mindfulness
Many therapeutic parents have found online guided meditations a really fantastic way to de-stress and take a little time for themselves. Meditation and mindfulness help us to slow down and be in the moment a little more. It can help to stop catastrophic thinking and enable us to gain some perspective on current events.

Spa days

Okay, I know that strictly speaking this is not a therapy, but it *feels* like therapy. I mean, sitting in the hot tub, relaxing in the lovely, quiet, water-trickling room, having a head massage – sometimes that's all the therapy we need. As long as there are nice snacks and no phone coverage, obviously.

See strategies: Brain Breaks, Essential Maintenance, Havening, Switching Off, Triggers (Managing), Yoga, Zen

 TIMESAVERS

Here's my list of favourite timesavers:

- Put the children's shoes in the car the night before (if travelling to school by car; obviously, it would be ridiculous to put their shoes in the car and then forget where they are, if you walk to school).
- Sort the children's clothes into a tidy pile, in the order they need to be put on, and the right way round. Keep the piles in your room if they are likely to be sabotaged.
- Do absolutely everything else you can the night before (even at weekends). I know it's a pain, but you don't know what kind of night or morning you are going to have. It feels like a bit of nurture for us to come down to find the table is set, the dog food is already in the bowl, your clothes are laid out, chosen and colour matched, and the children's school bags are already packed, with their lunch boxes in the fridge waiting to go in. It means you're able to have that much-needed cup of tea or coffee. (And yes, it's too early for wine.)
- For a really quick meal that looks as if you put in lots of effort, and seems to be wholesome and nurturing, keep some tins of macaroni cheese and ravioli in the cupboard. You can

pour these into a casserole dish, cover with grated cheese and put in the oven for 15 minutes. Hey presto! Home-baked pasta surprise. The children never cottoned on.

- Keep yogurts, tins of custard and tubs of instant jelly handy. Pour them into a bowl together and call it a trifle. This can also be low sugar too, as an extra bonus.
- If you have more than one child, do their washing on different days. This means their clothes don't get tangled up and it saves lots of time sorting clothes out from each other.
- Buy socks and underwear in the same colour for a particular child – pink for one, yellow for another. Not only does this cut down arguing and mean that what belongs to who is easily identifiable, but it also reduces the amount of time your children will go out in unmatching socks. (For my children, it was the majority of the time anyway, as they used to steal each other's.)
- Stop answering emails that just annoy you. You'll find that people eventually stop writing to you.
- Sometimes it can be quicker, and less effort, to walk to school. If you have dogs, you can combine this into a dog walk, and it also lowers the children's cortisol levels (and yours for that matter), making everyone feel better. On the return, you have a walk afterwards in blissful silence.
- Stop doing homework (see 'Homework (Not Doing)').
- Use permanent ink to write initials on clothing – not on the labels as they can be cut out, but actually on the waist bands or bottoms of the cuff. This means you don't have to spend hours designing/ordering/sewing/ironing on name tapes when that jumper will be lost within two hours anyway.
- Invest in some realistic-looking fake flowers (unbreakable obviously). You can put these out around the house. That way, you never have to bother buying flowers, sorting them out, getting the vases, watching the vases of water going black over the next two weeks when you haven't got time to

change the water, and then having depressing vases of dead flowers littered all over the house.

- Invest in hardwood floors and washable rugs, which practically cover the floor. This saves hours of housework.
- If you have a child who struggles with bedwetting, use pull-ups rather than having to keep washing all the sheets. Your child isn't ready yet, and frankly you have more important things to worry about. It is unlikely they will still be wetting the bed at 25. Don't get into washing sheets every day in the mistaken belief that being in wet sheets will 'help them learn not to wet the bed'. It is a fallacy. It just makes your house stink of wee, fills up the washing machine all day long, and depresses you.
- Save hours by stopping yourself from asking pointless questions like 'Well, where is the other one?' or 'Where is your lunch box?' or, worst ever, 'Why did you do that?'
- Fill the paddling pool with warm water, call it a hot tub and double it up as a regulating bath for the children. (NB: Make sure you do not even *joke* about 'putting the vacuum cleaner on to blow, to create bubbles'. It does not end well.)

See strategies: Losing Things, Routine, X-ing Out (Crossing Out)

TOP TRUMP PARENTING

Also see Catastrophic Thinking, Diagnoses, Eeyore Parenting, Friendships, Perfect Parents

'Top Trump parenting' can be a race to the bottom *or* the top!

The good news is that Top Trump parenting happens everywhere. Any parent of securely attached children, living a pretty straightforward life, will come across the Top Trump parent boasting and showing off about their child's remarkable achievements. You can make the most innocuous observation or impart a little piece of news, and the Top Trump parent will immediately trump you with something like this...

You to child: Come on, Jo, let's get your shoes on...

Top Trump parent: Oh, are you teaching shoelaces? It's tricky, isn't it? I was so lucky with Casper, he just seemed to do it on his own. I think he's going to be an engineer as he just seems to have that kind of brain!

You: Um, no. Jo has slip-ons...

Top Trump parent: (*patronizing face*)

It can be just as draining in reverse. The negative 'Eeyore Parent' is determined to prove that their child has more difficulties than yours, and that therefore their life is *so much harder*, so by definition they are automatically doing much better than everyone else.

I used to come across this all the time. I think it was because I had five adopted children, so Top Trump parents had their noses put out of joint as I was already 'winning' in the number of children category. With negative Top Trumps (Bottom Trumps maybe), the parent is often overwhelmed or has compassion fatigue and the top trumping is a symptom of this. Here are some of the things that are said:

- The therapist/social worker says my child is the most extreme child they have ever dealt with.
- My child has 17 different disabilities and it's completely hopeless.
- The school say they have never worked with such a difficult child. They don't know how I cope.

On our therapeutic parenting Facebook page, we frequently see parents listing diagnoses and descriptions of 'hopeless' children.

Even when positive encouragement is given, with examples of better outcomes, the Top Trump parent is unable to accept this, and continues to recite the number of Top Trumps they have.

If you recognize yourself as a Top Trump parent, think about which of *your* needs are not being met. Is there an important issue which you need others to really listen to and be aware of? (Only about 1000 probably.)

If you are dealing with a Top Trump parent, this can be really draining. It's worthwhile tackling it head on and being straightforward about competitions you will not be joining in with: 'Oh, I see what you did there... I mentioned about Marie going to after-school club and you told me how you do meaningful after-school activities with Casper. I am sure you didn't mean to make me feel bad, when you already know how difficult our lives are. I am sure Marie would love to join in your activities with Casper, though; she may enjoy it more than after-school club' (*expectant smile*).

*See strategies: **One Step at a Time, Paddington Hard-Stare, Pointy-Eyebrow Death Stare, Protecting Self, Sarcasm, Useful Phrases***

TRAILBLAZING

Also see Criticism, Empowerment, PIEs

Trailblazing is born from lonely despair, and a drive to find answers. As Plato said, 'Necessity is the mother of invention.' I needed to find a way my children could:

- communicate
- attach
- cope with school
- stop fighting
- manage their trauma.

And no other bugger was giving me any ideas!

It is true that many therapeutic parents are trailblazers. I've often been referred to as a 'trailblazer' myself. I suppose it's valid. I've *had to* create new pathways; I've had to invent new ways of working, communicating and resolving trauma. I would have been quite happy to use methods that worked. I just couldn't find easily accessible ones.

When we see a problem, we can become really creative about finding the solution if the traditional methods don't work. This is what makes us trailblazers. Other people will see it perhaps as rude or stroppy or deluded. They don't realize that our drive forwards is born from quiet desperation, not a wish to create a whole new set of rules.

I understand that being a trailblazer can feel very lonely and also be really tiring. We get to the point of thinking, 'Do I really need to explain this *again*? Do I have to sort this out *again*? Is there really only me that can do this, or who cares enough to do this?' Sadly, it's time to have some cake and carry on, because trailblazing is a full-time occupation and our children will thank us for it in the end.

The people who used to criticize my methods and ideas, the ones who would condemn our efforts to resolve our difficulties as a family – well, I hope they have been to my training now. I hope they have read the books. But most of all, I hope they have stopped dismissing other therapeutic parents and are now supporting them.

At the start, I felt as if I was in a trailblazing club of one. Now, however, with all of our organizations and resources, the brilliant and devoted parents, teachers, social workers and therapists and other experts in the field (all trailblazers in their own right), we are indeed *all* trailblazing a huge fiery path together.

See strategies: Essential Maintenance, Expectations (Managing), Protecting Self, School Strategies, Useful Phrases, Valuing

 **TRAINING**

Training can be the bane of your life, or it can be one of the best things that's ever happened to you, if you feel you gain understanding, and therefore improve your life. Here is a handy checklist so you can identify training that is going to work for you, and training that you need to avoid (or at least reduce).

Pointless training	Relevant training
The trainer has unrelated experience but links everything to that experience. For example, you want to know how to stop your child smearing poo on the walls, and the trainer (gifted in DIY) explains to you how to redecorate your home.	The trainer has relevant, shared experiences. When you ask a question, they can answer it because they have been in the same situation, and they now have tried and trusted methods that work, saving you hours of trial and error.
You are forced to go to training that you know you will never need in your life. For example, you live in a flat, but you are being told you have to go on training around 'health and safety in the garden'.	The training relates to your current situation and the needs of your children. For example, you have three siblings under five and the training is specific to sibling groups and the trauma bond.
When you, or indeed anyone, asks any questions, the trainer replies with 'Yes that's very difficult', and then doesn't answer the question.	Questions are answered with real-life strategies, or you are signposted to where you can get the answers.
The PowerPoints are completely filled up with tiny writing, clearly copied and pasted from a textbook, that the trainer then reads out loud to you, unable to offer any context, and appearing baffled by their own slides.	The PowerPoint is interesting with memorable bullet points, pictures and engaging videos to illustrate certain points.

At the Centre of Excellence in Child Trauma, we have ensured that all our training is now fully accessible, whatever hour of the day or night you need it. This does not mean that I stay up all night in case someone logs in. We realized that what parents actually *need* is training and information that is video-based without relying on lots of tests and reading. Here are the key foundations that *everyone* working in this field needs to understand:

- The impact of trauma on children.
- The reasons our children behave the way they do.
- Why traditional parenting models don't work.
- How allegations can be better understood and managed.
- What we can do instead.

If you are struggling to get a supporting professional, partner or family member to understand what it is you are doing and why, point them in the direction of our online training. You can also access some short, free videos which explain the basics:

- *Understanding Your Traumatized Child*
- *What is Therapeutic Parenting?*

Many therapeutic parents have given *The A–Z of Therapeutic Parenting* or *The Quick Guide to Therapeutic Parenting* to their own parents and extended family to help them to understand why there are differences in our children. You can just encourage them to look at the first couple of sections in *The A–Z of Therapeutic Parenting*, especially the sections around why traditional parenting doesn't work and why our children behave the way they do. Alternatively, they can access The Therapeutic Parenting Podcast for free, and just choose the episode most relevant to them. There are episodes specifically for family and friends of therapeutic parents.

You can find information on all our training and podcasts for parents, schools and supporting professionals at www.coect.co.uk and www.inspiretraininggroup.com.

See strategies: Brain Breaks, Essential Maintenance, Podcasts, Protecting Self, Reflecting, Understanding

TRIGGERS (MANAGING)

It's worthwhile taking a moment to think about what your triggers are. They might be reasonable, but you might feel they are unreasonable or puzzling ('I don't know why it annoys me so much!').

Other people might feel your triggers are unreasonable and accuse you of 'overreacting'. Well, if they can't actually help you then they don't need to be involved in general criticism really. If you have a trigger, you have a trigger, and that's all there is to it.

At the Centre of Excellence in Child Trauma, we use Havening to de-link triggers so that you don't have an overwhelming, uncomfortable reaction anymore (see the 'Havening' section).

Before looking at Havening (or other useful therapeutic interventions that deal with triggers), it might be useful to just do a bit of exploration around the trigger.

In order to help you to identify and manage your triggers, try answering the following questions to gain some insight into your responses:

- Is there a particular time of day/week/month/year when you are more likely to be triggered?
- What action provokes a negative reaction in you?
- What is the best word you can find to describe that reaction (e.g. anger, irritation, sadness, frustration)?
- Where do you feel that in your body (e.g. chest, stomach, brain)?
- Do you recognize that feeling/response from another time/ action?
- What else has made you feel that way?
- When was it?

- What happened?

Now look to see if there is a pattern. For example, it might be that this always happens at the table when people are eating around you, or there might be a particular anniversary which comes up related to a season or an actual date. I always feel sad on Armistice Day. I now know this is because it is the anniversary of the day I had to move my foster children to their adopters, on my own, on a Sunday. Although this is nearly 30 years ago now, my body still remembers the sadness of that day, even if my brain has parked it!

Once you've identified some patterns, you can start to see emerging themes relating to people, times and activities when you're feeling triggered. There *will* be a root cause for this. It might well be that you've written it off in the past as 'Someone's just being an idiot and irritated me', but that's still a trigger. Some people are able to handle that really well, because patronizing idiots *don't* trigger them. Their own self-worth is high enough, and they feel that they will be able to resolve whatever it is. So, therefore, if being spoken to in a patronizing way *is* a trigger for you, it may have made you feel ignored and unimportant. What made you feel that way in the past? Where did it come from?

In this way, you can link triggers appropriately and find the real home for them. This can really help with managing your child's behaviour *and* managing yourself. Just using 'pausing' is really effective in identifying triggers. If you can catch yourself in the moment, just as you start to feel angry or anxious, try to ask yourself, 'What is it *right now* that's making me feel this way?'

One thing you can be sure of, if you *are* triggered the children will know it. They will be thrilled to see the big red button marked 'push'. They will keep pushing it until the battery runs out.

See strategies: Brain Breaks, Essential Maintenance, Havening, Pausing, Reflecting, Understanding

U

UNAPPRECIATED

Also see Disappointment, Eeyore Parenting,
Forgotten, Pity, Resilience, Valuing

Your children are not grateful, yet. They may never be. That is a hard fact, and one which drives us to look for appreciation elsewhere. I found it in chocolate and the TV soap opera *Emmerdale*. I appreciated what a great job I had done that day.

Know this though: *I* appreciate the efforts you make. I see it in your faces when we meet at training. When you say you have 'had a bad day', I know what that really means. I know what you have given up. I know how tired you get and how you feel as if you are all alone. I know how relentless it feels sometimes. I appreciate you. All of you. And do you know what? Lots of people appreciate what you do too. The whole team at the Centre of Excellence in Child Trauma for a start! You may be unaware of it, but one day, when it's safe, people will appear and say things like 'I don't know how you did it' or 'You did an incredible job there'. It *will* happen.

And, best of all, it's very likely that one day your children *will* appreciate all you did for them. If it isn't spoken, it's still obvious. There will be a dawning realization of the sacrifices you made, the immense efforts you went to for them, because you love them and want the best for them. And *then* you will be appreciated, and it is the most wonderful feeling in the world.

See strategies: Brain Breaks, Celebrating, Essential Maintenance, Natural Consequences (Allowing), Protecting Self, Valuing

 # UNDERSTANDING

Understanding what is behind the behaviours of others helps us to stop taking it personally. We get quite good at doing this with our children, but it's really handy applying that to adults too. In the 'Support' section, I mentioned about feeling ill-prepared, as if you have been taught to paint, but realize you need to build the wall before you get to the painting. When we develop true understanding, it isn't about suddenly having all the right tools, it's about knowing we don't have them and making a plan to get them.

Often, I have been asked to problem-solve in teams where things are going a bit wrong. By applying a little bit of understanding and taking the perspective of others, most issues are resolved quickly. For example, a blame culture is frequently rife in care settings, because blame absolves the blamer of responsibility. We see this pattern in families too, especially where we have our wonderful, unique children indulging in hourly blame-fests.

I might go into a team where there is a lot of finger pointing. By simply saying 'That's interesting, I wonder why she did that?' or 'I wonder what he had experienced *before* that day to make him behave in this way', we get a shift of perspective.

If I ask the 'blamed' person these exact questions, the dawning light of realization appears, shining brightly on the team. By just shining an 'understanding' light on the experiences and motivation *behind* the exhibited behaviours we become wise, empathic people.

And yes, I know, you wish someone would apply this to you too.

People don't/won't understand our perspective for several reasons:

- They choose not to.

- It's irrelevant to *their* life.
- It will create work for them if they understand your perspective.
- They don't believe you.
- They have more important things to do.
- It's at odds with their own belief system.

When you know that someone is capable of understanding and they are choosing not to, you can waste many hours trying to convince them. There's no point to this. You can send a nice long email with lots of web links and resources, but they won't read it. Have some chocolate instead. If they *choose* not to understand, you can't make them.

Through reflection, pausing, training and empathic listening we can gain more understanding of our children and our responses. When we gain a true understanding of our children's behaviour and have insight, there are knock-on, positive benefits:

- It's very empowering.
- It stops us feeling as if everything's personal.
- It helps us to get the right resources for children.
- It takes some pressure off us.
- It helps us re-evaluate who's helping us and who isn't.

We can also start to plan long-term and have some *real goals* in mind when we finally have the tool list for the supplies we are going to need, identify what is missing, and have a plan about how we are going to complete the task.

See strategies: Brain Breaks, Empathic Listening, Essential Maintenance, Forgiving Yourself, Pausing, Reflecting, Self-Regulation, Training, Triggers (Managing), Useful Phrases

☼ USEFUL PHRASES

Shortly after I had adopted all five children and had suddenly became a single parent, living on a building site, my tolerance of other people's stupidity reduced dramatically. This helped me to develop some handy time-saving phrases for fast communication.

Early on, I heard a saying which went, 'Behold the field in which I grow my fucks. Lay thine eyes upon it and thou shall see that it is barren.' After saying this a few times, I only needed to start off with 'Behold the field...' and I didn't even need to get to the swearing. They just shut up and started urgently packing up their things.

Here are some more handy phrases you can use, depending on the situation and person you are dealing with.

For arguments with partners

Antecedent	Instead of	Say
Not helping.	You are so lazy!	I know sometimes we can all be a bit lazy, however...
Partner comes home complaining of hard day at work.	What do you mean you've had a bad day?! You've been to work! You've had a lunch break! I've been stuck here dealing with poo and shoplifting, and that prat of a therapist unbottling everything, spilling it all over the floor, and leaving me to clean it up!	Cup of tea? Then we can both hear about the other's day.

cont.

Antecedent	Instead of	Say
Accusation of being 'too strict' with child, who is triangulating.	Of course, I am not being 'too hard on her'! She's got you sucked in, wrapped round her little finger! Are you bloody stupid?	I think there's some 'splitting' going on here. Here's some information about that. If you read it when you have a chance, you will see that's what is happening.
Coming home from work to stressed-out partner, who immediately starts shouting at you about the children's behaviour.	Well bloody well ring up social services and say you don't want them if it's that difficult!	Let's put the kettle on, then you can tell me all about it.
Partner insists that child 'must learn' to 'tell the truth'. Stuck in traditional parenting.	Are you actually an idiot? Of course, he is not going to be able to admit the truth to you, when you keep banging on like some arsehole of a sergeant major!	Let me deal with this. We will discuss it later.
Partner forgets important event or decides you 'won't mind' being overlooked.	Fine then...I'll just carry on doing everything then, shall I? After all, why would I even care that you have forgotten my birthday/ Christmas present or my Valentines/special event? No NOTHING is wrong. Everything is ABSOLUTELY FINE! (Crashing noises).	NO, actually I DO mind. I know you didn't mean to hurt my feelings, but you have. How can we put this right, so we both feel better?
Partner undermines you with child.	Oh, that's right! Brilliant! Spectacular! Well done for making our child feel insecure! Idiot!	I see what happened – you didn't realize I had already said x. We can sort it out later. Meanwhile let's...

For schools

Antecedent	Instead of	Say
School phones and says they are excluding your child.	You can't bloody exclude him again! It's ridiculous! You haven't got a clue, have you? Just bloody admit it!	Before we discuss this, I need to be absolutely clear that I will be wanting proof that our written plan has been adhered to and that he was not sabotaged by the school. Again.
Teacher says, 'I'm sorry to tell you that your child has been on the (sad face emoji) all day. I am very disappointed.'	Get my child's name off that fucking reward chart right now! (Tearing and stamping noises)	Ah yes! I forgot that I haven't given you that handy information resource explaining why reward charts don't work for children with developmental trauma. I'll pop it in tomorrow.
He is fine in school! We don't have any issues!	So, what are you saying? You manage everything just fine, so it must be just me who is crap and can't cope? Fine. Book him in to every single club: breakfast club, after-school club and school holiday camp for the next two years, then see how you get on!	Aah, that's a shame (sad face). Hopefully one day he will feel safe enough at school to stop masking his real feelings and fears. I am so pleased he is comfortable enough to do this with me now.

cont.

294 THE A–Z OF SURVIVAL STRATEGIES FOR THERAPEUTIC PARENTS

Antecedent	Instead of	Say
School phones and says your child has a detention and you need to 'speak to them' about their poor behaviour.	Don't ask me to support you in your crap, irrelevant punishment detentions! I only have your version to go on. You have proved time and again that you have no idea about trauma triggers. So no, I won't be having any kind of discussion with him about your perceived bad behaviour.	Lovely! Of course, I will be delighted to discuss with my child what happened. I may even be able to rustle up a disappointed face. I will do this as soon as someone from the school comes round to ask him why he hasn't tidied his bedroom. I've asked several times now.
Teacher says your child has failed to do their homework and is sending home extra work.	Have you any fucking idea what it is like in our house between end of school and bedtime? I am lucky if we don't have crap on the walls, let alone making sure everyone actually gets to eat without stabbing each other.	Oh, sorry, didn't you know? I am a therapeutic parent, and we don't do homework. This is because our children cannot manage the change in me from 'parent' to 'teacher'. It can be very distressing for us all. Would you like some literature explaining this? I am, however, more than happy for them to stay on at school and attend the homework club.
Teacher tells you, 'She will be fine on the school trip. You are a bit of a worrier, aren't you?'	And you are a bit of a patronizing git, aren't you?	You are quite right. Take them on the school trip. Oh, did I mention what happened last time? Probably best to take out extra insurance, just as a precaution…

I am very worried about how hungry Sophie is. She has been stealing out of lunch boxes. Would you like our fact sheet on how to make a healthy packed lunch?	Yes, I would be thrilled to have your fact sheet. I can make good use of this in my craft box for the children. Clearly, you think I am some kind of fuckwit who, despite the fact that all of my children are growing healthily, needs some kind of nanny state intervention to explain to me how to feed them. Feel free to phone social services if you think there is a need.	I'm very concerned about the lack of supervision this suggests to me. I've mentioned before that due to Sophie's developmental trauma she does not recognize feelings of hunger. I would like a written plan from you outlining how you will help her to manage that in school. Also, just a reminder that obviously she does tend to be driven to find and eat the unhealthy things because she's addicted to sugar. This is normal for children with high cortisol levels. Would you like an information sheet on this?
Teacher joyfully informs you that the class are doing 'family tree' work and everyone needs to bring in 'cute little baby photos' which she knows you don't have.	(Pointy-Eyebrow Death Stare, followed by very awkward pause.)	And how will you be ensuring inclusion in this topic? I will be really interested to see how you can do that, because as you know, my child does not have any photos before the age of two.

For PIEs

Antecedent	Instead of	Say
He's been with you a long time now and won't remember anything. So, the behaviours are really down to you.	You really are astonishingly ignorant for someone in your job. Get out of my house now.	Oh, what a shame! They didn't teach you about attachment at university either, did they? Never mind. What would you like to know?
I don't think there's anything particularly wrong with your child. They just get a little bit anxious sometimes. This is normal.	And what are you basing that opinion on? Yet another pathetic comparison to your securely attached seven-year-old and their normal anxiety about going to the dentist? No. I am talking about screaming, dragging their siblings away and hiding. So, not really 'anxiety' then. Prat.	That's an interesting point of view; however, you may not be aware how children with developmental trauma mask their feelings. Of course we see anxiety, but there is a lot more going on here. Would you like information about this?
We are going to do an assessment to see what kind of support we can put in place.	Bloody marvellous! Last time you did an 'assessment' it was just a 'let's blame the parent' fest masquerading as a 'support package'. I don't need constant bloody criticism and interference from someone who has not a Scooby Doo about trauma, attachment and therapeutic parenting. I've got a good idea! How about you actually listen to what we need as a family, then help me to put that in place?	That's a great idea as long as the process can include my supporter, and we have clearly understood and agreed outcomes. After all, there's no point doing an assessment for the sake of it, is there? We've had quite enough of those. (NB: Check if you have to have an assessment. Often, they are not mandatory and require your consent.)

Have you tried talking to them?	(Paddington Hard-Stare) What a wonderful idea! Do you know? Talking to my children had actually never even crossed my mind until you cleverly pointed it out.	The difficulty with having lengthy conversations with children with developmental trauma is that they cannot take in and retain the information. Therapeutic parenting uses reflection, empathy and naming the need. This changes behaviours and builds synapses in the brain. This is proven to be much more effective than any kind of talking about behaviours, which is more likely to invoke shame. Would you like a fact sheet on this?
You are doing a marvellous job.	And you know that because…? Oh, I see, you want to withdraw support, so you are bigging me up first.	I know you mean well, but I find that difficult to hear unless it is evidence-based.
My child is just the same. I do understand what it's like.	Brilliant! Our children can have playdates and you will understand entirely when all the terrible behaviours surface. No? Thought not. So, your child is not just like mine. Your child is seven and securely attached. Don't be so bloody patronizing.	Oh, I am so sorry! I did not realize your child also had special/ additional needs/ developmental trauma (delete as appropriate). What happened?

cont.

298 THE A–Z OF SURVIVAL STRATEGIES FOR THERAPEUTIC PARENTS

Antecedent	Instead of	Say
I know you believe that your child has developmental trauma, but no experts have assessed them yet, so we don't think that's correct. It's probably just a touch of attention deficit hyperactivity disorder (ADHD).	What the actual fuck? What is a 'touch' of ADHD? Is that like having a 'bit of a missing leg'? Have you actually read any of my reports/emails/letters? Have you seen the referral from my GP/ social worker?	That's a shame, it looks as if you're not aware about the link between high cortisol levels and the condition looking as if the child has ADHD. Obviously, high cortisol levels are one of the symptoms of developmental trauma. Dr Bruce Perry and Dr Bessel van der Kolk have written extensively on this. You can easily find them by doing a search on google. It's good, though, as my MP was really interested when I sent him all the information on this and what we are trying to achieve. Would you like me to send you a fact sheet too?

For family/friends/Perfect Parents

Antecedent	Instead of	Say
So, what happened to their real parents then?	Don't be so bloody nosey! And what do you mean by 'real parents'? So bloody rude!	So, how's your sex life at present? (Pause for shocked face.) Well, what you just asked me is about as personal as that.

You do too much! Have a little break.	Yes, you are right... I am actually 'overdoing it'. I am bloody exhausted. What do you suggest I do? Go and sit in the bath with headphones on? So, you're going to bloody well look after them, are you? No? Thought not.	Thank you for noticing how tired I am. Lots of people don't. I'd appreciate some practical help with...
They are so naughty. Can't you just send them back?	Oh yes, great idea. Because that wouldn't make everything a million times worse for everyone would it? Back where? Where is 'back'? Do you think there is some kind of Wizard of Oz house over the fucking rainbow, waiting to house sad little failed adoptees?	Great idea! I know, let's send your kids/ partner/dog off at the same time! They can treat it as a little holiday. Like evacuees in the war!
You think they'd be grateful!	Of course, they should be grateful! Can't imagine why I didn't think of that before. I must sit them down and remind them how grateful they should be for having been abused in their early life/ having disabilities to struggle with (delete as appropriate).	Do you know, it's really fascinating that some people (not you obviously) believe that the children should actually be grateful for the experiences they suffered in early life... (tinkly laugh, Pointy-Eyebrow Death Stare)

cont.

Antecedent	Instead of	Say
Do you have any real children? I mean blood, you know?	Let me see. I'll just see if I can find some lurking under the sofa. I think I only have pretend children today. They are not real children as they do not poo or eat, obviously. Are you actually stupid?	Goodness me, that is an outdated expression! The term would be 'biological or birth' children. Also, it is really safer to ask, 'Do you have any other children?' That way you can avoid discriminatory language. Other people might be more offended than me.
So, what cakes can I put you down for the school fete? Or would you rather look after one of the stalls?	(Mute, incredulous stare, then Paddington Hard-Stare, then Pointy-Eyebrow Death Stare.)	Well, let's see who is going to help me with childcare, then I will be delighted to have an afternoon sitting about on a cake stall. Where do I sign?
My child is so clever... He has just passed his maths test a whole year early! We are so lucky, and he is so good!	Well, whoopy doo... Do you just say this type of crap to piss me off? Do you actually have any clue how difficult life is, just getting the children to school?	That's brilliant! And guess what? Harry didn't wet the bed last night AND Lily hasn't even tried to punch me ALL day! We are so lucky, aren't we?
(Any patronizing critical suggestion.)	Oh sorry! You are mistaking me for someone who gives a shit.	That's an interesting point of view. Pity it's wrong.
Oh, poor you! Aren't you doing a wonderful job, despite everything?	Please take your pity face elsewhere. Immediately.	I understand that you think you are being kind but what I really need is practical help, not pity.

See strategies: Natural Consequences (Allowing), Paddington Hard-Stare, Pointy-Eyebrow Death Stare, Protecting Self, Sarcasm, School Strategies, Top Trump Parenting, Vanishing Helpers

V

VALUING

*Also see Boundaries, Empathy, Forgotten,
Resilience, Unappreciated*

Valuing ourselves

Sometimes, therapeutic parents spend so much time putting their needs last that they completely forget that they are valuable. We overlook this because we're so focused on the needs of others. This is further magnified when our efforts are unappreciated or criticized by others.

One of the central themes of this book has been around the importance of recognizing, accepting and *meeting* our own needs. It comes down to self-respect really. If you don't respect yourself, then you can't really expect others, including your children, to value you. This is easier said than done in our busy lives, and a lot of it is around learning to say no, delegation, and stating clearly what our expectations *are*.

Even if you are a pretty feisty person, well known for being clear about your own needs and expectations, you may still find yourself sighing inwardly and saying, 'It's fine!' When it clearly isn't. Why do we do this? Well for me it was normally about efficiency and speed. If I did it, I knew it was definitely done and done properly. I felt I'd rather complete the task than wait and hope for someone else to do it. I didn't want or need the uncertainty in my life.

Delegation is the key, but in order to delegate you have to have:

- someone to delegate to
- time to show them what to do
- the trust that they will do it
- the patience not to kill them when they forget to do it.

Valuing special times

Nowadays, I look back and value a lot of the times we had as a family:

- Finally skiing down a mountain all together with no arguing.
- The lovely snowball fight.
- The first birthday cards and Mother's Day cards, which were written from the heart.
- The first evidence of the children developing empathy.
- Bouncing on the bouncy castle together and laughing *so* much.
- Picking strawberries at a 'pick your own' farm and laughing at the amount they were stuffing in their faces.

It's much easier to value those times in retrospect. At the time, I was probably focused on avoiding arguments, checking no one had wet themselves and getting them all home in one piece, in time for tea.

But I wish now... I wish I had just stopped for a moment and valued that time, that space, that event. The last time the children were all together, I didn't *know* that would be the last time for five years. How I would have valued that day more, committed more to memory if only I had known.

It makes it easier to place special value on the times which I know are coming. The weekends with grandchildren, the planned holidays with some of my adult children. These will be valued before, during and after, because now I have the time and the peace of mind to be *in* the moment with them.

See strategies: Celebrating, Essential Maintenance, Forgiving Yourself, Krispy Kreme Donuts, Looking Good, Protecting Self, Reflecting, Useful Phrases

 ## VANISHING HELPERS

When people offer to help but then do nothing whatsoever to *actually* help, they need to be tackled. You know the people I'm talking about:

- The school gate mum who offers to look after your children, then recoils in horror when it looks as if you might take her up on the offer.
- The extended family member who says they *would* babysit but unfortunately they have to be home by 6pm.
- The partner who promised to come home on time but fails to materialize or answer their phone.
- The social worker who has promised you they *definitely will* write the report to help get the resources your children need, but then forgets to write it and then forgets to visit.
- The 'helpful' supporting professional who tells you that 'you *really must* take a break or go for a walk', but then is unable to provide you with any practical means of achieving this. They are then unavailable for the next fortnight while they go away on their holiday.

These people simply have to be confronted. It makes us feel much better when we call them out on it. A straightforward smile with a little sarcasm goes a long way. I would say things like, 'Oh that's so funny! You wouldn't *believe* the number of people who have offered to help and then I never see them again! (*tinkly laugh through gritted teeth*).

Don't be afraid to just say it how it is: 'I know you *mean* well, but if you can't *actually* help then please don't offer, because otherwise I do start to think that there might be some relief where there isn't any' (*sad martyr face, quivering lip*). This makes it more likely that the person will be guilt tripped into actually helping you.

The words 'official complaint' can go quite a long way to stop a helper vanishing. You clearly can't use this with the well-meaning school gate mum: 'I'd like to make an official complaint that on Friday 22 June you distinctly offered to have Mohammed and Arthur round to play for the afternoon. It is now 28 July and you have failed to deliver. I would like to file an official complaint about your behaviour. Where is the form?' You can, however, use it with the 'forgetful' supporting professional: 'I know that you've got a lot on your plate, and you have forgotten to write the report, but we *really do* need those resources. By the way, what is the official complaints procedure for your team?'

See strategies: Essential Maintenance, Paddington Hard-Stare, Picking Your Battles, Protecting Self, Sarcasm, Useful Phrases

 ## VANISHING TREATS

Part of essential maintenance is making sure that when we have treats for ourselves, we safeguard them. You might think that you're being clever by hiding the lovely biscuits at the back of the cupboard, but I assure you, your children will hunt them down and inhale them before you even notice they are in the kitchen. If you choose a locking box, the entire box will disappear, and you will find it crowbarred open at the bottom of the garden. I used to hide my treats in the shed, but this stopped when the mice got them.

The only really secure places to keep my treats were either in my bum bag (carrying round at all times) or in the safe. Now, there are very limited numbers of treats you can fit in a bum bag when you've already got your quick exit kit in there – phone, keys and credit cards. Also, chocolate can get a bit melted, and wine does not fit.

In the winter, you can also use the boot of your car providing you make sure that the treats are hidden under an old dog blanket or something. (NB: Make sure you move these before putting the dog in the car. Lesson learned.)

The safe always worked out best for me, and so what if people thought I was mad having doughnuts in my safe. Needs must.

See strategies: Cake, Chocolate, Coffee, Essential Maintenance, Krispy Kreme Donuts, Protecting Self, Tea (Cups of, Cream)

VIEWS

I found that one of the best ways of losing a load of guilt or anger was by dumping it somewhere.

When I found myself frustrated or angry, unable to think straight due to that kind of overload, I would walk up to the top of a hill, lowering my cortisol levels on the way naturally, and find a focal point in the distance. I would then allow myself to feel the anger and then imagine placing that anger onto the focal point in the distance. Sometimes this would be a power station, and it felt really appropriate to put some anger there. It was actually very liberating and freeing, and as I walked down the hill I felt lighter.

Using visualizations combined with a wonderful view can be a very powerful way of putting unwanted emotions to one side.

If you can make yourself stop, just for 20 seconds, and look at the view – a different view, something away from your hectic life – it will give you some perspective. It will also help you to calm a little bit and remember that there is a whole world out there.

Sometimes I have combined Havening with views (see 'Havening'). I've visualized my favourite view while Self-Havening and imagined losing the anger or perhaps even setting fire to some bits of paper with unwanted emotions on them. This can be a very powerful release. Be careful, though, if you decide to start setting small fires in real life on National Trust hills on hot summer days – you will be told off.

See strategies: Brain Breaks, Havening, Self-Regulation, Switching Off, Walking

W

💡 WALKING

Walking is a really great strategy to help us to think clearly. I know when the children were younger, unhelpful others often used to say, 'Why don't you take yourself off for a little walk?' They would be met with my mutinous stare and the question, 'So, you will look after the children while I do that then will you?' (*Hurrying off sounds.*)

'Going for a walk' felt like a massive waste of time to me. I just didn't think I could bear to spend even 20 minutes walking, when there was washing to do, attachments to make, children to calm and tea to drink.

In the last two years, I have suddenly got it. Walking is absolutely brilliant because it:

- gets you away from tension
- lowers your levels of cortisol and adrenaline
- enables you to think clearly after the first few minutes
- changes your perspective
- does actually make you fitter, with virtually no effort.

Since walking more, I have transformed from an unfit, stressed-out blob who used to gasp her way up the slightest of inclines, into someone who can easily manage steep hills, has greatly reduced stress levels, is more productive and looks forward to long walks (with picnics, obviously). Yes, I *know*! 'Looks forward to long walks'...who'd have thought?

The trick with walking is to start off with something manageable and stick to it. A slightly longer walk with the dog, a walk to work or school instead of driving. You will be surprised at the mental health benefits which you feel very quickly. For me, these hugely outweighed the other physical health benefits.

I now realize that when I felt unable to go for walks when the children were younger, this was not really due to the fact that there was 'no one to look after the children'. Of course, there were times when the children were at school. There were times when I was walking the dogs, when I could have walked longer. I could have parked my car a bit further away from work and walked in, giving myself a little built-in time between home and work. The *real* problem was that I lacked the motivation and nurtured the perception that I was 'too busy'. Well, I *was* very busy indeed, but the washing, arguing children and stress would still have been waiting for me when I got home. It's just that I would have been in a much better frame of mind to deal with it all.

All my best ideas and breakthrough moments happen on my walks. I do not ever answer the phone while walking. I keep my brain free for thoughts and inspiration or working through a complex problem. Although I don't answer my phone on a walk, I do take it with me. This means that when I get a great idea, or a solution, I make a quick voice recording so I don't forget it when I return home and the clutter of life descends.

Nowadays, I regularly walk up and down the garden or kitchen when on the phone. I have encouraged my children to do this too. It really helps to keep your thought processes clear. If you are dealing with a PIE or an automated queue recording, the pacing also keeps anger at bay. On a long call, you can rack up 5000 steps without even thinking about it! That's a lot of calories and certainly deserves at least a bit of chocolate.

*See strategies: Brain Breaks, Self-Regulation, Switching Off, Views,
Woods*

 ## WEIGHTED BLANKET

Go on, treat yourself! You know you want one...and it feels like a
hug. You don't need to keep stealing your child's.

See strategies: Audio Books, Essential Maintenance, Podcasts

 ## WOODS

When my children all lived at home, we would always go for a long
walk every Sunday. This was easily the most regulating activity we
ever did together. We would always go somewhere different, with
low levels of stimulation. I am not advocating a nice long walk
around Disneyland. A walk in the woods with a handy stream for
calming down, and regular snack injections, was our best bet for
an uneventful Sunday.

I used to find it much easier to sneak sweets or chocolate into
my pocket and eat them surreptitiously when the children were
running on ahead, as they didn't hear the rustling noises.

The best times were when we joined other families with 'unique'
children. There was something about being in the woods and all
following the same path that made interactions and conflicts less
intense. And besides, if something dreadful happened there was
virtually no audience.

There is something very grounding about just being in the
woods that seems to really help our children to feel calm. Obviously
ground rules are needed:

- No picking up big sticks and swinging them round so you 'accidentally hit someone'.
- We will all start and finish the walk together.
- Hiding in the woods is not funny.
- No trying to fit down badger holes.
- For the adults, no leaving your children in the woods to find their way out, while you sit in the car with a nice thermos of tea. It will be frowned on.

See strategies: Brain Breaks, Switching Off, Views, Walking

X

 ## X-ING OUT (CROSSING OUT)

Yes, I understand that this should really be under 'C' for crossing out, but I was struggling. I didn't feel I could really write anything about xylophones and x-ray machines, other than the fact that you might get a little brain break in an x-ray machine.

When my life was very busy working as a social worker and I was juggling lots of different priorities, I was taught a really good list system. This ensured that I never forgot anything and could easily reference back and find when a task had happened, or a conversation had taken place. I used this with my children as well.

The great thing about this system is that it makes you feel successful every day! The simple strategy adds in that extra little psychological win, of 'crossing out', so that you can feel a sense of satisfaction, even on bad days.

The system deliberately does not rely on any technology. There is something reassuring and grounding about having a go-to system which is always reliable. The last thing we need is the stress of trying to access an important list or note, when technology fails, and we are pressed for time. This is how it works:

- Obtain an A4-lined pad with a margin, a normal pen and red, green and yellow highlighter pens.
- Write the date at the top of the first page.

- Write down your to-do list for that day, numbered in the margin. Don't think about the order of importance.
- Once the list is written, first, in the margin, add initials related to the task. So if, for example, the social worker's initials are AC, then every time there's an interaction or something to do with that social worker, you write AC in the margin. That way you can quickly find anything relating to interactions with that person.
- Second, prioritize. Go down the list using the red highlighter and strike through the number relating to any point you think is important. So, if, for example, you have written 'Prepare notes for meeting tomorrow' as point 4, and that is something you absolutely *must do* today, strike the no. 4 through with the red highlighter. As you get emails or receive/make calls during the day, the list will change. That's okay, you just add further points with numbers and highlight as appropriate.
- Make notes as you go along in your day, completing tasks, with the initials relating to the task in the margin.
- Highlight in yellow any really important events or conversations that you may need to easily find in the future.
- Revisit the list frequently and check what you have completed. Prioritize those points with the red highlighter.
- As you progress, strike through in green any completed points.
- At the end of the day, look back at the list. Make sure that all the points which were originally marked red now also have a green highlight through them too. This gives you a great sense of satisfaction and you can see at a glance that all the important stuff got done.
- Draw a line under all the notes and events from the day.
- Write the date for tomorrow and transfer over any uncompleted tasks for the next day that you don't want to forget.

This makes it easier to switch off, as you won't be worrying about forgetting something important.

- Keep the book next to your bed at night to make a quick note if you wake up in the middle of the night and need to jot something down. This is much better than switching on your phone to add a reminder and seeing 27 missed calls at 3am.

If you do a list and have made everything red, then seriously, you need to have a word with yourself. Everything is *not* a priority.

See strategies: Losing Things, Tech Control, Timesavers

Y

🔆 YOGA

No thank you.

Look I know, I have seen wispy women contorting themselves into odd shapes and then claiming it's relaxing. I believe you. But when I did it there was no wispiness. Just screeching and horrific muscle ache. (Yes, I know, I was doing it wrong.) I needed a doughnut to recover, so that's probably not the idea.

So anyway, yes, apparently yoga is relaxing. I couldn't possibly comment.

YOUTHFULNESS

Children help us to stay young, don't they? Um well, not for me! I got fat and old. Happy news, though – as my children got older, not only did I discover Boots No7, which miraculously took away all my crow's feet and worry lines, but I also had time to move around more, lose weight and eat better. As my cortisol levels lowered, I stopped eating sugar. This resulted in me looking and feeling younger and healthier *after* the children had left home. All is not lost! If you are currently feeling old and tired, your youth will find you again.

Z

ZEN

Also see Yoga

It *is* possible to achieve a Zen-like state. I remember the day when I did this. I was lying in bed; it was early morning. I had a cup of tea, the sun was shining, and the dogs were snoozing peacefully around me. I was playing Zen music to help me with mindfulness and also using Self-Havening for calm. I was overcome with a feeling of calm and tranquillity. There had been no incidents (to my knowledge) for the past week. All was well. I could make plans for the day and be confident the plans would come to pass.

Oh, did I mention? The children had moved out five years previously...

See strategies: Brain Breaks, Protecting Self, Reading, Switching Off, Therapy (For Parents), Views, Walking, Yoga

ZOMBIFICATION

Also see Compassion Fatigue, Drained (Feeling), Exhaustion, Motivation, Overwhelm

The definition of zombification is 'a psychological condition in which patients believe their body is enslaved while their awareness is kept in a bottle or jar'. Yep! I'd say that just about sums it up for about 75 per cent of the time. In fact, I quite like the idea of having a little jar which I can pop my awareness into. It can stay there for safe keeping, ready for when I get my life back and there's a point to noticing things again and feeling like I might have a little rest.

And as for my body being enslaved... Hmm, well yes I suppose it is, although I *did* choose this 'enslavement'. I'm not exactly a forced slave, I'm a voluntary one, so I can't really complain *too* much. I know the saying goes 'Be careful what you wish for', but I'm glad I wished for it, and if I *am* 'enslaved' as a therapeutic parent, then as long as my awareness gets cake sometimes, I think I can cope.

See strategies: Brain Breaks, Empathic Listening, Essential Maintenance, Faith, One Step at a Time, Protecting Self

ZONES

I found it saved me a lot of hassle in my life if I established zones in the house. The central living area had lots of soft furnishings which were easily washable, laminate flooring (easily wipeable) and washable rugs. Another, smaller lounge had lots of breakables within it and cherished photographs. The children spent the majority of their time with me in the 'unbreakable zone'. This zone also had lots of handy ornaments which were easily replaceable and hard to break. This created a nurturing, warm environment which was able to stay more or less free of damage.

Dividing your home and your life up into these zones is quite liberating. You can relax in areas where the breakables are replaceable (because, let's face it, we cannot supervise our children 24/7).

Obviously, we don't want to live as if we are in Fort Knox! But at the same time, we do have to promote a nice, homely environment where we have the right to keep special things safe. If you have a special photo or piece of jewellery, put it in the 'safe zone'. Do not set your children up to fail – you don't need that heartache.

See strategy: Space

Afterword

As I wrote this book, I have shared freely the ups and downs, the heartaches, joys and sorrows we have faced as a family. I have naturally reflected on these times and relived them during the writing.

I want you all to know that I would not lose a single second of the heartbreak, frustration and trauma we have shared, because those times also gave me the privilege and joys of parenthood and grandparenthood, and for that, I am eternally grateful and humble.

Index

Sub–entries refer to strategies for issues/problems